THE RED ARISTOCRATS: MICHAEL AND CATHERINE KAROLYI

Also by the author:

Fiction:

MUCKALUCK

ON THE RUN: THE FABULIST STORY OF
    FELIX CARVAJAL

STRAIGHT CUT DITCH

THE RELUCTANT HERO: A FICTIONAL HISTORY
    OF ROBERT GOULD SHAW
    AND THE MASSACHUSETTS 54TH

Non Fiction:

ARRANGING DECK CHAIRS ON THE TITANIC:
    CRISES IN EDUCATION

ROBERT COOVER

THE WRITE STUFF: A PRACTICAL GUIDE TO
    STYLE AND MECHANICS

WILLIAM GOLDMAN

WRITING THAT WORKS: A PRACTICAL GUIDE
    FOR BUSINESSAND CREATIVE PEOPLE

THE RED ARISTOCRATS: MICHAEL AND CATHERINE KAROLYI

by Richard Andersen

AMANA BOOKS
58 Elliot Street
Brattleboro, Vermont 05301

Photo on back cover is by:
HELENE HINIS

ISBN 0-915597-85-3

AMANA BOOKS
58 Elliot Street
Brattleboro, Vermont 05301

Cover design by: SARA PUBLISHING

For: HELENE HINIS

INCRODUCCION

I hadn't been at the Karolyi Foundation for more than a few hours when a note arrived from the countess: "Would you be so kind as to accompany me to the Cannes Film Festival? Come by around seven."

I didn't know it then, but the question was purely rhetorical. If the countess wanted something, there was never a reason why she shouldn't have it. She called and you went. It never mattered where—to meet a young admirer in Tourrettes or to surrender her pistol to the police—you went.

"What brings you to the Foundation?" Catherine asked on the road to Cannes.

I told her I had always wanted to live in Europe. An advance from a novel and her accepting me as a Writer-in-Residence had made that possible.

Did I know anything about her husband?

All I knew was what I had read in an encyclopedia: Michael Karolyi had been kicked out of Hungary for being a socialist.

"That's correct," Catherine replied, though she knew it wasn't. I think she was grateful that at least I knew Michael was Hungarian and a socialist. But then again, it was her way not to correct, and she'd have the months ahead to educate me. No one ever left the

i

Karolyi Foundation without everything they needed to
spread the word.

The line wasn't long by Cannes' standards: a
couple of Mercedes, a Rolls, and us in a Bug. When I
pulled up before the big red carpet, the doorman put his
nose into the air as only a French doorman can and
impatiently snapped his fingers for me to keep my foot
on the gas.

I got out and opened the door for Catherine.

When the doorman saw we weren't wearing
evening clothes, he turned his back and walked away.

Or maybe he was carried away by the crowd. I
didn't see where all the people came from because I was
helping Catherine out of the car. But when I turned
around, there they were. I know now that there
couldn't have been more than fifty or sixty of them, but
at the time they seemed like several hundred. Kneeling
and reaching out to kiss Catherine's hands, they
mumbled words in a language I'd never heard. Some
pressed their foreheads to the backs of her hands.

And more were coming. From under the police
ropes and down the steps of the festival hall, they
rushed to pay homage. And those who had already
kissed her hands were running to the back of the line to
kneel, kiss, and mumble some more.

Flashbulbs threw so much light into the sky
Catherine had to stop and put on her sunglasses. Who
was she? the *papparazzi* wanted to know. Mary
Pickford? Lillian Gish?

As I got back in the car, a reporter jumped in on
the other side and locked the door. "Who is she?" he
demanded.

I told him.

He called me a liar. Then he begged me to have
a heart. This was the break he needed to get on the
regular staff at *Nice Matin*. I had to tell him WHO
SHE WAS.

I told him again.

When we got out of the car, he told the reporters

who had run after us that the old lady and I were exploiting the press for all the publicity we could get. If they weren't from a big paper, they could forget it.

But the reporters hadn't run all of a block and a half for nothing. If it was publicity we were after, all I had to do was tell them whether the old woman was Marlene Dietrich or Greta Garbo.

I began to wonder. A lot of famous people were living in and around Vence: James Baldwin, Simone Signoret, Marc Chagall. D.H. Lawrence and Henri Matisse had died there. It wasn't impossible for someone like Mary Pickford or Greta Garbo, long out of the public eye, to wind up in a sophisticatedly sleepy place like Vence. But then someone long out of the public eye wouldn't have to hide out. And if she was hiding out, she certainly wasn't going to risk exposing herself by showing up at the Cannes Film Festival in a Volkswagen.

Unless, of course, it really was a publicity stunt.

"Who are you?" I asked Catherine when seated next to her.

She just smiled and signaled for the movie to begin.

For the next nine months, I drove Catherine wherever she wanted to go. And wherever we went was usually more interesting than anyplace I could have gone by myself. She introduced me to all her friends, and I was given a view of France's international community that wouldn't have been possible on my own. One day we ran into Madame Chagall shopping for groceries. She was leaving Marc, she said. He'd become too rich and too famous. There was no more room for improvement, no further need to struggle. She had found a *real* artist—a twenty-seven-year-old photographer from Paris. Catherine explained afterwards that Madame Chagall was eighty-five and people did crazy things when they were eighty-five.

Eighty-five was the most difficult year of anybody unlucky enough to live that long. Eighty-five was one of the reasons a lot of people didn't reach ninety.

From the shopkeepers, former residents of the Foundation, and people who used to work for Catherine, I heard other stories: that she was an alcoholic and a drug addict, that she never paid her bills, that many of the town's businesses boycotted her, and that she really wasn't Michael Karolyi's wife but an actress he had picked up in England. The real Countess Karolyi had refused to follow her husband into exile and died fighting the Russians in the 1956 Revolution. Others said Catherine was the real countess but had gotten her husband kicked out of Hungary for the role she played in the murder of the Prime Minister, Stephen Tisza. I heard that she had shot her parents, made love to Gordon Craig while her husband lay dying in the next room, and robbed her children of all their father had left them in order to start a colony for naive artists who waited on her hand and foot.

And her husband wasn't all history made him out to be either. He had stolen millions of florins from the Hungarian people and never gave so much as a franc to the city of Vence. Marc Chagall said he cheated at chess, and a Romanoff from Tourrettes claimed Karolyi was responsible for the White Terror of the Horthy regime. "If there hadn't been a Karolyi," he told me, "there'd never have been a Hitler." I didn't know what to think. Catherine did take thirteen different kinds of pills every day and she did speak English without any trace of an accent, but French doctors are notorious overprescribers and Catherine also spoke French and German without an accent. On the other hand, if there was one language that gave her trouble, it was Hungarian. Did that mean she really wasn't a Karolyi? And just because her house was filled with drawings by Gordon Craig, did that mean they had been lovers? She had works by Andre Kertesz and

iv

Gustav Klimt. Had they been lovers too?

I found it hard to believe that Michael Karolyi was responsible for Hitler, but there *were* monthly statements from a bank in Switzerland and a broker in London. He may very well have taken money from Hungary. On the other hand, Catherine didn't seem to have a whole lot of money. Even the clothes she wore to receive the Order of the Flag came from Prisunic.

The only accusation I could be sure of was that the artists did wait on her hand and foot. But even then she gave more than she received. We never went anywhere or did anything without her teaching me something about her husband's role in history. One day I'd be traveling with her and George Bernard Shaw to a conference in Moscow; the next day I'd be riding up Pacific Coast Highway with Michael and Charlie Chaplin. Chaplin is going to enter a Charlie Chaplin Look-Alike Contest. He comes in seventh.

The evenings I spent reading the Karolyis' memoirs, letters, speeches, articles, plays, and novels. I also read anything I could find on the Karolyi Revolution and its short-lived government.

Both Michael and Catherine were early disappointments to their class: Michael for refusing to beat his servants, rape his peasants, or leave a single book in the family library unread. Catherine for wanting to be independent. Her signing up for a bookkeeping course at the age of eighteen made national headlines. A countess wanting to work? It was unheard of.

The newspapers interpreted Catherine's decision as a sign that her parents wanted her to marry someone she didn't love. Michael knew something more important was a stake. He had found in Catherine someone who would support his calls for universal suffrage, land reform, and equal representation.

By the time I left Vence, Catherine had become a close friend and inspiring mentor. Together we had collected the Karolyis' papers and memorabilia for deposit in museums in France, Hungary, and the United States. The weeks that it took to complete this work were the most intense learning experience of my life. No longer was I just reading or hearing about the roles two people played in history. I was vicariously living through Catherine the fall of the Hapsburg dynasty and the rise of Eastern Europe's first democratic government. I especially remember coming across a pile of telegrams originating from the United States Senate. The messages relayed the momentum of a debate that would determine whether Michael would be given a visa to visit Catherine, who was dying of typhoid fever in New York. As I read the telegrams, the anxiety with which those messages were received in London was dramatically recreated in France. I became so involved I almost cheered as the vote swung in the Karolyis' favor and was profoundly embarrassed and depressed when the final tally came out against them.

And that wasn't the end of it. The time with Catherine set off a spark that took me everywhere the Karolyis had been. From London to Leningrad and Berlin to Budapest, I interviewed everyone from the KGB agent assigned to monitor Catherine's activities to the present leader of the Hungarian underground.

But it is to Catherine that I owe my deepest appreciation. To Katus, who taught me that "happiness should not be our aim in life, but rather that we should live intensely and completely and be ready to accept suffering; that we are all, every one of us, responsible for the evil happenings in the world, and we all, every one of us, must work to mitigate them."

Richard Andersen
Amherst, Massachusetts

1.
EXPECTATIONS
DENIED

Michael and Catherine were disappointments from the very beginning.

Michael was so small his father didn't even see him nestled in his mother's arms. He kept waiting for a nurse to bring his heir in from another room. When Georgina Karolyi realized what her husband was doing, she raised Michael higher on her arm and pulled his covers farther away from his face.

Julius shuddered at what he saw. The boy looked so weak and sickly. Not at all like a Karolyi. And the head! He had never seen anything like it. So narrow and so pinched at the temples Julius wondered if a forceps had been used. "Do you think it could be brain damaged?" he asked his wife.

Catherine's reception was even worse. Her grandmother, thinking she had seen something that wasn't there, shouted, "It's a boy!"

"It's a boy!" the nurse told the servant in the hall.

"It's a boy! the servant shouted to the maid on her way to the kitchen.

1

"It's a boy!" passed from the kitchen to the servants' quarters to the gardeners' cottages to the stables and to the fields. Cheers rose for the heir who would keep their families from being divided among new jobs, new masters, and possibly even new homes. Thanks to the new Andrassy baby, everything was going to stay the same.

It was the village doctor who broke the bad news: Ella Andrassy had given birth to her third girl. Cousin Sandor, who stood to inherit the Andrassy estate if Ella and Tivadar couldn't produce a boy, slept soundly for the first time in months.

And yet, given their centuries-old history of disappointing people, you'd think the Karolyis and Andrassys would be used to reversals. Take the year 1660, for example. Turkey ruled the Danubian Basin then and the Hungarians wanted them out. But the Turks weren't about to hand over the land they had stolen fair and square, so the Hungarians sought help from their Austrian neighbors.

The Austrians, headed by the House of Hapsburg, wouldn't have waited much longer for an invitation. They hadn't been too keen on the Infidels controlling all that trade on the Danube and saw in the Hungarian rebellion a divine calling to save the country for Christ.

Only the Austrians didn't leave once the Moslems were gone. Almost overnight, they went from being liberators to occupiers.

Francis Rakoczi was the first Hungarian to rebel against the new masters, but his country's aristocrats refused to support him. Led by Baron Alexander Karolyi, the aristocrats claimed the Hapsburgs were too strong and the Hungarians needed their protection against Turkey. Not only that but the Austrians were savages. Had Rakoczi forgotten how they had made the Moslem leaders sit on white hot thrones while their lieutenants waited to have the charred flesh stuffed down their throats?

Rakoczi argued that the Hapsburgs wouldn't burn Christian flesh, but no aristocrat wanted to test them. Especially Baron Karolyi. So Rakoczi went to the people. His first recruits were hajduks, cowboys really, who had given up driving cattle when the peasants began protecting their crops with muskets. Having no other skills, these *hajduks* became bandits, overseers for the aristocrats, or, when Rakoczi came along, crusaders against the Holy Roman Emperor.

The irony was not lost on Rakoczi. He changed the name of his *hajduks* to *kurocks*—meaning "crossbearers"—and the name of his enemy to *Labancoks*—a word derived from a German expression meaning "Run Hans!"

And run Hans did. All the way back to the Austrian border.

Baron Karolyi and the aristocrats reconsidered their decision to side with the Hapsburgs. If they didn't join Rakoczi soon, they might find themselves the subjects of a new expression meaning "Run Laszlo!"

Rakoczi's victory was short-lived, however. More than a little disturbed by the thought of Hungarian cowboys riding through the streets of Vienna, the Hapsburgs signed a treaty with their major rival in the West, the French, and rushed every soldier they could muster to the Hungarian border.

Rakoczi rallied his *kurocks*, but his hopes for an independent Hungary were cut short by a cook. Waking up in the middle of the night, the man found himself sweating and shivering at the same time. Shortly afterwards, a guard with the same symptoms asked to be relieved at his station. Both the cook and the guard had swollen necks.

The aristocrats knew what this meant: the revolution was over. Led by Alexander Karolyi, they sued for peace.

The Hapsburgs also knew how to interpret the plague: they could die. Led by anyone who had a say in the matter, they accepted Baron Karolyi's proposal to make everything the way it was before the revolution. The Catholic Church, who knew better than anybody what to make of the plague, offered to act as the aristocrats' and Hapsburgs' agent. Priests all over Hungary began telling their faithful that if God had wanted them to have a democracy He would have given them one. Rakoczi and his *kurocks* had committed the sin of pride, the same sin that had driven Satan from heaven and Adam and Eve from Eden. To return to the Eden that God had created for them in the Danubian Basin, the Hungarians had to get back into their Savior's good graces. That meant eliminating the temptation that had led them to sin (Rakoczi), asking forgiveness from God's secular representatives on earth (the Holy Roman Hapsburgs), and doing penance for their transgressions (the plague). Failure to reform would invite an even more horrible fate.

What this fate might be, no Hungarian could imagine. The plague had already taken more lives than the whole Austrian army. But the Hungarians weren't about to kill their beloved Rakoczi. Doing a little interpreting of their own, they helped him escape the Church, the aristocrats, and the Hapsburgs. By the time the revolutionary reached the court of Louis XIV, the Hapsburgs had made Baron Alexander a count with the right to wear eleven points on his crown instead of the usual nine. The Karolyis are the only Hungarians to have this honor.

When Michael Karolyi read one morning in 1906 that the Hapsburgs no longer bore a grudge against Rakoczi and were allowing his remains to be brought back to Hungary, he couldn't help thinking about the pattern Rakoczi had established for all the revolutionaries who had followed him. Even the most recent Revolution of 1848 was a blueprint of Rakoczi's: the Hapsburgs' attention had been diverted by the French, the Hungarians saw a chance to rebel, the

aristocrats claimed they needed Austria's
protection—only this time it was against their own
peasants rather than the Turks—and a hero by the
name of Louis Kossuth came out of nowhere to score
seemingly impossible victories in battle, announce
sweeping reforms in government, suffer defeat from
causes beyond his control, and die in exile.

The Karolyis played a role in this revolution
too. Michael's grandmother, Caroline Zichy, was
threatened with flogging for associating with a known
revolutionary: her brother-in-law Louis Batthyani.
Before she fled to France, however, Caroline smuggled a
dagger with the inscription *Ora et Semper* into the
prison where Louis was waiting to be hanged. He had
served as Kossuth's Prime Minister but refused to go
into exile or renounce his revolutionary ideals. Nor was
he willing to give the Austrian Emperor the satisfaction
of seeing him swing from a rope. Once on the scaffold,
he drew the dagger from his vest, shouted "Now and
Forever," and stabbed himself in the neck.

If it hadn't been for the rest of the family, the
Karolyis might have lost those extra two points on their
crown. As it was, only Michael's grandmother and uncle
had sided with Kossuth. All the rest of the Karolyis not
only remained loyal to Austria, they sent guides to lead
the Russian army into Hungary when the Hapsburgs
failed to defeat Kossuth by themselves.

Catherine's family also played a role in the
Revolution of 1848. They had been relatively quiet since
their ancestor King Arpad had led his tribe out of the
Ural Mountains and into the Danubian Basin in 898,
but Julius Andrassy, Catherine's grandfather, was
prepared to make up for lost time. Like Louis
Batthyani, Julius started out on Kossuth's side, but fled
to Paris as soon as he heard the Russians were coming.
A rude waiter at the Place de l'Opera got him to
thinking about the hundreds of friendly servants he
had left behind, however, and he was soon back in
Budapest crowning the very man who had signed his

death warrant: Emperor Franz-Joseph.

Michael was nineteen when Kossuth's body was brought back from Turkey and thirty when Rakoczi's remains were finally laid to rest. Between those years he had earned his law degree and run unsuccessfully for Parliament on a ticket headed by Kossuth's son. Did he draw any parallels between himself and Hungary's two greatest revolutionaries?

Probably not. Michael may have had *Ora et Semper* tattoed on his arm, but his difficulty in passing the bar and his reputation as a *bon vivant* blurred whatever promise he may have shown even to himself.

Like most aristocrats, Michael was spoiled—a condition made worse by poor health and his having been diagnosed early on as a "slow learner." But Michael wasn't so much "slow" as "off." He had trouble making connections. Or at least the connections people expected him to make. As a baby, for example, he was taught to warn his nurses when he was about to wet his diapers. He managed this well enough—if only during the day—but he failed to associate what came out at one end of his body with what came out at the other. His nurses called him "Never Wet But Always Dirty."

Then, when Michael was three years old, his mother died. Julius Karolyi remarried quickly, but he just as quickly lost what little interest he had in his children. Elizabeth, who was three years older than Michael, maintained the status she had always shared with girls in her class: beautiful perhaps to the man who eventually married her but something of a white elephant until then. All she needed to get her to her wedding day—a name, rank, and bank account number—had been there for her since the day she was born.

Michael, on the other hand, couldn't be ignored. Physically weak, frequently running at the nose, chronically wetting his bed, and unable to keep anything stronger than paprika in his stomach, he made his father look bad. The unfortunate youngster even had a lisp.

To isolate Michael from anyone who might judge the father by the boy, Julius sent his son and Elizabeth to live with their Grandmother Clarisse. Her palace at Foth, with its Doric columns, endless galleries, winding staircases, huge fireplace, three-hundred-acre park, eighty-thousand-volume library, and tremendous lake was just what Julius needed to keep his reputation intact. Frequently impotent —except when he could sodomize—Julius made Clarisse sign a contract allowing her to raise her daughter's children as long as she kept them from speaking to people who didn't live and work at the estate. Considering the fact that aristocrats only learned enough Hungarian to give orders, that didn't leave many people.

The private tutors Julius hired increased Michael and Elizabeth's isolation even more. They learned that aristocrats were God's favored pets and that His divine will insured their wealth and comfort as well as that of all their descendants. In return, the aristocrats were expected to help those beneath them but not so much as to make them forget their places. Social progress, even for the sake of human rights, was a sin.

Julius occasionally dropped by to see how his old family was doing—he never brought the new one—but he rarely liked what he saw. Michael always looked as if he hadn't seen the sun in weeks and, for all his talk about the good books in Clarisse's library, he hadn't read one about stalking deer, flushing boar, or trapping trout.

To offset the influence of writers such as Jules Verne, Julius hired the head of Hungary's Veterinary College to teach Michael something about horses. His first lesson—how to insert an enema—not only diminished any interest Michael might have developed in horses, it practically eliminated his appreciation of country life altogether. But every time he asked his father to send him to a school in Budapest, Julius would only reply, "You can't hunt on Andrassy Avenue."

Twenty years younger than Michael, Catherine Andrassy was almost his complete opposite. She realized before she was five what a disappointment she had been to her parents, but she wasn't the kind to retreat to a library. For years she struggled to be the boy her parents had wanted. After hearing the story of Adam and Eve, she counted her ribs as many times as was necessary to come up with the right number. When that failed to get her into pants, she began adopting boys as her role models. By the time she was a teenager, she could out sail, out ride, and out shoot every boy she knew.

Like Michael, however, Catherine had a parent she could never please: her mother. Strikingly beautiful but physically unaffectionate, Ella Andrassy rarely saw her children except to allow them to kiss her hands in the morning and again in the evening. A third occasion was just before the opening of the winter season. Catherine and her sisters were allowed to sit in Ella's dressing room and watch a gaggle of dressmakers parade the latest fashions from Paris. Ella, who was a different kind of Zichy than Michael's Grandmother Caroline, would try on dozens of gowns while her children looked on in awe. A new costume was ordered for every ball and opening, and Catherine saw her mother leave the house as everyone from Empress Theodora carried on a silver throne to Maid Marian riding a white horse whose saddle was laced with gold brocade.

Ella was seventeen when she married the son of Austria-Hungary's Prime Minister. Newspapers called the match "The Wedding of the Century," but for Ella, who believed that babies came from little seeds which grew under women's hearts, her first night with Tivadar was a shocking and terrifying experience. She couldn't believe what the son of the Foreign Minister who had written the treaty which united Austria and Hungary was doing to her. In fact, she had to keep telling herself "This is Julius Andrassy's son! This is Julius Andrassy's son" to keep from screaming.

A profound sense of humiliation came with the morning. Convinced that her love-making had brought about a physical change which everyone could read in her face, Ella stayed in her marriage bed for two weeks. Months passed before she set foot outside of her house. And she only left then because Tivadar had given her the idea of wearing a veil. Years afterward, she still only looked children in the eye, and the thought that she had been conceived by the "Beast With Two Backs" was something she never got over.

Instead of helping her children avoid the same cruel and embarrassing predicament, however, Ella did all she could to keep Catherine and her sisters completely ignorant of anything that had to do with sex. Not only couldn't they read any books she hadn't approved, the ones she did approve had words such as "marriage bed" and "natural son" put in brackets so the governesses could read to the children aloud without making any suspicious pauses. Ella also protected her daughters by sewing together any pages where the word "love" appeared. As a result, Catherine never read a love story and rarely went to a movie, ballet, or opera.

Michael, on the other hand, got to pick and choose from a library that rivaled the University of Budapest's. Jules Verne was his first great passion, followed by Wilkie Collins. But no early influence exceeded that of the family encyclopedia. Almost every interest Michael ever developed had its roots there. And no piece had as wide-ranging or as devastating an impact as Voltaire's entry on God. Could it be, Michael found himself wondering, that in spite of the churches his family had built, the confessors they had appointed, and their close friendship with Cardinal Samassa, the Karolyis might not be among God's chosen favorites? Could it be that there might not even be a God? That what Michael thought was God was really a fiction which a few men used to control a great many others? These questions shook the foundation of Michael's strongly-held Catholic beliefs. Everything from the aristocrats being allowed to eat meat on Friday to Michael's belief in the Virgin Mary became suspect.

There were no such questions in Catherine's childhood. There was no time. Her mother, an atheist who practiced all the latest child-rearing theories with the zeal of a missionary, prevented questions and a lot more from entering her children's minds by filling their lives with constant activities: four minutes after each meal for washing and drying of hands; three minutes after each meal for brushing of teeth; six minutes for brushing hair after every waking, fifteen before going to bed in the evening.

Catherine and her three sisters had a cold, five-minute bath to wake them up in the morning and a ten-minute warm one to ready them for bed at night. While the maids washed, dried, and dressed the children, governesses made sure everyone kept to Ella's schedule.

Ella also had a theory about colds: children who are kept the same temperature as their surroundings don't get sick. Catherine often had her diapers changed outdoors and, when she was old enough to walk, ran barefoot with her sisters through a nearby stream. This early morning "stimulation exercise" was expanded to include the distance between the water and the house whenever snow was on the ground. The time spent in purple feet and legs, however, remained the same: ten minutes. Remarkably, or perhaps miraculously, the Andrassy children were never ill.

Michael, of course, was rarely well. He not only
managed to catch every childhood disease, he was often
the first to come down with any virus. Then, after he
had passed it on to everyone he knew, he got it back
again. His father nicknamed him "The Plague" and
suggested he ring a bell to let people know when he was
coming.

In spite of this treatment, or perhaps because of
it, Michael was able to discover and develop many of
the virtues for which he later became famous. When he
was fourteen, for example, he read about an operation
that might correct the defect in his palate that was
causing him to lisp. The operation had never been done,
however, because no patient was willing to take the
risk. If it failed, Michael would never speak again.
There was a good chance he would die.

Julius Karolyi didn't think it was a good idea
for an aristocrat to undergo an operation that hadn't
been sufficiently tested on peasants, but he had to
admire how forcefully Michael argued in favor of it. The
boy said he'd rather not speak at all than have to
continue living the way he had. People mistook his
handicap for stupidity. If he was completely dumb, at
least nobody would question his intelligence. And he
could still communicate in writing or in sign language.
"Even death is better than this half-life," he told his
father.

"You can't hunt when you're dead," Julius
warned.

"Then the operation can't be a complete failure,"
Michael countered.

But Michael was a lot more frightened than he
had let on. The dead didn't hunt, but they didn't read
either. And at last count he still had a good 78,000
books waiting for him in his grandmother's library.

Lying on the operating table, Michael wondered
what would happen if he really did die. What if Voltaire
was wrong? The philosopher hadn't actually said there
was no God, but he also made it clear that if there was

a God, he wasn't anything like the one man imagined.
And what if his family, the Church, and 2,000 years of
history were right? There had to be dozens of people in
that time—Augustine, Aquinas, St. Paul—who were at
least as smart as Voltaire.

Michael decided not to take any chances. Or at
least as few as possible. He made a deal with the God
he knew from Church and the Bible. If that God proved
His existence by correcting the defect in Michael's
palate, Michael would forsake Voltaire. Not only that
but he would devote his new voice and rest of his new
life to serving Jesus as a priest in the Mystical Body of
Christ.

Had Catherine known Michael then, she
probably wouldn't have liked him. Or even what to
make of him. Her family was secular to the point of
being anti-clerical. And whereas Michael spent most of
his childhood evenings praying for guidance in the
Karolyi Chapel—the estate had its own priest as
well—the young Catherine joined her family in a salon
purposely set aside for discussions of art, history,
philosophy, and politics. Whatever range she may have
lacked in her reading was made up for here. The
newspapers printed few stories about Hungary's artists,
writers, scholars, and politicians who weren't also
houseguests at one time or another.

Catherine learned from them all, but her great
ability to listen to what others had to say and to detect
what they really meant came from another source: her
father's office. To the side of his desk was secret room
hidden by a curtain. Whenever anyone visited Tivadar
on an official or politically sensitive mission, the
Andrassy women listened from behind the curtain.
Then, when the visitor left, the curtain was pulled aside
and the family discussed whatever issues had ben
raised in the meeting.

The Andrassys had as many different opinions

about the subjects they debated as there were
Andrassys, but two emotions always united them: their
deep affection for the Empress Elizabeth of
Austria—Tivadar called her "The Guardian Angel of the
Hungarians"—and their hatred for her husband, Franz-
Joseph. Cruel, selfish, and almost unbelievably
heartless, the Emperor made his wife miserable with
the demands he continually placed on her. Whatever he
didn't want to read, he made her read for him; whatever
he didn't want to write, she had to prepare for his
signature; whomever he didn't wish to meet, she had to
meet in his place. The Emperor's job, as he saw it, was
to delegate responsibility, make the big decisions, and
keep up his image as strong leader. Unfortunately, he
carried this image into his private life, and his son
killed himself when he couldn't take it any longer.

At least that's how the Andrassys saw it.
Catherine's grandfather was at his desk in the Foreign
Ministry when he heard about Rudolph's suicide. The
first to arrive at Franz-Joseph's side, he was shocked to
discover the Emperor calmly carrying out his everyday
duties. Nothing in Julius Andrassy's career—not his
support for Louis Kossuth, his exile in Paris, his
crowning Franz Joseph, or his writing the treaty that
united Austria and Hungary—affected him more. Years
later, when the Empress sought him as a lover, he had
come to understand what her life was like and opened
his heart to her.

Franz-Joseph and Elizabeth were also friends of
the Karolyis, but Michael was under his father's strict
orders to kiss their hands and make himself scarce.
While the royal couple rode over the grounds at
Foth—the Empress's favorite course—Michael
concentrated on keeping his promise to God. He studied
Latin in the morning, read collections of saints' lives in
the afternoon, and devoted his evenings to discussing
religious issues with the estate's confessor: What would

happen if a Moslem ate a consecrated host? Would the host remain consecrated? Would God allow Himself to be chewed up by an Infidel?

Then, when Michael was fifteen, his father suddenly died of a heart attack. There had never been much love between them—Michael doesn't even record his father's first name in the index to his memoirs—but he took the loss hard and in a way no one had expected. He felt as if God had betrayed him, taken away his opportunity to prove himself in a way that had nothing to do with guns or horses. What Michael didn't realize was that he had already proved himself. Every time the boy spoke, Julius wondered if he would have had the courage to undergo the operation and painful rehabilitation exercises Michael had endured. Unfortunately, Julius never shared this thought with his son. That he left to Uncle Alexander.

Alexander Karolyi had been a sort of surrogate father for Michael ever since he found out they both loved books. Michael also discovered he could talk with his uncle about things he wouldn't even mention to his father, and he appreciated how his uncle asked him questions instead of always telling him how life was. Alexander also listened, which made Michael feel as if he was being taken seriously. Perhaps most important, however, was Alexander's not thinking Michael was genetically flawed because he didn't like to hunt or ride. In fact, one of their closest initial bonds was their mutual hatred of polo. Michael, of course, had a deep and abiding resentment for anything to do with horses, but Alexander believed the game was an accurate measurement of just how far the ruling classes had allowed their responsibilities as Christians to slide.

Alexander Karolyi was known as a liberal and a hard worker, but these rare qualities were not necessarily admired by the Hungarian ruling classes. Like Michael, Uncle Alexander was considered a little "slow." He believed, for example, that political independence from Austria made no sense unless Hungary was economically independent as well. As long as the Hapsburgs determined what prices they paid for Hungary's raw materials and what prices the Hungarians paid for Austria's manufactured goods, Hungary's real status in the world would remain fixed.

Nobody argued with that. Hungary was politically and economically dependent on Austria. Hungary was also militarily dependent and looked to Austria as a guiding light in the arts as well. The point Alexander missed was that most of Hungary's aristocrats wanted it that way. Their holdings were so large, they still made a ton of money on the prices Austria set. If there was a bad year, they'd pass the loss on to the peasants by cutting their wages. And if one of the gentry went under every once in a while, well, there was always an aristocrat who could absorb the estate and pay off a portion of its debts. True, the Hungarians had given up some of their political freedoms—the right to determine their own future, for example—but they felt what they got in return was worth the sacrifice. Who could say when Turkey regained its strength or Greece threatened to export its democratic ideas or the Hungarian peasants decided they'd had enough of poverty and exploitation? Who would the aristocrats turn to then? And what would happen to Hungary's "historic class" if the country were overthrown? Where would they dance or eat chocolate? In Budapest? They might as well go live in America.

But Alexander wasn't worried about the power Hungary had given Austria. Nor was he concerned about the Turks or the Greeks. His focus was on the aristocrats themselves. They were unconsciously giving away a power base that even the Hapsburgs couldn't return to them. And they were giving it away to an older and more desperate enemy than either the Moslems or the democrats: the Jews.

According to Alexander, the aristocrats were

God's chosen class. They transcended national boundaries to form a kind of multi-national club to which pedigree was the only criterion for membership. This pedigree had been bestowed on them by God to be passed on from generation to generation. But membership in the club had its responsibilities as well as its privileges. God expected the aristocrats to help those less fortunate than themselves. To improve the quality of life for everyone in God's Great Chain of Being without disturbing its delicate balance. That was what the ruling classes had been put on earth to do. Rule. Not just dance, eat chocolate, and play polo.

This wasn't a new idea. Most aristocrats had been hearing some form of it all their lives. What was new was Alexander's application. He claimed the aristocrats had shirked their responsibility as Christians. Instead of helping their less fortunate brothers improve their impoverished condition, the aristocrats had kept the peasants who worked for them as poor and as undereducated as they could. This meant more money for the landowners and more time for dancing in Vienna, but it also meant a widening of the gap separating the two classes. That gap—combined with the nobles' penchant for spending most of their time in Paris, Rome, and London—had created a power vacuum which was quickly being filled by a class of lawyers, doctors, and businessmen. Ordinarily this wouldn't have been so bad—these professional types only made more money and less work for the aristocrats—except that this new, rising, and increasingly more powerful class was made up almost exclusively of Christ-killers. They hadn't made many demands yet, but they kept carving out larger chunks of Hungary's economic pie for themselves. Once they had enough to form a base of power, it would only be a matter of time before they introduced their so-called "progressive ideas," which anybody with any sense could see were only other words for "socialism." And the Austrians wouldn't be able to stop them because

they depended as much on banks and merchants as the
Hungarians. In short, the Jews were making
themselves indispensable to the survival of the nation.
People who did business in the capital were already
calling it "Judapest."

To combat this growing influence of the Jews,
Alexander proposed a series of leadership schools.
These schools would be based on economic principles
and traditional Christian values. Their graduates
wouldn't know exactly how to go about investing
capital—that would be beneath them—but they
wouldn't be completely dependent on the bankers,
brokers, and lawyers either. And with the extra money
they'd earn from the Jews no longer being able to take
advantage of their ignorance, the aristocrats could help
those in the less fortunate peasant class.

As an example of what he had in mind,
Alexander founded Hungary's first cooperative.
Financed by an aristocrat (him), managed by a board of
directors (only the treasurer was a Jew), and run by
peasants, the cooperative was designed to make more
money for the investor, keep the Jews in their place,
and raise the peasants' standard of living.

It did just the opposite. Because Alexander
didn't understand the peasant mentality—life was pain
and anyone who said differently was trying to put
something over on you—and because he made arbitrary
decisions based on his own vision of what a cooperative
should be—it only lasted as long as it did because of the
Jewish treasurer—the cooperative had little basis in
reality. Alexander soon discovered that nature had
more influence over the peasants' schedules than the
board of directors, and businessmen in the city didn't
share any vision which cut into their profit margin.
When the peasants discovered they could make more
money hiring themselves out as field hands, the board
discovered it no longer had a cooperative to direct.
Alexander was left with a building no one had any use
for.

Nevertheless, Michael was impressed by his uncle's ideals. And he probably would have helped put more of them into action if he hadn't been studying so hard for the priesthood. Or rather, pretending to study. The truth was he still preferred Voltaire to Aquinas and, as time increased his distance from the operation on his palate, he found more and more reasons to read what he shouldn't.

As Michael's enthusiasm for the seminary waned, however, his desire to find a mission in life increased. Uncle Alexander recognized this idealistic streak—he had it himself—and tried to win the boy to his side. Never one to dogmatize, he further undermined Michael's vocation by suggesting books on the theories of Darwin and the *laissez-faire* school of economics. In the discussions that followed, Alexander encouraged Michael to discover for himself the value of combining his Christian ideals with practices that not only saved souls but improved conditions for the living as well.

Unfortunately for Alexander, Michael was too much his uncle's nephew to grasp the point that had been set up for him. He agreed, for example, with everything Marx had to say about the anarchy of capitalism—the lesson Alexander had wanted him to learn—but failed to see how his uncle's system of cooperatives was better than what Marx offered. Nevertheless, the hours Michael spent reading *Das Kapital* and discussing it with Alexander determined his whole career. He realized with all the fervor of a calling that poverty was a crime. Perhaps the worst crime because so many others stemmed from it. Consequently no work could be more important than delivering the poor and oppressed from their misery. This conviction, though clouded at times by the carefree existence of aristocratic life, was never extinguished and, after World War I, exploded into the primary reason for Michael's existence.

Catherine's greatest influence before meeting Michael was also an uncle. Until her father died when she was thirteen, most of her childhood had been determined by "the seasons." Winter and spring were centered in the Andrassy palace on the Buda side of the Danube, while summer was reserved for the country estate at Terebes in northeast Hungary. The shooting season opened at Dubrin—a mere "shooting box" able to accomodate only fifty servants—the fox hunting season took place back at Terebes, and what was left of the year was passed at Tisza-Dobb, the Loire-like chateau where Catherine was born.

Catherine liked the shooting box best. From its balcony, she could look down into the valleys of the Transylvania Mountains and across silvery streams to the dark forests on the opposite slopes. A special wildness in the air and ruggedness in the landscape made her imagine the spirits of ancestors dancing in the night.

Few people lived in this remote, rock-ridden region, and those who did looked less human than their beasts. At least that's how Catherine was taught to see them. Somewhere between noble savages and child-like candidates for civilization, they were good enough to service your every need but not evolved enough to behave responsibly without the promise of reward or the threat of punishment.

Like most aristocrats, Catherine was forbidden to mix with these people. In fact, the aristocrats rarely associated with anyone who spoke Hungarian. Hungarian was a barbaric language. Unless they were giving orders, the members of God's chosen class spoke French, English, or German.

In addition to having to accept their status—or perhaps to augment it—the peasants were expected to donate their best fruit, vegetables, poultry, livestock, dairy products, and so many days of free labor each year if they wanted the aristocrats to hire them for the planting and harvesting seasons. Is it any wonder, then, that Catherine could describe the trout served to her under the pergola at Dubrin as the "biggest and bluest and most curled up" she had ever eaten? Or that the beef portioned by her father wasn't the "most savory of any in the world"?

No pleasure at the shooting box, however, equalled the family picnic. Half the Andrassy staff, which included houseboys, cooks, butlers, footmen, and maids, left before dawn for a prearranged spot high in the mountains. The other half would help the Andrassys wake, bathe, dress, and eat. Then, with an army of grooms waiting midway with a team of fresh horses, Tivadar led a procession that included his wife, his brother, and his four daughters. The children's governesses followed in what was called "nursery etiquette": the governess of the oldest child first, the governess of the next oldest second, and so on down the line. Another set of grooms with horses, guns, and ammunition took up the rear.

When they arrived at the picnic site, the Andrassys found a delicious meal just being taken from open fires and displayed on an extravagantly decorated table. Unless, of course, Tivadar happened to shoot a deer or a boar. In these cases, the cooked food was packed away and a new meal was prepared. Because some food went with deer and other food went with boar and still other food went with beef, the servants had to carry as many different kinds of food as there were animals to kill. Sometimes as many as four meals were prepared for any one the Andrassys chose to eat.

What the Andrassys didn't finish was then divided among the people who waited on them. According to "servant etiquette," those who worked in the house and closest to Tivadar ate first; those outside the house but closest to the horses began the second wave. The farther down the scale you were, the more you hoped Tivadar would shoot a large animal.

But etiquette wasn't the sole reason for these hopes. Only the aristocrats had the right to kill certain species of animals. This meant, for example, that the servants couldn't eat any deer that hadn't been killed by Tivadar or his brother. A peasant who killed a deer—no matter how hungry his family—was a poacher. And because property was valued more highly than all but one class of people, the aristocrats also had the right to kill poachers.

Or have them killed. The Andrassys' best gamekeeper had been hired specifically for this reason. Reputed to have murdered dozens of hungry peasants, he eventually wound up with a bullet in his head.

That same day the police caught a boy leading a wounded man on horseback into the valley. The man, who had a gaping hole in his stomach, died shortly after his arrest. The boy was brought back to the Andrassys for questioning. There, the police hanged him by his thumbs, whipped him, and broke one of his kneecaps, but the boy wouldn't confess.

The police wondered if a few electric shocks would loosen his tongue.

When Catherine heard the screams—the boy hadn't made a sound until then—she pleaded with her father to make the police stop. Tivadar went to the officer in charge. He said the gamekeeper could easily be replaced. Why not let the boy go? Now that he'd never walk again, surely all the deer would be safe. But the officer explained that the situation involved more than the deer or the gamekeeper. If those responsible for the poaching and the murder were not brought to justice, others would think they could get away with stealing and killing too. Who could say where it would end? Even good aristocrats like the Andrassys would be in danger.

The torture continued, the boy died, and the mystery went unsolved, but it left Catherine with a question that haunted her for years: why was it murder to kill a gamekeeper and not a poacher?

Her Uncle Duci had the answer: "Gamekeepers and poachers are not of the same class."

21

Uncle Duci. Brother of Tivadar, namesake of the
famous Julius, and a favorite of the Andrassy family,
Uncle Duci was to Catherine what Uncle Alexander
was to Michael: someone who knew, cared, and
inspired.

He was also like Uncle Alexander in that he
was never one to force his ideas on others. Instead of
passing around books, however, he listened to all the
sides of any story before reaching a conclusion. And
because he listened, his advice was almost always
heeded. In the matter of the gamekeeper and the
poacher, Uncle Duci explained how the lower classes
had a pecking order that was just as rigid as the
aristocrats'. In the same way that Catherine could
never marry someone from the gentry or professional
classes, so too would a peasant who owned land be
shunned by his people if he married the daughter of a
harvest worker. Similarly, the daughter of a harvest
worker couldn't marry a land laborer, a land laborer's
daughter couldn't marry a shepherd, no shepherd could
marry the daughter of a swineherd, and a swineherd's
daughter couldn't marry anyone but a swineherd.
Gamekeepers ranked high on the pecking order. Their
contribution to society placed them right up there with
harvest workers. Poachers, on the other hand, were
criminals, lower than the lowest swineherd. To kill a
poacher was to rid society of a parasite.

This made sense to Catherine not so much
because of what Uncle Duci said but the way that he
had said it. Gentle, kind, and wise, he helped her
understand her problems and solve them in ways that
made her feel confident, secure, and right. In other
words, he put her world in order. It was his order, but it
worked for Catherine because everything had its place.

One thing which had no place in Uncle Duci's
world was marriage. This worried his father—especially
when his other son's wife only gave birth to girls—but

Catherine interpreted Uncle Duci's decision as another sign of his intelligence. By going just about everywhere the Andrassys went, he was able to enjoy all the advantages of family life without having to suffer any of the inconveniences. Never, for example, was he called on to scold a child, slap a maid, or whip a servant.

Catherine's mother did most of the beating in the Andrassy family. An ivory pen knife was her weapon when the children were young, a cane was called into service as they got older. Once, when two maids burst into tears as they held Catherine bare-bottomed across a chair, Ella had Catherine whip the two women.

Michael, on the other hand, was never beaten and only once struck someone else. Coming across a group of servants laughing at something their dog had run up a tree, Michael looked up to see a crouched, bleeding form staring down at him. Someone had skinned a cat and set a dog on it. When Michael found the man who was responsible, he whipped him until he couldn't lift his arm anymore.

But ivory pens, canes, and whips weren't the worst punishments known to aristocratic children. Far worse for Catherine was being locked in a closet with a painting of Elizabeth Bathory. Known as the "Bloody Countess," Elizabeth was famous for torturing, sexually abusing, and finally killing dozens of servant girls whom she'd recruited for their youth and beauty. Her instrument of death was a pressing machine that enabled her to bathe in her victims' blood as the life drained out of them. One of these victims visits Elizabeth in the painting, but Catherine was always told that she would be the victim's revenge.

As Catherine grew older, her punishments

23

became increasingly more humiliating. Kneeling on her hands by the dining room table while her parents and their guests ate was not uncommon. Rather than curb Catherine's behavior, however, these punishments only made her stubborn and violent. Once, when placed in a vacant area between two walls, she banged her head from one to the other until she knocked herself out. The doctor who had to be called was told the girl had fallen from a horse—an unlikely story as Catherine had won almost a dozen hunts before she was eight.

Refusing to participate in this domestic violence, Uncle Duci became a source of affection for everyone: children when they had been beaten, parents when they weren't appreciated by their spouses, even servants who had been misunderstood. Heated arguments could be taking place all around him and Uncle Duci would continue reading a book or writing a letter as if he was in his dark, heavily cushioned study on the Danube Embankment.

A connoisseur of Italian Renaissance art, Uncle Duci's extensive collection also included a self-portrait by Rembrandt as well as works by Millet, Corot, Turner, and Lawrence. The easels on which his paintings stood throughout his house—precious Oriental rugs hung on the walls—were for Catherine the counterpart of Michael's library at Foth: a place to escape and learn.

Uncle Duci also collected painters. Co-founder with Tivadar of the National Salon, he helped many struggling Impressionists before the school had become fashionable in Hungary. The most promising—many of whom Catherine remembered as having long hair, shabby clothes, and dirty fingernails—were invited to spend their summers at one of the Andrassy palaces.

Uncle Duci's favorite painter was an Austrian named Zich. A great fan of Corot, Zich covered the walls of Tisza-Dob with imitations for which Uncle Duci paid extravagant prices. When asked why he allowed himself to be taken advantage of, Uncle Duci replied, "Because young artists need confidence if they are ever to become great."

Like so many artists whose egos resent charity after it is accepted, however, Zich soon began to bite the hand that fed him. He claimed Uncle Duci had paid pennies for the works of a genius, exploited the best artist of the century for his own advancement, and owed Hungary's greatest talent vast sums of money.

Zich finally stormed out of Tisza-Dob after a frappe he had sent back to the kitchen still wasn't to his liking. He claimed the chef couldn't stand a talent greater than his own under the same roof and was trying to insult him. This was true, but it didn't lessen Uncle Duci's disappointment: Zich had taken all his paintings with him. Ella, however, was relieved. Her eldest daughter, Ilona, was becoming a little too interested in the best artist of the century.

A series of letters followed in which Uncle Duci was called names and accused of behavior that did more credit to Zich's imagination than any of his paintings. Shortly after they stopped, Ilona came across Zich begging on a streetcar. She told her uncle, who brought the prodigal imitator back to the overloaded tables, sprawling lawns, shady parks, and blank canvases of Tisza-Dob. All was forgiven because, in Uncle Duci's words, "Artists are often mad and must be permitted behavior others are not if they are ever to flourish."

In January of 1905, Catherine's father came down with pneumonia while canvassing for Uncle Duci in the general elections. The family left Budapest under doctors' orders for the castle at Terebes, but the move only made Tivadar's condition worse. At Terebes, the daughters took turns reading to their father while he lay in bed. It was the first time that any of them had been allowed to get close to him. He praised Catherine for being so grown-up and taking good care of her mother while he was ill.

In March, the doctors recommended a warmer

climate—the Istrian coast where Julius Andrassy had died was the most accessible—but Tivadar never made it past Budapest. The last time he saw Catherine, he scolded her for letting his illness distract her from her lessons.

Although her father had played a major role in her life only during his final days, Catherine suffered with the knowledge that he was gone forever and that someday she too would die. Uncle Duci, who knew Catherine's secular upbringing contained no promise of an afterlife, helped her recognize the value of life on earth. Yes, she was going to die just like her father, he told her, but that should only give her more reasons to live and to respect the lives of others.

Ella Andrassy required a different kind of comforting. Entailed property could not be passed on to women, and most of the Andrassy wealth had been established by Tivadar's father. Uncle Duci suggested she marry him. There would be some difficulties—only the Catholic Church had the authority to perform marriages, no couple could wed without having been to confession, and Uncle Duci refused to participate in anything he didn't believe in—but there wasn't anything that couldn't be overcome with time and patience.

Uncle Duci got around the confession requirement by sending the manager of his estate in his place. When the manager returned absolved of Uncle Duci's sins, Uncle Duci realized there were more advantages to being a Catholic aristocrat than not having to eat meat on Friday. Years later, when one of his cousins wanted to divorce her husband and marry his brother, Uncle Duci was able to have the marriage annulled on the grounds that it was never consumated. That the married couple had three children didn't matter. The Church got richer, the woman was married, and Uncle Duci won the respect, admiration, and gratitude of everyone concerned. Except the children. The Church declared them non-existent.

11.
WALKING THE WORLD

While Catherine divided her "seasons" among Budapest, Terebes, Dubrin, and Tisza-Dob, Michael spread is over Budapest, Paris, and London with an occasional side-trip to Ceylon or San Francisco. How far he traveled usually depended on how badly his heart had been broken.

Michael loved older women. Serially. He would meet them at balls and openings, and they would be flattered by his attention, but they balked when he insisted they leave their husbands for him. That they were all old enough to be his mother was no excuse. He knew from the eager way they snuck him into their bedrooms at any time of the day or night how they really felt. But once they had chosen to prefer their husbands, he rarely gave them a second chance.

Paris was about as far as Michael would go the first time he'd suffer any rejection. There were so many of these first times, however, that Paris became something of a second home. From his Uncle Ladislaus' mansion on the Quai d'Orsay—Ladislaus had traded a Caribbean island complete with slaves for it—Michael sought the distractions he needed to forget his pain. He found them in the Follies Bergere, the Moulin Rouge, and in Madame de Thebes' crystal ball.

"You will have a high position in life," Madame de Thebes told him. "Higher than the Prime Minister. But you will lose it and all your money as well. You will experience tremendous ups and downs. You will know what it means to be destitute, but toward the end, for you will live long, your star will rise again. After you die, it will shine brighter than ever, thanks in large part to the woman you marry: a girl much younger than you whose most striking feature will be her eyes."

Michael suppressed a laugh. You had to be a Hapsburg to hold the only position higher than Prime Minister, and he couldn't imagine a life without more money than he could ever spend. Nor what he could do to lose it. In Hungary, only the Esterhauzys and the Catholic Church owned more. And as for marrying a woman younger than himself, even the women his own age were too young.

Age made no difference to Catherine, however. She had often heard Michael's name mentioned as a possible match for one of her older sisters. The Andrassys couldn't figure him out though. His family's position and wealth made him one of Hungary's most attractive bachelors, but his notorious affairs with older women, his beard—which reminded Catherine's mother of Svengali—and his progressive ideas about such things as the secret ballot puzzled them. Uncle Duci said Michael was a phony.

Catherine got a chance to decide for herself when she was sixteen. Her mother had taken her to Parliament to hear a debate on the new armament program. No one really supported the bill, but those who were voting for it said they had no choice. Berlin had insisted that Austria-Hungary play a larger role in maintaining the stability of Central Europe. In other words, more guns had to be ordered from Germany's growing munitions industry. Opponents of the bill, led

by Michael, argued that the money could be better
spent developing Hungarian industries and that
Parliament wouldn't be in this position if the country
wasn't allied with Austria.

Stephen Tisza, the Speaker of the House, tried
to shift the focus of the debate back on arms, but his
adversaries wouldn't let him. They blamed the country's
circumstances on the alliance with Austria and called
Tisza everything from a marionette to a traitor.

Tisza responded by calling the police.

The opposition parties were removed, a vote
was taken, and the bill passed with only a few
abstentions, but Michael couldn't believe what had just
happened. Tisza had removed his opponents from
Parliament and nobody had objected.

The next day, Michael resigned in protest from
his position as President of the National Hungarian
Agricultural Society—Hungary's most powerful political
organization.

That ruined any chance he might have had with
Boji or Ilona Andrassy, but it only made Catherine more
curious. Michael was only thirty-five. Why would he
give up such an important position for a principle?

Uncle Duci said it was a publicity stunt, a way
for Michael to get his name in the papers.

But Catherine wasn't so sure. She began cutting
Michael Karolyi stories out of the newspapers and
pasting them in her diary. Together they make
interesting reading. While Catherine describes Francis
Esterhauzy catching and eating a fly for her
amusement, the papers record a brilliant ball given by
Michael in his historic palace. The ballroom is lit by
thousands of candles because Michael refuses to have
electricity installed. He thinks it's cheap and vulgar.

On another page, Catherine lists her brother-in-
law's advice on how to be a successful woman:

A. Never argue about ideas, books, or abstract
   subjects.

B. Never appear intellectually superior to a man.
C. Never make enemies of women.
D. Always stick to small talk.

Facing the quotation is a story about Michael leaping from a speeding train to rendezvous with a mysterious woman.

The diary entries and newspaper stories are best, however, when they have to do with the same event. Such as the time Stephen Tisza ordered the police to throw his adversaries out of Parliament. He later runs into Michael at the exclusive National Casino and greets him as if nothing had happened.

Michael puts his hand behind his back and keeps on walking.

"Didn't you hear me?" Tisza says. "I asked how you were."

"I heard you," Michael replies. "But after what you did today, I don't care to know you."

Tisza's seconds call on Michael that evening.

At this point in the story, Catherine writes in the margin of her diary: "Tisza is a champion fencer who practices every day."

Tisza is also practically blind. It takes him thirty-four bouts lasting more than an hour to scratch Michael's arm. Nevertheless, Catherine writes: "Michael fought like a lion. Even though he was wounded, he refused to give up. He had to be dragged off by his seconds, completely exhausted."

There was no reconciliation.

But there was a triumph. Catherine writes: "Today Michael Karolyi became my hero. Greater even than Rakoczi."

Just how great that was can be measured by an earlier diary entry. Catherine is standing on the front lawn of the Andrassy palace in Thebes. A wave of clouds blows overhead. She can see giant horses with wild manes galloping toward her. Then she notices *hajduks* with their long drawn swords. Leading them is Rakoczi.

Catherine tells the revolutionary how she's always loved him and how sorry she is that they weren't born in the same time. She would have been such a help to his cause.

Rakoczi smiles and gallops down from the sky. "You are my chosen daughter," he tells Catherine. "I have given you my spirit. You will achieve my aims because I am no longer of this world. From now on, you are me on earth."

Rakoczi then presses his cold lips to Catherine's forehead and she faints. When she comes to, she wonders how her mother would feel if she knew her daughter carried the soul of the great Rakoczi in her heart.

Shortly after Rakoczi has to make room for another hero, the newspapers report that Michael has been killed in an automobile accident. "What rotten luck!" Catherine records telling her mother. "Had he lived, he would have been my husband."

"*You!*" Ella replies. "Why on earth would he want to marry *you!*"

When not dancing with women, jumping from trains to return to their beds, or racing in his car to rendezvous with them, Michael tried to get over them. His escapes to other countries were largely unsuccessful, however, because everywhere he went was similar to his life in Hungary. The distractions just weren't distracting enough.

Except in the United States. Not even the Waldorf-Astoria and New York's select "Four Hundred" could save him from a series of experiences that often left him confused and frustrated. He couldn't tell the difference, for example, between "Mayflowers" and people who had made their fortunes in the past fifty or a hundred years. They all seemed loud and

undereducated to him. And proud of it in the sense that
the world had little to offer that couldn't also be found
in Yonkers or Schenectady or some other place he'd
never heard of. At the same time, and much to his
embarrassment, Michael was often deferred to in ways
Americans imagined royalty expected. At dinner
parties, for example, he was often seated on a throne
above all the other tables while black people danced at
his feet and white people kept asking him what it felt
like to have blue blood.

American women were especially disturbing.
They could all date without a chaperone, but Michael
could not distinguish between those he could invite out
alone and those he couldn't. In Europe, a respectable
woman received invitations through her parents; in
New York, a woman could dine alone with you in a
restaurant, ride alone with you in a cab, and then be
outraged if you misunderstood her intentions.

Nevertheless, Michael was impressed by
America's sense of democracy. His valet was less so.
When a waiter in San Francisco seated them both at
the same table, Bakos was furious. Michael told him to
relax and enjoy his dinner, but the servant could not
contain himself. He insisted on a separate table. Did
the Americans think he had no pride?

The New World may have been different, but it
didn't remove Michael from the old problems that had
brought him there. So when he returned to Budapest,
his family greeted him with a distraction that was sure
to put his mind back on track: Uncle Laszlo's Annual
Shooting Party.

If there was one thing Michael loathed more
than having to get up at the crack of dawn to go squat
in the woods until some innocent deer came along, it
was pulling a trigger. Fortunately, he had learned long
ago what to do: stretch a rug on the ground in some
isolated spot and read or sleep until it was time to go
home.

The evenings posed a different sort of problem.

Now Michael was the prey. Every night a different
peasant girl waited for him in his bed. When Uncle
Laszlo found out that Michael had asked them all to
leave, he knew his nephew was in serious trouble. Just
how serious became clear when Michael explained his
reason. Uncle Laszlo couldn't make any sense out of it.
What did loving one woman have to do with sleeping
with another? Weren't they all the same once you stood
them on their heads?

Michael didn't think so.

Uncle Laszlo called a meeting of the uncles. A
conspiracy was formed. Everywhere Michael went, a
woman who had been paid in advance would throw
herself at him.

Michael slept with more of these women than
he cared to admit—these weren't peasant girls after all;
some were even older than he
—but the mornings usually found him more depressed
than ever. He knew whom he really wanted to sleep
with. She just preferred to sleep with her husband.

Law was Michael's next escape. Moving with
Bakos into his family's empty seventy-two room palace
in Budapest, he plunged into his studies. Day and night
he kept his mind off women and his body at home. He
even managed to go a whole year without spending his
entire pocket allowance. Not that hard to do, perhaps,
when your spending money exceeds your Prime
Minister's annual salary, but no one in Michael's family
had done anything like this before. Nor could they
believe it when their "scholar" failed his bar exam. That
hadn't been done before either.

Uncle Laszlo threatened to have the examiner
sacked.

Michael stopped him. Even though aristocrats
were entitled to read the questions beforehand and
submit answers that had been prepared in advance,

Michael wanted to pass the exam on his own.

Now Uncle Laszlo knew what was wrong with his nephew: he was crazy.

Michael had a different reaction. After he had undergone the surgery to correct the defect in his palate, he practiced painful theraputic exercises several hours a day for months. Now he'd have to study with the same discipline and determination to pass the bar.

The next time he took the exam, Michael became the first aristocrat to pass without having previously submitted his answers.

His family couldn't believe it.

Catherine's education was much more traditional by today's standards but downright radical by her own: she went to a school. Her parents hoped the good sisters of Notre Dame de Sion could discipline their child better than any of her governesses, but the sisters, or rather the ways of the school, intimidated Catherine. She had never been made to memorize passages and recite them in front of a class, for example, a practice that left her shy, diffident, and a great disappointment to Sister Berthe, who was eager to show off her only titled student.

To improve her performance, Catherine was seated next to the best student in the class: a converted Jew with a first-rate memory and impeccable elocution. As the Order of Sion had been founded to convert Jews, this student was also something of a trophy.

Catherine became even more intimidated. Her marks for the first term were "Excellent" for behavior but only "She does her best" for everything else.

Catherine wasn't too keen on the other girls either. They behaved like . . . well, girls. They giggled among themselves, passed silly notes to one another, idolized Sister Berthe to the point of copying her most unattractive manners, and, when catechism class was conducted by the convent's handsome young confessor, vied with each other for his attention.

Catherine wanted to slap all their faces. Not one of them could ride a horse, sail into a gale, or drop a bird on the fly if her life depended on it. The worst part of it, however, was the nagging thought that, if these Catholics were right, Catherine's father was in hell. Not only that but Catherine was supposed to work toward getting into a place that closed its gates on everyone else in her family too. In her mind, this contradicted everything heaven was supposed to be. Heaven couldn't possibly be heaven without the people she loved, and hell couldn't possibly be hell if that's where her father was. And if that's where her father was, it was better to be in hell with him than in heaven with a bunch of giggling girls. That really was hell.

Sister Berthe told Catherine God would make her so happy in heaven she would forget all about her family.

Catherine held that not even God had that much power.

"Heretic!" Sister Berthe cried and, in the manner of Stephen Tisza, told the students to drop to their knees. "There's a soul that needs praying for."

Catherine refused to kneel.

Sister Berthe called on God for help.

Catherine rushed from the room and didn't stop running until she was in Uncle Duci's office on the Danube Embankment. She told him she was never going back. Notre Dame de Sion was a terrible place and all the Andrassys were going to hell.

Uncle Duci calmed her down. Then he explained that the Andrassys—he and Ella anyway—were going to Egypt. Catherine would not only have to return to the convent, she'd have to board the whole winter there.

The first night was a disaster. The Jewish convert lassoed her with a rosary, and the nun in charge of the dormitory called on God for a miracle. Nevertheless, Catherine quickly learned to enjoy living with thirty girls her own age. All that riding and shooting and sailing helped her become a leader in games, and she soon discovered she had a talent for mischief as well. For years she thought she'd invented the short-sheeted bed.

Catherine also discovered she was more interesting than any of the girls and most of the nuns. They could sit and listen for hours to hear her tell stories about people they had only read about in the newspapers. Everything from her Uncle Geza's introducing polo to Hungary to the food Franz-Joseph left in his moustache increased her popularity.

Her views on universal suffrage, however, were less well-received. In a class discussion on the subject, Catherine repeated the aristocrats' view that freeing the vote would eliminate the ruling classes. Hungary's greatest heroes were aristocrats. If there were no more aristocrats, Hungary would have no more heroes.

The students, coming mostly from the homes of military officers and civil servants, argued that the lower classes had never been given a chance to produce any heroes. How could Catherine say what they were capable of?

Catherine couldn't answer this one, and, as the students' appeals for fairness mounted, she found herself sounding more and more like that narrow-minded God who kept her family out of heaven. Frustrated, embarrassed, and feeling very much alone—but unable to admit she might be wrong—Catherine ended the debate by grabbing a bust of Franz-Joseph from Sister Berthe's desk and smashing it against the wall.

"Jesus wasn't an aristocrat," Sister Berthe added quietly after all the pieces had settled on the floor. "Let us pray for those who crucified Him because He was not of the same class."

Despite her being seen as the kind of person who would kill Jesus, Catherine was still the school's major attraction for snobs, and Sister Berthe made sure she stood at the head of the class the next time the students lined Andrassy Avenue to welcome Franz-Joseph to Budapest. The Emperor smiled down benevolently at the enraptured girls, and, one by one, their skirts swept the street.

All except Catherine's.

Franz-Joseph gave her his best grandfatherly smile, even a tiny wave of his hand, but she refused to curtsy.

Sister Berthe, who didn't know of the Andrassys' hatred for the Emperor, thought she'd die of embarrassment. The students felt personally insulted. Even the parents wondered what Franz-Joseph would think of Notre Dame de Sion now. In fact, everyone was so upset with Catherine, they didn't notice another rebel standing right next to her. The two became immediate friends and, united by their sense of independence, searched for other ways to distinguish themselves.

One venture was an underground newspaper with Catherine writing the fiction and Helen Kallay the editorials. Sister Berthe soon discovered them, however, confiscated their back issues, and, in accordance with a policy to discourage strong friendships among the students, began searching for a way to separate the two rebels.

She found it in a game of hide-and-seek. The next morning, Sister Berthe announced in class that she wasn't naming any names, but two girls committed sins of impurity while hiding in the lavatory during the previous day's recess. Catherine didn't know what Sister Berthe was talking about—Helen had sat on a sink while Catherine described the seekers' movements from a window sill—but there was no doubt *whom* she was talking about. While Helen buried her face in her hands, Catherine tried to defend them. "Would it have made a difference," she asked, pretending to know what she was talking about, "if one of us was a boy?"

"Ne soyez pas hypocrite," Sister Berthe hissed. But something in Catherine's innocent eyes stopped her from saying anything more. Years later, she apologized. She said she had spent too much time among the mixed classes in Beirut.

Catherine was fifteen by then, but she still had no idea what Sister Berthe was talking about. Besides, her relationship with Helen Kallay was a thing of the past. She had a new interest now: Sister Nathaniel.

Catherine did everything she could to get the nun's attention—even get in trouble. And Sister Nathaniel encouraged the girl by never punishing her. She even went so far as to dig up the love poems Catherine had written for her and buried in the meditation garden.

Knowing the Mother Superior of the Convent of the Sacre-Cour of the Order of Notre Dame de Sion was reading *her* poems with soiled fingernails drove Catherine wild with ecstacy. Everything in her life came to center on this new emotion. The outside world simply ceased to exist.

The outside world continued to make its presence felt on Michael, however. At the age of twenty-six—and a good five years before Catherine was sent to school—he ran for office as a member of the Independence Party. The Independence Party, which had little to do anymore with independence from Austria or even independent thinking for that matter, supported the government, which, to get that support, promised to reform the country's electoral abuses.

The problem was where to begin. Only six percent of the Hungarian people had the right to vote, and the electoral districts were distributed in such a way that it took ten times as many votes for the opposition parties to elect someone as it took the party in power. In districts where the voters were "reliable," only one hundred votes were needed to seat a deputy;

"unreliable" districts, on the other hand, needed ten thousand. Eighty thousand voters in "dangerous" Budapest elected nine representatives while ninety thousand "safe" Transylvanians elected seventy-four.

And just to be sure there were no slip-ups, the voting itself was rigged. Opposition candidates were often forbidden from speaking and opposition voters were kept from the polls. Government supporters, meanwhile, were transported to the polls at public cost. "Undesirable" candidates weren't listed at all the polls, the voting wasn't secret, bribes were commonplace, the police counted the votes, and some people were made so drunk they couldn't fill out their ballots. When these measure failed, the polling booths were destroyed by "irresponsible elements" that could never be found.

Michael took the government's promise of reform seriously, however, and ran under a slogan that quickly became the biggest joke of the 1901 campaign: "Clean Elections!" Less than twenty-four hours into the race, he received a call from his agent in Zilah. Money was needed for "constitutional expenses."

Michael knew what this meant and telephoned the Prime Minister. "What should I do?" the candidate asked.

"Pay!"

Michael, of course, didn't and, of course, lost the election.

This led to some serious second thoughts. The Independence Party was led by Louis Kossuth's son, Francis, and Michael's liberal uncle, Albert Apponyi, but they weren't nearly as progressive as they wanted some people to believe. While using the famous Kossuth name to rally sentimental nationalists around the idea of independence from Austria, they traded his human rights vision for government seats.

Michael confronted them on this and was told to be realistic. How much longer had he expected them to rant and rave about Hungarian independence and not get elected?

Michael couldn't say, but his image of Francis
Kossuth shrunk to that of a great man's small son.
Kossuth's Italian manners, which he picked up in exile
and which once seemed romantic and cosmopolitan,
now looked theatrical and ostentatious. And what once
seemed like self-confidence and determination now
came off as vanity and megalomania. Kossuth
confirmed these new views—at least in Michael's
mind—when he was not only delighted to receive a
medal from the Emperor who had overthrown his father
but had it added to a portrait which had been painted
before the award was given.

Uncle Albert was a different story. Michael had
been raised to look up to him as a great man, and, to
hear him speak, it would be hard to think otherwise.
Now, however, Michael realized that Uncle Albert didn't
speak so much from convictions but from what his
listeners wanted to hear. A self-proclaimed pacifist who
regularly attended international peace conferences, he
gave the Hungarian people their rallying cry when war
broke out in 1914: "At Last!"

But the Independents also had something going
for them: a great thinker by the name of Julius Justh.
Having no sense of vanity or personal ambition,he had
lost the party leadership to Kossuth and Apponyi. Still,
his ability to see through appearances ranks him
among the first to recognize the force that most
threatened Hungary: its people were deluding
themselves.

On February 13th, 1896, thousands of
Hungarians turned out to celebrate their kingdon's one-
thousandth anniversary but, as Justh delighted in
reminding them, there was no kingdom. As late as
1526, much what the people celebrated as Hungary was
made up of independent fiefdoms. The Turks had
controlled central Hungary until the end of the
seventeenth century, and most of the country's
minorities had been ruled by their co-nationals. Even
Budapest had been in the hands of Vienna for longer

than many people wanted to think about.

This myth of the sovereign state was created for Hungary in an agreement the aristocrats signed with the Hapsburgs in 1867. Unsure of his ability to control a rising tide of nationalism in Hungary and not wanting to give away a part of his empire every time he called on Russia for help, Franz-Joseph offered to "return" to the Hungarian aristocrats the freedom Louis Kossuth had won for them in the Revolution of 1848. The catch was that they had to pledge their allegiance to him.

The aristocrats thought this a small price to pay to be able to associate themselves with the Hapsburgs' long and acquiring—if not exactly glorious—history. Especially as the aristocrats' loyalty had never been to Hungary in the first place. They were too busy exploiting the poor, gaining power, and having a good time. The result was a country in which 87% of all the peasant families had fewer than ten acres of land while a handful of aristocrats grew fat on 45% of all Hungary. The Karolyi family alone accounted for 186,000 acres. And they, like the other aristocrats, chose their servants and laborers from a pool of one-and-one-half million landless peasants who had to work for the aristocrats for free in the winter if they wanted to work for them for money in the spring, summer, and fall. While Michael was campaigning for "Clean Elections," his farm workers' annual wage averaged about $16, from which he deducted $10 in lodging and "wear and tear" on the equipment they used. Most of what was left went to taxes. The ruling classes, of course, paid no taxes. Not even on their estates. And Michael's was conservatively estimated at the turn of the century to be worth 55 million pounds. Sterling.

Life in the cities wasn't much different. Workers had to labor from five in the morning to six or seven at night and were prohibited by law from quitting their jobs. One quarter of those living in Budapest spent their nights in windowless cellars where they rented beds. Outside of the cities, many workers—including some employed by the Karolyi glass factory—lived in caves. And those not lucky enough to find caves left for work every morning from holes they had dug in the ground.

By 1905, the workers had had enough. They demanded a five-cent increase in their daily wage.

The owners refused.

Some of the workers went on strike.

The government sent in the cavalry. Literally.

That ended the strike and, by 1907, anyone who refused to work for any reason could be thrown in jail for sixty days. But that wasn't good enough for the aristocrats; they wanted coolies too. Then they discovered that coolies were entitled to holidays and religious days of rest, that their workday was limited to ten hours, and that their employees were responsible for providing them with living quarters that contained kitchens.

The aristocrats weren't Hungary's only oppressors, however. The gentry, who were just below the aristocrats on the social scale but had equal voting rights, considered themselves to be Hungary's real rulers ever since they crushed a peasant uprising in the sixteenth century. That they couldn't afford to travel abroad and return only to check on things at their estates confirmed in their own minds this false sense of importance.

The truth was the gentry lost most of their political influence—and much of their earning power as well—to the aristocrats who kept close ties with Vienna. As a result, the gentry retreated to their farms and, under the banner of protecting Hungary's national character from foreign influence, did everything they could to maintain their country's feudal structure. The peasants, in turn, began leaving the country in droves. From 1871 to 1898, the number of yearly emigrants jumped from 119 to 270,000.

The absence of the aristocrats, the

retrenchment of the gentry, and the evacuation of the peasants left a vacuum of industrialists, bankers, and tradesmen that was filled to a significant degree by Jews fleeing religious persecution in Russia and Romania. Their little shops became the stepping stones that, by the turn of the century, would make Hungary a leader in banking, sugar refining, flour milling, textiles, and metallurgy. Rather than form a middle class with some power of their own, however, the Jews opted to assimilate with the gentry. Many became more Hungarian than the Hungarians.

The result of all this was not a land of freedom, harmony, and progress but of tension, scorn, and distrust. The aristocrats looked down on the gentry as provincial. The gentry saw the aristocrats as parasites and took out their frustration on the peasants. The peasants bristled under the gentry's dominance and resented the landless peasants who serviced the large estates. The landless peasants also got it from the city workers for taking their jobs and keeping wages down. But the landless peasants got to give some headaches of their own because almost everybody depended on them for cheap labor. In short, there was only one issue that all Hungarians could agree on: the minorities.

The problem here was that there were no Hungarians. The proper name for the people of Hungary is "Magyar," which comes from "Megyeri," the name of one of the ten tribes that migrated from Southern Siberia to the Danubian basin sometime in the ninth century. The early alliance of these ten tribes was called "Onogur," which means "ten arrows" in the language of the ancient Magyars. It was from this term that Latin derived and passed on to us its name for these people, calling them "Hungaricus" or "Ungherus."

Nevertheless, "Magyar" is the name of the language and the people who live in what we call "Hungary." They were joined throughout history by Slavs, Germans, Turks, Tartars, Romanians, and, yes, even Celts. Eventually, the Magyars found themselves ruling a land of many Irelands instead of just one. They couldn't give any power to these other nationalities without losing some of their own. And the more repressive they became, the more dependent they grew on Austria for protection.

The Hapsburgs capitalized on this situation by threatening the Magyars with universal suffrage and minority rights every time they balked at supporting one of Vienna's policies. As a result, Hungary developed not into a melting pot but a country where everybody stuck to their own kind and harbored fear and resentment toward everybody else. Which might not have been so bad if they were all equal, but the Magyars kept the minorities divided among themselves by favoring some nationalities over others. These favored nationalities thought themselves as far above the other minorities as the Magyars thought themselves above everybody except the Austrians who were above everybody except the Germans whom they depended on for much the same reason the Magyars depended on the Austrians and the favored nationalities depended on the Magyars: protection.

What Hungary had to do, according to Julius Justh, was break away from the Hapsburgs. Or at least show enough independence to have some say in the direction Franz-Joseph was leading them. The best way to do this was to reach an understanding with the minorities so the Hapsburgs couldn't use them as leverage every time they didn't get their own way.

The aristocrats and the gentry couldn't have agreed with Justh more, but they weren't about to follow his suggestion of giving full voting rights to all the people of Hungary. Keeping the poor and oppressed disfranchised was the only way they knew of maintaining their own supremacy. Anything less than that was unacceptable.

Michael was torn between the two. He didn't want to deprive anybody of their basic human rights, but he didn't want the Magyars overthrown by the

numerically superior minorities either. So, like a good
politician, he did nothing, and, like a good politician, he
was rewarded for it.

When Alexander Karolyi died, Michael was
asked to help get his uncle's failed cooperative back off
the ground. To this end, he traveled to England, France,
Belgium, and Italy to study the movement's more
successful operations. But little came from these travels
and, as a result, Hungary's most powerful political
society asked him to become its president. Had Michael
done anything to improve the cooperative, the National
Hungarian Agricultural Society (read: the biggest
landowners in the country) wouldn't have had any
confidence in him. Obviously, he was opposed to his
uncle's "socialist" experiment; obviously he was on the
landowners' hugely conservative side. No one ever
asked him how he felt.

On the strength of his connection with
Hungary's wealthiest landowners, Michael ran again
for Parliament on the Independent ticket. This time he
supported the landowners' stand against universal
suffrage, touted the gentry's program to "Magyarize"
the minorities, and kept any ideas about independence
from Austria to himself. He even learned to enjoy polo.

He won in a landslide.

Michael was still for "Clean Elections," however,
and made the secret ballot his first bill in Parliament.
It was defeated by over 400 votes. In fact, Michael, the
president of the most powerful voting bloc in the
country, could rally only one vote for his bill: his own.

What were the aristocrats and gentry afraid of?
They were the only ones with the right to vote. That
was less than 6% of the population. If the government
couldn't give a secret ballot to that small number, what
chance did those not represented in Parliament have?
Who but those who needed it least would ever benefit
from the government's idea of social reform?

Michael got his answer to these questions when
Stephen Tisza threw out of Parliament anyone who had

argued against his armament program. Although he wasn't one of the deputies and understood the program was being forced on Tisza by Vienna and Berlin, Michael was outraged at Parliament's passive response to the ejection. The next day, he resigned as President of the National Hungarian Agricultural Society.

A lot of people—including Uncle Duci—believed that the real reason why Michael resigned was that the landowners had voted unanimously against his bill for a secret ballot. Tisza's action gave him the opportunity to turn what he must have interpreted as a vote of no confidence into a protest.

Though his inability to get a single vote from the landowners no doubt entered into his thinking, Michael also realized that Julius Justh had been right. It wasn't enough to be autonomous or even free from Austria. Independence had to be linked with democracy if Hungary was to flourish.

The minorities had come to the same conclusion as early as 1848 when they offered to support Louis Kossuth's revolution against the Hapsburgs, but Kossuth turned them down. Later, defeated and exiled, he realized his mistake. He also came up with a solution: a Danubian confederation in which each nationality retained its own autonomy.

Unfortunately no Magyar would go for it. As long as Kossuth called for freedom from Austria, he was a hero; once he got into his United States of Hungary theme, he was considered out of touch. The Magyars simply refused to recognize the aliens within their borders as equals. And yet, they could never free themselves from Austrian control without the minorities' cooperation, a situation that eventually proved disastrous.

The first warning of what was to come appeared in 1912 when Greece, Bulgaria, and Serbia rebelled against their Turkish rulers. Hungary, which had fought for its own freedom against the Moslems, sympathized with the rebels, but Austria followed

Germany's lead and backed Turkey. This time the issue was not so much Moslem versus Christian as feudalism versus democracy. If Greece, Bulgaria, and Serbia became democratic, it would only be a matter of time before Austria-Hungary also fell. Franz-Joseph called it "The Domino Theory."

Michael's small group within the Independence Party was the government's only opposition. Led by Justh, they argued that the best way to keep Hungary out of a Balkan war was to take an independent line. The more closely Austria-Hungary allied itself with Germany, the more aggresssive Germany would become. And the more aggressive Germany became, the more Hunagary had to lose. Being closest to the conflict, Hungarians would be the first sent into battle. If, on the other hand, Hungary could reach an agreement with the minorities and become democratic, Parliament could exert a stronger influence on Austria's role in the alliance with Germany.

Hungary's first step toward self-preservation, then, had to be universal suffrage, a step made virtually impossible by the minorities holding only eight of four hundred and fourteen seats in Parliament and Stephen Tisza's insistence that ten million non-Magyars be thoroughly Magyarized before any talk about free elections could begin.

Turkey eventually lost to the revolutionaries—a significant setback to Germany—and, when Julius Justh retired because of poor health, his popular protege was elected President of the Independence Party. This was not the blow to party leadership that Michael's supporters imagined, however. The reality was that Michael was only window dressing. He could espouse all of the party's traditional rhetoric about independence from Austria but was prevented from taking any action by a committee whose members represented as many shades of opinion as there was members of the committee. Because Francis Kossuth and Albert Appony still had the most followers, however, they still had the most influence.

The committee also decided not to give their populist leader any responsibility on the grounds that he was only thirty-six and still considered something of a dilettante—an impression Michael did little to correct. Once, while traveling with the committee on the Vienna Express, Michael received word that the conference they planned to attend had been cancelled. Rather than ride all the way to Vienna just to turn around and ride back, he waited until the train slowed for a turn, jumped off, and hurried to surprise the woman he'd spent the night with. Not that this was a bad thing in and of itself. Others on the train might have done the same. The problem was that Michael hadn't told anyone he was leaving. When his colleagues couldn't find him, they pulled the alarm. Over the breakfast the next morning, Michael and his lover read in the newspaper that he had fallen off a train and been killed.

Catherine dutifully recorded the announcement of Michael's death. It was the first of many. Too many. But the pages of her diary also reveal a rival. Out of the convent at sixteen, she searched for someone to replace Sister Nathaniel and found the object of her desire in a man of just about the same age as the Mother Superior: Uncle Duci.

She had always been a little in love with him, but her imagination and experiences in the convent combined to create a passion which soon bordered on obsession. That Uncle Duci didn't return her love, that he didn't even know about it, was of no consequence. At least at first. What was more important was that she had someone to love, an object to provide her with the emotional outlet that she needed.

Catherine's initial reaction to her newly discovered feelings was to deny their existence. As her love for her stepfather increased, however, they began to possess her. She started competing with her mother for his attention and, as might be expected, she lost more often than she won. Still, her instincts told her that Uncle Duci was no longer totally indifferent to her. Unlike her father, he was accessible, and, like Sister Nathaniel, he encouraged her by making sure she was always the closest person to him: at the table, in the carriage, on the hunt, whatever. He also spoiled her with gifts—clothes, jewelry, perfume—and he did something he never did for anyone else: he taught her to play chess.

As Catherine became closer to Uncle Duci, her demonstrations for affection became bolder. Now it was not good enough to be next to Uncle Duci in the salon, she had to sit on his lap. Uncle Duci didn't mind, but Ella did. How could he discuss the possible consequences of Ilona's marrying Winston Churchill—he had taken her rowing at Blenheim—with a sixteen-year-old in his lap?

It wasn't long before fierce quarrels, unpredictable scenes, even physical violence became commonplace. And yet it was everything outside of this context that seemed senseless and boring. Because happiness was unattainable within this context, however, Catherine's everyday life was miserable and hopeless. Her mother insisted on treating her like a child—especially when Uncle Duci was around—and seemed to take every opportunity to run her down. If it wasn't her hair or her teeth, it was the bad manners or stupid ideas she'd picked up in the convent. And because Ella was the kind of person who let herself be carried way by her own words, she often would finish up with an exaggerated litany of her daughter's shortcomings. Trapped in this web of sterility and wretchedness, Catherine eventually took her mother's criticism to heart.   "You seem," Ella told Catherine after one argument, "to be living in another world."

Not a particularly withering statement, but Catherine dwelled on it. Perhaps her mother was right.

But whatever world that was, it was still too close to the one her parents inhabited. To cut herself completely off from them seemed to be the only way of finding relief. For them as well as her.

Ella kept a small revolver in her nightstand. Remembering this, Catherine ran up the winding stairs of the Buda palace. Her mood shifted from depression to a mixture of curiosity and detachment with each step. She'd soon know if there was a heaven and a hell.

Quietly she opened the drawer and removed the gun. Its pearl handle and engravings matched Ella's opera glasses.

Catherine took the gun into her mother's bathroom and shut the door. She lifted the old-fashioned catch, aimed the barrel at her heart, and pulled the trigger.

Silence.

A bullet was missing.

Catherine rearranged the bullets in the chamber, took aim, and fired. A sharp bang, a blow to the chest, and . . .

Nothing more.

Catherine walked to a mirror on the other side of the room. She wanted to see as well as feel what it was like to die.

Only there wasn't any pain.

Catherine grabbed her heart and staggered like the characters she had seen in movies.

Still nothing.

Bored with waiting to die, she went downstairs.

"My God!" Ella cried. "What have you done!"

Uncle Duci, who had heard Ella's scream, arrived just in time to catch Catherine from hitting the floor. When she came to, he was carrying her up the stairs to her room. She was glad she hadn't died alone. So glad, in fact, that she didn't associate her parents' pale faces with anything she'd done.

Ella told the doctor that Catherine had been playing with the gun when it went off accidentally. But the doctor knew better. "She made no mistake where her heart lay," he told Uncle Duci. "Fortunately, the bullet only ran along her ribs and lodged under the skin. A simple operation will extract it."

The operation had to be performed in a hospital, however, and that meant the press would ask all kinds of embarrassing questions. Ella feared that no man would marry her daughter now. They'd suspect that she had lost her innocence.

When the truth did come out, no one believed it. Everyone was certain that this was another case of a young girl being forced to marry a man she didn't love. Hundreds of letters poured in from all over the country offering Catherine advice and encouragement. The best suggestion came from her brother-in-law, Gyuri Pallavicini: "By all means kill yourself, but not with a pistol. Upper-class people don't shoot themselves. It just isn't done. If you want to die, do it right: rent a plane and jump out of it over Tisza-Dob. Your way was decidedly middle-class."

When Catherine was released from the hospital, her parents sent her to the Pallavicini farm where her sister Boji knew just the cure for suicidal tendencies: pasta. Pasta was the one thing her happy husband, his happy family, and all the happy Italians she knew had in common. Without it, they were miserable.

Every morning Boji sat Catherine at an outdoor table where she ate a huge bowl of spaghetti and watched happy farm animals copulating in the sun. Spaghetti was also served with tea and in the evening before going to bed. By the time of her "coming out" ball, Catherine had gotten over Uncle Duci and blossomed into a beautiful, if slightly overweight, young woman.

The Hungarian words for "coming out" mean "walking the world" and, in Catherine's time, the path was very straight and very narrow. An awesome gauntlet of mothers lined the walls of every ballroom. Nothing escaped their collective eye. To dance the cotillion twice during the season with the same partner was considered the prelude to an engagement. Otherwise, the girl had been "compromised," and the man had not "behaved like a gentleman." To talk while dancing was considered "rude," and any girl who sat at a table where a man was present had "a bad reputation."

During the cotillion, the men were expected to present expensive bouquets to the young women they danced with—Catherine never went home without a car full—as well as make sure that each girl had her share of dances. Invitations were sent out weeks in advance and many hours were devoted to whom to accept, whom to reject, and whom to keep in suspense. The diplomacy needed to replace an accepted partner with a more desirable prospect made Stephen Tisza look like an amateur.

And you couldn't dance with anyone you liked even if you did receive an invitation. There was class to consider, and no class was as exclusive as Catherine's. Male aristocrats could dance with gentry women, but gentry men couldn't dance with aristocrat women, whom the aristocrats treated like little sisters and made sure no one from the "second society" became "familiar." To make the gentry men appear less attractive than they may already have been, aristocrat men told jokes about them to the aristocrat women. Such as the time a lady offered the corner of her handkerchief to a gentry man so she wouldn't have to suffer his kissing her gloved hand. The gentry man was so unsophisticated, he took the handkerchief, blew his nose into it, and gratefully returned it.

Every woman—gentry and aristocrat—had three seasons to attract a suitor or be banished forever to Spinsterville. Catherine, of course, had more suitors than she knew what to do with, but none of them interested her. She was used to conversing with people like Sister Nathaniel and Uncle Duci. The men she met at the balls, though considerably older than she, were still too young. Conventional, non-thinking clones of one another, they had nothing to offer her but uneventful security.

Michael Karolyi, whose name begins appearing regularly again in Catherine's diary, was different. He may have said disagreeable things in Parliament from time to time, but he seemed sincere about them. At least to Catherine. If only his interest in politics allowed him some time on the dance floor!

Uncle Duci claimed all Michael's talk about democracy was a way to get his name in the papers, but Catherine couldn't help wondering if Michael might be right. What if the world really did change and her life of hunts and balls came to an end? With no marketable skills, she'd be what Michael called "a living anachronism."

Catherine decided to see how the other 94% lived. She would become a bookkeeper. That way she'd have a skill if she needed it. Only no such thing had ever been done. Aristocrats didn't earn their money; they inherited it!

Nevertheless, Catherine's parents didn't object. Who could say how she would react if they did? If she was lucky—if they all were lucky—maybe someone would come along and marry her. In the meantime, bookkeeping and pasta would keep her out of trouble.

But not out of the newspapers. Catherine's passing the first of three qualifying exams made national headlines. Elkan Brothers, a fancy fur shop on Andrassy Avenue, printed an offer to hire her immediately—a proposal Catherine's parents thought impertinent.

The press was taken by the idea, however, and besieged Catherine wherever she went. They wanted to know her reason for breaking with tradition. She told them the truth: "I want to be independent."

"I want to be independent" became the punch

line for dozens of anti-aristocratic jokes all over the country, and the press made its usual response to a woman's unconventional behavior: an affair of the heart. But there was one person in Hungary who took Catherine's statement seriously. Could he have discovered a kindred spirit?

111.
KINDRED SPIRITS

If Michael ever needed a friend, it was in the summer of 1913. Here he was President of the Independence Party and the only independent person in it. Albert Apponyi and Francis Kossuth, the party's real leaders, wanted to form a coalition with the other party opposed to Austria's close ties with Berlin. Michael didn't object to forming a coalition—the Independents needed all the help they could get—but their would-be ally, the Constitutional Party, stood for everything the Independents were against.

The "Forty-Eighters," as the Independents were called, favored the complete separation from Austria that Louis Kossuth had fought for in 1848. The "Sixty-Seveners," on the other hand, supported the Compromise of 1867 that gave Hungary home rule but retained its allegiance to Austria. The Forty-Eighters believed the compromise limited the Hungarians' influence on foreign policy and made them subject to Vienna's will; the Constitutional Party argued that a small country in the midst of giants was bound to be crushed or absorbed unless one of the giants protected it. Austria protected Hungary not only from Turkey and possibly Russia but from its growing minority population as well.

Michael argued that Austrian "protection" was only another word for "exploitation" and "control." To form a coalition with the party responsible for Hungary's condition would only weaken the Independents' credibility. Who would believe they were sincere about minority rights after they allied themselves with the minorities' strongest opponent?

Uncle Albert told Michael to forget about minority rights. As long as the Independence Party lacked power, minority rights weren't "negotiable." Nor were any of the party's other programs. If the Independents wanted to oppose the government and influence its policies, they needed a share of the power base. To get that share, Michael was going to have to reach an agreement with the President of the Constitutional Party: Julius Andrassy, Jr.

Not much was expected from the talks. The Andrassys and the Karolyis weren't exactly enemies, but they weren't anywhere close to being friends either. The Andrassys were anti-clerical and nationalist; the Karolyis were Catholic and cosmopolitan. Julius Andrassy, Sr., who had co-authored the Compromise of 1867, had been a liberal, but the party that now supported the treaty was conservative. Michael, on the other hand, was a radical whose roots were so reactionary his family was still known as "The Guides of the Russians." Nevertheless, Michael had more than political reasons to hope for an agreement—something the Andrassys were quick to notice.

While Michael and Uncle Duci sipped iced coffee, ate apricots, and talked on a balcony overlooking one of the gardens at Tisza-Dob, Catherine studied bookkeeping in a strategically placed hammock below. Sometimes Michael would be so distracted, he'd have to excuse himself to join Catherine under the acacia trees or invite her for a row on the river.

Uncle Duci didn't mind. He knew when he had an advantage. And who could say? Perhaps families as well as parties might someday be united.

Catherine gave the better chance to the parties. Here at last was someone she could admire and respect who wasn't a nun or a parent, but she disagreed with practically every one of Michael's political views. First, he wanted to abolish her grandfather's historic compromise. Then he wanted to overthrow the ruling classes—her heroic classes—by giving ignorant people the right to vote. And then, just to make sure the best in Hungary was history, he wanted the aristocrats to give 75% of their land to the people who worked it. Michael wasn't a politician; he was a masochist.

Uncle Duci told Catherine not to worry. Michael couldn't possibly be sincere about his democratic views. He was the kind who wielded power, not gave it to others to wield for him.

Uncle Duci's colleagues couldn't have agreed more. They knew Michael had only joined the Independence Party because it was the smallest and the weakest and he could control it faster and easier than any of the other parties. He didn't give a fig for its philosophy. Talented and ambitious to the point of being dangerous, Michael would do anything—even form a coalition with his enemy—to achieve his own aims.

Many Independents felt the same way. Michael's frequent visits to Tisza-Dob and the gossip linking him with Catherine made them wonder if he wasn't using the party to his own advantage. The Karolyis, after all, had a three-hundred-year history of betrayals.

Both sides decided to undermine him.

The Independents struck first. They leaked reports to the press that Michael was being unfaithful to the woman he was having an affair with: the wife of a leading Constitutionalist. Then they insisted he stop seeing Catherine unless he intended to marry her.

Knowing that marriage to an Andrassy would create a conflict of interest and raise calls for his resignation, Michael claimed he had no intention of marrying anybody.

The Constitutionalists then demanded that he stop seeing Catherine under false pretenses. She was only a child and already deeply involved. Had he no conscience?

Catherine read Michael's supposed reply in a newspaper: "Affairs with flappers should not be taken seriously."

Uncle Duci immediately suspended the negotiations. What kind of person, he asked himself, would use an innocent girl to further his own political ends?

Michael responded to this crisis the same way he responded to all his other failed affairs: he packed his suitcase. This time he escaped to Tunisia. Pictures of him with dancing girls and heavily tasseled camels were sent to all the Hungarian papers. Independents and Constitutionalists alike shook their heads in disapproval.

Only Catherine remained loyal. She had clipped enough newspaper stories to know Michael's politics and his ways with women were wrong, but love, rather than make her blind, had opened her eyes to qualities that others didn't see. Here was a man who, like herself, believed that facts were often the enemy of truth. When Ilona's husband, Paul Esterhauzy, called Catherine's studying bookkeeping "idiotic," Michael defended her. "The effort to acquire knowledge can be called many things," he said, "but 'idiotic' is not one of them." Moreover, Michael showed an interest in what interested Catherine. And he could do it without being condescending or superior—a feat Catherine interpreted as a sign of his maturity.

Nevertheless, all those pictures of Michael running around the desert with underdressed women puzzled her and, when she tried to find excuses for him, her parents accused her of having no pride. Unable to run away to Tunisia or anywhere else, she locked herself in her room and wrote countless love letters

she'd never have the courage to send. In them she
argues that she and Michael understand each other
despite their differences of opinion. They are the two
halves of Rakoczi's great soul and destined to complete
his work. She is also willing to live with him without
being married if he fears a marriage would compromise
his relationship with his lover. Catherine even goes so
far as to say she loves him all the more for being so
considerate to the wife of a political opponent.

Catherine doesn't go so far as to believe she can
win Michael's love without a scheme, however. When
the Independent returned from Tunisia, Catherine
arranged to run into him at the fancy and exclusive
Park Club. Once he felt relaxed, she asked her prepared
question: "Will you give me some advice, Count
Karolyi?" Aristocrats addressed each other formally
until they were married. "I have a friend who loves a
married man but doesn't know if he loves her. Another
man loves my friend and wants to marry her. Would it
be wrong for my friend to marry the man who loves her
even though she loves someone else?"

Michael was silent. It didn't take a genius to
figure out what Catherine was doing, but this was just
the kind of drama he had hoped to avoid by going to
Tunisia. "If your friend really loves one man," he told
Catherine, "she could not possibly marry another."

"But if her love is hopeless, doesn't she have to
get rid of the infatuation?"

Another silence. This was real teenage stuff,
but how was he going to get out of it?

Catherine watched some couples wrestle with
the newly introduced one-step.

"It's hell when a married man falls in love with
a girl," Michael told her.

Catherine's heart leapt. Michael had
understood. He was the married man; she was the girl.

But then he said, "Tell your friend to marry the
man who loves her. The married one will only make her
miserable."

Now it was Catherine's turn to squirm.
"You said the man your friend loves is already
married, didn't you?" Michael asked.
What could she say? "Thank you, Count
Karolyi. I think you are right. My friend will do as you
say. Now, will you dance with me?"
"I don't want to dance. The one-step isn't good
for us. Nothing is good for us anymore."
Catherine walked toward the dance floor.
Three men approached her at the same time.
She chose the one she knew best. "Pull yourself
together," he told her. "Everyone has been watching
you."
Michael stood near the edge of the dance floor.
His arms folded, his eyes following Catherine wherever
she went, he wasn't very happy. *His* scheme was
backfiring all over the Park Club.
They didn't speak for days. When they did
happen to run into each other, Michael was always in
the company of Catherine's cousin Ilma. Catherine
finally confronted her rival in a bathroom. She
demanded an explanation.
Ilma smiled. "The only thing we talk about is
you. Michael loves you and wants to marry you, but he's
in a very difficult dilemma. Can't you give him some
time to arrange his private life?"
Catherine wanted to know more about Michael's
private life.
What she got was: "Michael is the best of men.
Don't disappoint him. There's more to living up to such
a man than having your own way."
Later that night, a note was placed on
Catherine's table. "Meet me on the terrace off the main
staircase. Go through the pantry. It's safer."
Catherine had never been in a pantry, but she
wasn't going to let that stand in her way. When she
reached the top of the stairs, a Byronic figure stepped
into the stream of light coming from the banquet hall.
They fell into each other's arms. It was the first time

Catherine had ever kissed a man. "I love you frightfully," she said. "I will go off with you even if you can't marry me."

Michael laughed. "Of course we will marry. But we'll have to be patient. We cannot announce our engagement for two or three months. You have to trust me. It's a question of life or death."

"For God's sake! Catherine, are you mad!"

It was her sister, Ilona.

Michael slipped back into the shadows of the terrace.

"Uncle Duci is looking all over for you," Ilona told Catherine. He says he'll challenge Michael to a duel if he finds you with him. I came to warn you. The mothers saw your pink shoes going up the pantry stairs."

Catherine didn't care what they saw. Her great moment with Michael had been spoiled. Now he would have to marry her before he was ready. How often had she heard her mother and aunts say, "The poor man was caught; he had no choice."

An army of relatives waited at the foot of the main staircase. Some looked inquisitive or envious, but most were shocked and disapproving. Catherine felt like the kind of girl who kissed a boy behind a bush and then returned to the picnic disheveled. "Are you out of you mind!" Uncle Duci hissed. "Go brush your hair."

"It's a public scandal," Ella announced when the window separating them from their chauffeur had been rolled up. "I've never been so embarrassed in my life."

"Are you at least engaged?" Uncle Duci asked.

"No."

Catherine was exiled to her room. For days, she wondered if the phone would ever stop ringing. Aunt Clara told Ella she knew a friend of Michael's who had told her just how wicked he was. He not only saw several women at one time, he lied to every one of them. Constantly. Aunt Zenke said Catherine was the one who couldn't be trusted. If what she was doing with

Michael wasn't bad, why did it have to be done in the dark?

The uncles reached their own conclusion: the scandal had been planned by the woman Michael was having an affair with. Jealous of Catherine, she had masterminded the whole thing to compromise an innocent girl's reputation and score a political victory for the Constitutionalists.

The brothers-in-law didn't care who thought it up. The only thing worse than a girl who let herself be kissed was a man who kissed a girl who let herself be kissed.

Uncle Duci sharpened his sword.

But Ella thought Michael should be given a chance to propose marriage. To rush out and kill him would only confirm Catherine's dishonor. No one would marry her then.

Michael pleaded bankruptcy. He told the Andrassy family court that he was being forced to sell all his unentailed property. A man of his age, with his past, and now with no money was hardly the ideal husband for a young innocent girl.

The Andrassys thought so too, but they demanded satisfaction. Catherine's whole future was at stake.

Michael said he was leaving for America. If Catherine felt the same way about him when he returned, he would announce their engagement. If she changed her mind, he would still marry Catherine and then have the marriage annulled on the grounds that it was never consumated. That would not only restore Catherine's honor but make her eligible to marry someone else.

Uncle Duci told Catherine the good news. He said he didn't care if Michael didn't have any money. He had more than enough for everybody. The important thing was that his favorite niece and stepdaughter be happy.

Ella wanted Catherine to be happy too, but not

at the expense of the family's honor. "You'll marry Michael when he returns," she told her daughter. "And you'll stay married to him no matter what."

Michael's trip to America was duly reported in all the Hungarian newspapers, only this time the parties and the pretty women were a front. In fact, a lot of what Michael did these days was a front. Some of the things he did were outright lies. He wasn't really broke, for example. His entailed property—which he was forbidden by God and law to sell—still ranked him among Hungary's wealthiest landowners. Those who knew this figured Michael just wanted a last fling before settling down. A sort of extended bachelor's party.

And that's exactly what Michael wanted people to think. The real purpose of the trip was to strengthen his position in the Independence Party by securing money and alliances abroad. Basically, his thinking was this: although the name of Louis Kossuth and the idea of Hungarian independence could still bring fervent nationalists to their feet, the Independents were the weakest party in the country. Uncle Albert was right about that. But to form a coalition with the Constitutionalists only weakened them further. It undermined their credibility and still fell short of the numbers they needed to influence government policy.

Marrying Catherine would have the same effect. It created a conflict of interest that Michael didn't have the support to withstand. His political career would end the minute he said, "I do."

Unwilling to consider the prospects of an early retirement, Michael decided to look abroad for the support he lacked at home. If he could form an alliance with the countries Austria was most likely to come into conflict with, he would have a stronger lever in Parliament than any coalition with the Constitutionalists could provide.

Russia was the most likely candidate. It was the leading Slavic state and would have attacked German-supported Turkey if France hadn't influenced the Czar to show some restraint. But to approach the Czar from the position of Hungary's weakest leader didn't make much sense. Nor would it do much good to contact any of the parties in the Duma. The weather had more effect on Nicholas II than all of them put together.

The best way to reach St. Petersburg, then, was through Paris. The French had prevented a world war from breaking out in the Balkans, and many of Hungary's struggles for independence coincided with wars between the Bourbons and the Hapsburgs. Also, Michael felt more comfortable with the French. He spoke the language, knew the country's history and institutions, and was related by marriage to the Pommerys, the famous champagne manufacturers.

Michael planned to convince the French that many Hungarians opposed the alliance between Vienna and Berlin. He told President Poincare that if he could return to Hungary with French and Russian support and one hundred million francs to invest in domestic business and industry, he could free his country from its economic dependence on Austria, bring about a reconciliation with the minorities, weaken the alliance with Germany, and avert a world war.

This seemed like an awful lot for one hundred million francs, but Poincare encouraged Michael to meet with representatives from the heavy industries and consult with George Clemenceau.

Clemenceau told Michael that he was too late. The time for him to have acted was when Austria-Hungary had formed the alliance with Germany.

Michael pointed out that he was only four years old at the time, but Clemenceau wasn't listening. He was talking. "The Hapsburgs thought by signing a defense pact with Germany that Germany would protect them from their own minorities. Germany fanned this fear by exaggerating the democratic

revolutions against Turkey. If Turkey fell, Hungary
would be next and Austria would follow. What Franz-
Joseph didn't realize was that Hungary wasn't a buffer
zone against democracy. Hungary is Germany's
stepping stone to the Balkans."

"All the more reason for France and Russia to
act now," Michael said. "A strong Hungary will weaken
Austria's alliance with Berlin. War can be avoided by
balancing the power."

"War is inevitable," Clemencau told Michael.
"By supporting Turkey, Berlin has turned most of your
neighbors into your enemies. These countries have
nationals living within your borders who will rise
against your system of oppression. And Austria won't
be able to help you because Franz-Joseph will be too
busy fighting the enemies Berlin has made for him in
the West. It's all just a matter of time."

Michael didn't doubt a word of this, but he had
to do what he could to prevent his country's downfall:
he left immediately for the United States.

"The only way to influence Hungarian politics,"
Michael told his colleagues before they boarded at
Cherbourg, "is to break out of our provincialism and
become a force to be reckoned with. If we can't find the
support we need in our own country, we're going to have
to get what we can from Hungarians living abroad.
There are more than a half million in the United
States. Most of them fled intolerable conditions at
home. Now they can do something about it: they can
influence American opinion against the government
which perpetuates those conditions. Our job in America
will be to organize and channel that influence."

"Our job," as Michael's colleagues saw it, was to
interest American investors in Hungarian industry.
When word reached Budapest that they were forming
political blocs to undermine the government, they'd all
be declared outlaws.

A telegram interrupted their debate: "SERBS MURDER FERDINAND. RETURN IMMEDIATELY. UNCLE ALBERT."

Catherine, who was the only person in Hungary to know of Michael's plans to win foreign support for his domestic programs, decided to follow his example: she would form an alliance with the people her family was most likely to come into conflict with: the Karolyis. Her cousin Gyula, who had married Michael's half sister, warned Catherine of the malevolent scrutiny she would face and the difficulty of being judged worthy of Michael. But this was no news. The Karolyis' skeptical attitude toward strangers, their fastidious and distant manners, their rigid Catholicism, and their opinion that no one was good enough for them were all well known. What intimidated Catherine was their highbrow conversation about the arts and letters of eighteenth-century France. They were all experts on the period and looked down on anyone who wasn't.

Catherine was fluent in French, but what she knew about the Bourbons couldn't fill the bottom of a teacup. Gyula pleaded with her to spare him the humiliation of having a donkey for a cousin.

Catherine didn't know what to do. She wanted the Karolyis to like her and show their support for her when Michael returned, but she felt studying to confirm their enthusiasm for eighteenth-century France was hypocritical and self-abasing. After all, she was an Andrassy. Her ancestors had ridden with Arpad into the Danubian Basin, her grandfather had been a Prime Minister, her sister had married an Esterhauzy, her cousin was a Cartier, her aunt . . .

"Yes, Catherine," Gyula explained, "but in the Karolyis' minds, Arpad was a barbarian who tenderized his meat by carrying it under his saddle, your grandfather was responsible for selling Hungary's independence to Austria, the Esterhauzys weren't sophisticated enough to rescue Mozart, and Cartier has no taste. Stick to Aubosson carpets and Sevres vases; you'll be better off."

Uncle Duci proposed an idea that would help Catherine win over the Karolyis without losing her self-respect. Gyula would teach her what she needed to know about Louis Quinze and Louis Seize paintings and furnishings, a tutor would fill her in on the Karolyi family history, and Uncle Duci would show her how the Andrassys weren't as far apart from the Karolyis as the Constitutionalists were from the Independents.

Catherine already knew how the major part of the Karolyi estate had been awarded to Alexander Karolyi for betraying Rakoczi. She also knew about the Karolyis leading the Russians through the Carpathian passes against Louis Kossuth. These were major events in Hungarian history. Michael had told her about his Grandmother Caroline smuggling a dagger into Louis Batthyani's prison cell, Batthyani's public suicide, and Michael having his uncle's final words tattooed on his forearm. What Catherine didn't know was that *Ora et Semper* was also the family motto. Nor had Michael ever mentioned that his hated father played a small part in a revolution his grandfather Edward had planned in 1866.

Julius Karolyi had been given the task of bringing over from Italy 100,000 golden crowns to the Revolutionary Committee in Budapest. Unfortunately for Julius, the plot was discovered and Julius was arrested as stepped across the border. But Julius was no fool. He had a very clear idea of the privileges afforded rank in his day and asked if he could have something to eat before being interrogated. At a nearby restaurant, he took the opportunity of his guard's going to the bathroom to thrust the crowns into the lap of a man sitting at the next table. "Keep this safe for an hour and you will be well rewarded," Julius told the man. The stranger filled his pockets without a word, the police found nothing on Julius, and the young revolutionary returned to the restaurant to discover his depository was none other than Baron Nathaniel Rothschild.

Catherine thought this a most amusing story, but her tutor told her never to mention it in the Karolyi house. It was probably a good idea to stay away from Caroline Zichy and Louis Batthyani too. The family, with the obvious exception fo Michael, was extremely conservative. They upheld tradition and contributed more to the Catholic Church than anyone else in Hungary. If Catherine wanted to endear herself, the best approach was through her position as Uncle Duci's stepdaughter. The Karolyis may never have forgiven Julius Andrassy, Sr. for uniting Hungary with Austria, but they saw eye-to-eye with his son: Michael and his Independents were little more than a bunch of upstarts with no sense of history. That's what made them so dangerous. All their nonsense about minority rights and universal suffrage only gave hope to people where there wasn't any. Nothing good could come of it.

Catherine's tutor advised her to play the role of someone who could influence Michael in ways his family would approve. "You've been educated in a convent; you're the only Catholic in an anti-clerical family," he told her. "Espouse your stepfather's political views, which are your own as well, and throw in some of the things you learned from Sister Berthe. You'll win all the support you need to marry Michael."

Aunt Geraldine, Michael's stepmother, received Catherine in a house that looked like it had been imported from Faubourg St. Germain. Her first words to her future daughter-in-law were in a kind of broken Hungarian.

This was not a good beginning. In fact, it was an insult. It meant Geraldine was acting as if Catherine might not speak one of the aristocratic languages.

Undaunted, Catherine answered in French. She

also spoke knowingly about the soft *Bergeres, petit point* chairs, and *Guerdions* she passed on her way to the parlor.

Aunt Geraldine didn't have a chance.

And neither did Catherine. But it wasn't the furniture that won her over; it was Aunt Geraldine's obvious and genuine love for Michael. She said she hated giving him and his sister away right after her marriage to Julius Karolyi, but she had little choice. Grandmother Clarisse, who bitterly resented her son-in-law's remarrying, had insisted on it. Geraldine gave up the children in the hope that she'd someday be able to make peace with the grandmother. It never happened. The old woman wouldn't even let Michael and Elizabeth see their half-brother and two half-sisters.

Because he was a man, Michael was able to free himself from his grandmother's dominance without having to rebel. Elizabeth, however, lived in almost complete subordination until she was over thirty. Distinguished, elegant, and wealthy—she held the unentailed property of the Karolyi estate—she had dozens of suitors.

Grandma rejected all of them "An independent woman can pick and chose," she told Elizabeth. But Elizabeth, who was gentle and passive by nature as well as conditioning, let her grandmother do the choosing. If it wasn't the lack of pure Magyar blood or the size of their annual contribution to the Church, it was a look in the eye or a wart on the nose. Something was always wrong. "Imagine having to sit at breakfast with that face staring at you every morning," Grandma Clarisse said of more than one unhappy suitor. "It would ruin your appetite."

Then came Sigfried Pappenheim. A Protestant. Grandma wouldn't let him through the front door. He converted.

In the parlor, Sigfried's nationality became the issue.

Sigfried said he'd change his name.

"Don't be a fool," Clarisse told him. "Once a Pappenheim, always a Pappenheim."

But Sigfried wouldn't give up. Several times a year, he argued for Elizabeth's hand. "What's in a name?" he once asked Clarisse.

"Everything."

Elizabeth, meanwhile, was approaching forty. Something had to be done. Michael told Clarisse that he'd never speak to her again if she didn't consent to Elizabeth's marriage. The old woman, who obsessed about Michael even more than she fretted about Elizabeth, finally gave in.

Suzanne and Juliette, Michael's half-sisters, also married at late ages, but Aunt Geraldine blamed this on Clarisse too. She was the one responsible for the Karolyis' reputation that no family was good enough. Two whole countries knew what she put poor Pappenheim through.

For Michael's half-brother Joseph, no other family *was* good enough. He married his first cousin, Daisy Wenckheim.

Aunt Geraldine may not have been as hard on suitors as critics of the Karolyi family have claimed, but she could be a demon to those who disagreed with her on other issues. She and her circle of friends considered themselves the *gens pensants* of Budapest. A surprising number of others did too. Here were the trend-setters' major themes:

Most bad things in the world were the fault of either the Freemasons or the Jews.

All bankers and many ministers were Jewish agents.

The "Elders of Zion" had already penetrated the Royal Court in Vienna. If the aristocrats let down their guard, Hungary would be next.

Most "right thinkers" of this kind are smug, severe, and generally unhappy, but Catherine found none of these traits in her future mother-in-law. Perhaps because she so firmly believed she was right, Aunt Geraldine could maintain her opinions and still be kind and generous. Michael's beliefs, for example, conflicted with everything she held most dear, but she always defended him against the family's charges of being difficult, tyrannical, and capricious.

"Difficult," "tyrannical," and "capricious" were only three of the eptithets Michael's colleagues hurled at him. They had wanted to return to Hungary from Cherbourg, but Michael had convinced them to continue on to the United States. He claimed they could do more there to prevent war.

Now they were in a God-forsaken place called Cleveland, and they realized, once again, that Michael had only been thinking about himself. His affair with the Andrassy girl and his failure to reach an agreement with the Constitutionalists had taught him nothing. Ever since they'd arrived in America, he had been telling people how at odds he was with the Independence Party and how Hungary's expatriates should support his policies if they wanted peace and prosperity in Europe.

This wasn't a lecture tour; it was a campaign.

Then the news arrived that Austria blamed Serbia for Archduke Ferdinand's death. An ultimatum had been sent that Serbia could not possibly sign.

Michael condemned the ultimatum before a large group of Hungarian immigrants without telling anyone in his party that he even objected to it.

His colleagues were furious. When word got back to Budapest, the whole Independence Party would be arrested for treason. Michael had left them no choice but to return to Hungary immediately.

Michael agreed to return but only because he

hadn't rallied the support he had hoped for in the United States. In fact, the tour had been something of a shock. It hadn't dawned on him that most of the Hungarians he'd meet would think of themselves as Americans. Or that they might not want to return to Hungary. Or that they might no longer care what happened there. Or that some would even wish their homeland the worst.

Just off the French coast, the ship's captain informed Michael that war had been declared. The Commandant of Le Havre was waiting on the pier to capture his country's first prisoners and, as a description of the arrests had already been sent to the local papers, the Hungarians were to do exactly as they were told.

Michael didn't do anything to alter the newspapers' report but, remembering his father's story about the privileges available to aristocrats, he asked the commandant if his party could stay in a hotel rather than a jail. The commandant said Michael could but not his colleagues: they were only citizens.

Michael refused the preferential treatment and wired President Poincare. Could the Hungarians be released on the grounds that no actual fighting had broken out between France and Austria-Hungary? Poincare replied that as French bureaucracy was pretty much the same as it had been before Michael left for America, war hadn't even been declared yet. The Commandant at Le Havre was just looking for a way to get his name in the papers. The Hungarians were free to go.

They decided to take the first train to the border. Any border. Fast. But with the army requisitioning every car it could get its hands on, there wasn't much room for civilians. Especially enemy civilians.

Four days later, the Hungarians boarded the

Pomplona Express. This meant traveling from the
French border to Barcelona on Europe's worst trains,
sailing to Venice, and riding another series of trains to
Budapest, but they had little choice. Every minute
counted.

They missed their final connection in France by
seven.

France's first prisoners of the war could see the
train station from their cells in the Bordeaux prison,
but whenever they looked at what might have been for
them, they saw what was for others: weeping crowds,
endless embraces, and grim-faced soldiers. The prison
guards talked about pushing straight through to Berlin,
but there were no illusions about a quick, easy victory
with those who would be doing the fighting.

President Poincare apologized to Michael for
the French railway system—"If only we could do
everything as well as we bake"—and offered to have the
Hungarians paroled in a hotel if they promised never to
fight against France.

Michael refused. Though past the age for
military service, he wouldn't compromise his freedom.

His colleagues told him to wise up. He had
sailed for America when the party had ordered him
home; he had denounced the ultimatum and
endangered the lives of his colleagues in Budapest; now
he'd gone and compromised the very thing he wanted to
save: his freedom. Didn't he realize that oaths made to
an enemy weren't binding?

Michael claimed that all oaths were binding.

One Independent held that this one wasn't,
signed his pledge, and left for Budapest. But Poincare
was so impressed by the integrity of those who stayed,
he put them up in a hotel anyway. When word reached
Bordeaux that the Hungarian who left had enlisted,
however, the prisoners were returned to their cells.

And just in time. The war's first casualties
arrived the next day. People began looking for ways to
unleash their pain and anger. Some marched on the

prison. *"Celui-la a la tete a guillotiner,"* they shouted.

Many Hungarians also wanted the Independents' heads. Or at least Michael's. Not only had he condemned the ultimatum to Serbia, he'd *chosen* to remain in France. The man was either a coward or a traitor or both. Crowds demonstrated against him almost daily. Effigies burned outside his palace in Budapest and in the square in front of Parliament.

Catherine had to be sent to Tisza-Dob. Uncle Duci thought she might suffer a breakdown if the attacks on Michael got any worse. Mostly she was just confused. All she thought she knew now seemed to be the opposite of the way it really was. Or at least was supposed to be. No one had liked the assassinated archduke, but everyone thought the Serbs should be punished. No one was for war, but everyone wanted to start fighting as soon as possible. No one supported the man she loved, but everyone cheered Franz-Joseph's inflexible stand against Serbia. Even Cousin Leopold couldn't sleep the night he drafted his country's ultimatum. He was so afraid the Serbs might accept it, he kept getting out of bed to make changes.

And what was one way one day was another way the next. Stephen Tisza, like Michael, had denounced the ultimatum. How could anyone expect Serbia to dismiss whatever officials Franz-Joseph decided were responsible for the assassination? Or outlaw any organizations that opposed Hapsburg policy? The Serbs had no choice but to fight and Tisza, more than anybody, knew how ill-prepared Hungary was for war.

Germany changed his mind when Kaiser Wilhelm II guaranteed Romania's neutrality and promised to threaten Nicholas II if Russia mobilized.

Then Wilhelm did an about face of his own: he instructed Franz-Joseph to accept Serbia's answer to the ultimatum.

But Franz-Joseph wasn't about to show weakness to the country that had killed his heir even if he didn't like him very much. Twenty-four hours after receiving Wilhelm's letter, Franz-Joseph ordered the attack on Belgrade.

Now everybody claimed responsibility for the war. Wilhelm had made it possible; Franz-Joseph had saved face; Tisza had hesitated long enough to give Germany and Austria-Hungary time to prepare.

Public enthusiasm increased with the first victories. Catherine's brothers-in-law pranced about in new uniforms, her sisters ordered their fall gowns in the national colors, and her mother and aunts had themselves measured for stylish nursing outfits. Catherine felt as if her family was getting ready for a big hunting party. Everyone said the war would be over in a matter of weeks.

The train to Tisza-Dob presented Catherine with a different perspective. In station after station, the people who would do the actual fighting embraced their loved ones and climbed aboard. Catherine watched the faces of the women looking at the train. Hundreds of them in each of the dozen stops connecting Budapest with Tisza-Dob. Each face more desperate and tragic than the one before. These are the real victims, Catherine thought, the ones who are left behind. The men have each other and the war, but the women all stand alone. Unable to turn into heroes on the battlefield, they can only cry, tremble, and faint for those they love.

Compared to these women, the military bands and soldiers seemed disturbingly artificial, but Catherine was nothing if not patriotic and kept repeating to herself what she had heard Uncle Duci tell Prime Minister Tisza: "Our budget cannot afford mobilization without a war."

Hostilities broke out first among the governesses at Tisza-Dob. Mlle. Robert announced she was returning to Rouen to protect her furniture from the *Boches*. Fraulein Koestler told Mlle. Robert that Rouen would soon be German. Miss Cooney assured them both the English wouldn't interfere. They liked the Hungarians. Mlle. Robert said liking the Hungarians was the first thing wrong with the English and proceeded to list a dozen more. Fraulein Koestler agreed with everything Mlle. Robert said about the English, but she couldn't pass up the opportunity to secure an ally in Miss Cooney and attack France at the same time. "People who eat snails, frogs, and pigeons," she said, "cannot possibly be civilized."

Mlle. Robert thought this a low blow and announced her resignation. She could not bear to remain under the same roof as Fraulein Koestler. Fraulein Koestler, not to be outdone, also quit. Miss Cooney didn't understand why everything couldn't just continue the "nice" way it had been, but she also left when England entered the war on the side of France.

Catherine returned to Budapest, but everything was different now. An uninterrupted flow of war declarations had turned the grinning masks of the carnival days into the anxious faces of people preparing to wage war against England, France, Russia, and Belgium. With more to come. Even Montenegro wanted to do the Hungarians in. Who could've guessed that all these countries would want to fight on the side of the murderous Serbs?

Uncle Duci, who thought Russia wouldn't shame itself by backing the Serbs and that its mobilization was a bluff, was now singing a different tune. Echoing his father's censure of the annexation of Bosnia and Herzegovina, he said Hungary was responsible for arousing Serbia's hatred. Hungary had forced it to seek Russia's help to make sure more territory wasn't taken. Now Russia was standing by its ally. Did Vienna really think weak Serbia would take on the whole Hapsburg Empire? Tisza should have realized this and kept Hungary out of the war.

But the momentum couldn't be stopped. Priests

blessed guns, politicians prayed for victory, children
carried flags to class, and squadron after squadron
marched up Andrassy Avenue under a wave of patriotic
farewells.

The first to return arrived on their backs. Ella
and her sisters rushed to the river-landings to fight
with the other nurses over which hospital would receive
the casualties. They needn't have bothered. Hungary's
most elite calvary regiments, their sabres glistening in
the sun, had all been mowed down by machine guns.
The foot soldiers soon followed. So many casualty
barges filled the Danube, Ella wondered where they all
came from. Hundreds of private homes had to be turned
into temporary hospitals. Within six months, almost
every soldier who was in the army when the fighting
broke out was dead or wounded.

The government tried to compensate for the
growing disaster by flooding the newspapers with a
series of fictitious triumphs. The Serbs were on the run;
the Germans were marching on Paris; the French had
executed Michael Karolyi.

The Andrassys prevented the news about
Michael's death from reaching Catherine by keeping
her too busy to think let alone read. At the hospital
where Ella worked as a volunteer nurse, Catherine
helped ease the wounded soldiers' pain with games of
cards and chess. She also served meals and changed
beds but was forbidden by Ella to give baths or talk
with any officers.

Some of the soldiers were from Michael's estate.
When the nurse in charge told them Catherine had
been engaged to their master, they didn't believe her.
One said, "Our master would never lower himself to
marry a servant girl."

"She's not a servant girl," the nurse corrected.

"She's a countess."

"A real countess would not wait on people like us," the soldier argued. The others agreed.

But something about Catherine must have convinced them the nurse was right. When Catherine showed up the next day with her chess set, a picture of Michael had been cut out of a magazine and placed on a table in the middle of the room. Flowers and ribbons surrounded the picture. It never occurred to Catherine that she was looking at a memorial, and the soldiers were amazed by the countess's acceptance and courage.

Devoted to her work and freed from having to weigh the rights and wrongs of the conflict, Catherine's time at the hospital passed quickly. Nevertheless, the war continued to make itself felt in ways she hadn't expected. Her diary entry for October 12th, 1914, records what Catherine describes as "the cry of an animal in pain." But it is not an animal; it is the bloody mass of flesh and bone that once was a man. Doctors and nurses are walking back and forth. No one seems to care.

Catherine rushes to find her mother. "Something must be done," she tells her.

Ella asks a nearby surgeon for a sedative. The man reaches into his pocket and asks Catherine what is wrong. She tells the doctor about the man screaming in the ward.

"The sedative is not for you?"

"It's for the man in pain."

"Don't worry about him," the doctor explains. "He's a Bosnian. The Bosnians can't stand pain. There's no reason to waste any drugs on them."

After work, Catherine tells her stepfather what happened. He replies, "Suffering is sometimes necessary so people can be happy later on."

Ella announces at dinner that it was a dull day at the hospital. Nothing serious happened. Aunt Ilona says it's hypocritical to nurse prisoners who would have killed her husband if they had gotten the chance.

Aunt Ilona's husband, like many of the aristocrats of military age, had volunteered himself and his car for the "automobile corps," but the first time he heard gunfire he drove back to Budapest. A veteran now, he talked at dinner about the "beautiful wounds" the Russians' small, pointed bullets made and how General Tercsansky divided his prisoners into pairs, bound them face-to-face, ran bayonets through them, and tossed them into mass graves they had dug for themselves that morning. Many were buried alive.

Catherine couldn't take anymore. She told Uncle Duci and Uncle Gyuri that it was easy for them to talk. They hadn't suffered. They hadn't had to scream in pain in a hospital where the doctors and nurses kept all the sedatives for themselves. "It's horrible! It's ghastly! It's hellish at Mama's hospital!" she shouted as she ran to her room in tears.

Later, there was a knock at the door. It was Uncle Duci. He had good news. His letters to the French Foreign Minister had gotten through. Michael was on his way home.

A committee of Independents rushed to Vienna to tell the former prisoners how unpopular they'd become. To repair the damage and restore confidence in the party, they had to separate themselves from the anti-German statements Michael had made in Cleveland. Michael not only had to retract his statements, he also had to denounce the French for allowing Zouave guards to carry the heads of decapitated prisoners in their large pockets.

Michael asked the Independents what they knew about the Battle of the Marne.

They'd never heard of it.

"The Battle of the Marne will be to the French what the Battle of the Catalaunian Plains is to us."

Michael had obviously been brainwashed.

"We must initiate a peace movement based on mutual concessions," he told the Independents.

Peace movement? France couldn't hold out another two weeks. German reinforcements had already been sent to the Eastern front. The Hungarians were going to celebrate Christmas in St. Petersburg!

IV.
ADAM AND EVA

Michael and Catherine married on November 7th, 1914. There were no flowers, no hymns, and no bridesmaids. A symbol of the times to come, the wedding contrasted with the opulent Matyas Cathedral and the more optimistic marriages taking place everywhere else in Budapest. The Hungarians read daily in their newspapers about Serbs being routed or Russians being held. The Germans hadn't entered Paris yet, but the French people were about to revolt.

Michael's statements about the accuracy of these stories were presented in the papers as the ravings of a madman. For weeks he woke up with at least one window smashed in his palace.

Albert Apponyi suggested he resign as President of the Independence Party. Michael's time in prison and his preoccupation with the Battle of the Marne were no longer a matter of being out of touch. He was losing credibility. He hovered on the point of treason. Didn't he realize that the more loyal he was to the Crown the more grateful Franz-Joseph would be after the war?

Michael said he didn't think Franz-Joseph's gratitude was the kind of foundation on which he wanted to build his future. Or Hungary's.

Uncle Duci sided with Michael on this point, but he also thought his son-in-law should retire. All his programs—autonomy from Austria, stronger ties with the West, resistance to Berlin, cooperation with the minorities, even the secret ballot—had fallen through. If Michael couldn't contribute, he should get out.

There was no way Michael was going to get out of politics, but others could get him out if he wasn't careful. He decided to keep a low profile. Go to his villa in Parad. Keep his name out of the papers until his "lunatic notions" blew over or proved to be right. Take the honeymooon he and Catherine never had. Michael had been away for almost six months before they married. At Parad they could get to know each other better and plan a campaign which would influence Parliament and the press.

Few honeymoons, or even weekends in the country, began as ominously. Someone drove a nail into the fuel tank of the Karolyi's car, and the couple found themselves stranded on a deserted mountain road. Dragging Catherine's maid along with them—she had refused to stay with the chauffeur—they walked through a torrent of rain to the cottage of one of Michael's gameskeepers. There they waited until a carriage could be sent from the villa.

"Who owns this villa?" Catherine asked the gamekeeper when she noticed that he hadn't recognized Michael.

"It belongs to Count Karolyi."

"And what kind of man is this Count Karolyi?"

"We don't see much of him. He prefers foreign countries. But we hear he has money troubles and had to marry a rich woman."

Catherine decided not to wait for the carriage.

Michael told her she was being ridiculous.

Catherine didn't care. She was walking to Tisza-Dob.

"What does a gamekeeper know?" Michael asked as he followed Catherine through the rain.

"Apparently a lot more than I. But I'm not as naive as you like to think. I know you're immoral and sadistic and keep mistresses. Just don't beat me. I can't help it if I love you."

"I would think it would take more than a rumor to end our marriage."

That was all Michael said, but it was enough. Catherine was impressed by the fact that he hadn't protested or made extravagant promises. He was also right. And honest! Here was a man she could trust even if what he did was sometimes bad. She wasn't ready to give in yet, however, and used Michael's reputation as a way of discussing the differences that separated them.

The biggest of these differences was age: Michael was old enough to be her father. Which wouldn't have been so bad except that Michael was an old thirty-nine and Catherine was a young twenty-three. Two months before her wedding, she and her sister Caja were stretching ropes across the road in front of Tisza-Dob in a child-like attempt to stop the Russian army from reaching Serbia. While Michael argued in Parliament against German aggression, Catherine threw herself on a couch and sobbed because Uncle Duci wouldn't stop the war. Catherine couldn't compete intellectually with Michael's colleagues, and she couldn't compete emotionally with his mistresses. Most of them had as many years on Michael as he had on her. Competing with them would be like competing with her mother, and Catherine had suffered enough losses in the war over Uncle Duci to know the chances of a victory were not in her favor.

Michael said he considered Catherine his equal. What she lacked in some areas, she made up for in others. Her experience as a nurse, for example, had given her a view of the war that most politicians lacked. He had never seen any wounded people; he had never even *talked* to a soldier. Catherine, on the other hand, understood how much of a gap separated the war's victims from its advocates. She knew the difference between finishing a fight on a hospital bed and vowing to fight to the finish from the safety of a seat in Parliament.

It was just the kind of argument that someone of Michael's generation would think up and just the kind of argument that someone of Catherine's generation would believe.

Only Catherine didn't believe it. She knew that no matter what Michael said, she was still very young and immature. Nevertheless, she appreciated his not making her feel the years that separated them. Whereas another man would have dismissed her fears as womanish, Michael gave her confidence in her strengths. This brought out the best in Catherine, and the Karolyis found themselves becoming closer through what divided them.

Sometime in the middle of that long walk in the night, Michael turned Catherine away from Tisza-Dob and toward Parad. The welcome signs had been blown from the gate, the decorations were in shreds, and there was no light, but Michael and Catherine had reached an understanding that they would carry with them for the rest of their lives. They loved each other. Because of this love they would never lie or deceive each other in any way. If Michael fell in love with someone else, he would tell Catherine regardless of the pain. The same held for Catherine. Cowardice was a weapon of the weak, and the only sin they could commit would be to live together without love.

The next morning, the Karolyis discussed politics. And the next night. And all the days thereafter.

Catherine's allegiances were to the political traditions established by her grandfather. The Compromise of 1867 was infallible and fidelity to the Hapsburgs, even when they were wrong, was unquestionable. Hungary's stability depended on it. Independence was nonsense, democracy was demagoguery, and equal rights for the minorities was suicide. Power had to remain in the hands of the aristocrats for the best of what was Hungarian to continue.

Michael claimed that the privileged life that he and Catherine knew had become disconnected from the trunk of humanity. Parliament, which was run entirely by the aristocrats and gentry, was little more than an arena for interpreting historical facts and debating questions of national prestige. What had they ever done for the Hungarian people without the threat of a revolution hanging over their heads? When Michael had asked Stephen Tisza if he would reward the minorities for the sacrifices they were making during the war, the Prime Minister replied that the minorities who survived his plans for them would be too content to be back on their farms to worry about reforms. Even a well-meaning politician like Uncle Duci was a victim of the ruling class's narrow vision. How else could Catherine explain his comment that Hungary couldn't afford to mobilize without a war or that people had to suffer before they could be happy? What did he and Tisza think the Hungarian people had been doing for the past thousand years? Playing polo?

The business of government as Michael saw it, was to help people. To make life easier for everyone. He told Catherine how low the Hungarian standard of living was compared to France and England and how the ruling classes perpetuated Hungary's feudal system: three hundred and twenty four aristocrats got rich on 20% of Hungary's land, while 60% of the total population had no land at all. Michael admitted he was no exception—he owned 25,000 acres of forest, 35,000 acres of farmland, a coal mine, a spa, a glass factory, a villa in Parad, a palace and several houses in Budapest, a country estate in Sasvar, and a half-dozen shooting boxes—but at least he was ready to do something about it. Would Catherine join him? Would she participate in the struggle to weaken the nobles' domination of the poor and work to make life worth living for all Hungarians?

Catherine didn't know. The idea of working with Michael exhilarated her, but she had always thought of politics as a man's profession. Now Michael was offering her the opportunity to participate with him as an equal. What he wanted, however, went against Catherine's own plan to unite the Andrassys and Karolyis through their marriage. It meant overthrowing or at least freeing themselves from both families. It meant setting off on a path of their own. Where that path might lead frightened Catherine. She needed some time to think about it.

Michael suggested she read Tolstoy's *Resurrection*. He had just finished it and likened himself to the man who woke up to the sound of church bells on Easter morning to realize how empty his life had been.

Catherine read the book as an account of the author's spiritual awakening. As long as Tolstoy had acted in ways others approved of—even when he knew those ways were wrong—he was loved by all. As soon as he followed his own conscience, however, his best friends left him. The same was true for her and Michael. Their families loved them as long as they thought he was a fraud and her problems could be solved with a bowl of spaghetti. But the Andrassys didn't take her reaction to the wounded soldiers seriously, and the Karolyis turned against Michael when he dared to suggest peace instead of victory.

And where did the families' paths lead? The Karolyis feared the German Protestant influence that would follow the very victory they accused Michael of trying to undermine, and the Andrassys worried about the Jewish rise to power no matter who won.

The choice was obvious. The problem was how to act on that choice. What was the most effective way to make people aware of Michael's humanitarian policies without damaging his popularity?

The answer—and Catherine thought of it—was for Michael to enlist.

The big landowners were exempt from military service on the grounds that they had to manage their large estates or, as Uncle Duci put it, manage the bailiffs who managed the estates. But Paul Esterhauzy, Catherine's brother-in-law, had made a name for himself by refusing to take advantage of this privilege. "In the Battle of the Makacs against the Turks," he told the Hungarian press, "thirteen Esterhauzys remained on the field. This war deserves no less."

Perhaps Michael could make a name for himself also. To remain at home might make a stronger protest against the war, but, thanks to Esterhauzy, it also ran the risk of being labeled a coward. That plus Michael's reputation as a traitor might be too much to overcome in a future election.

Michael and Catherine discussed the possibility of becoming conscientious objectors and fighting the war of the militant anti-militant, but neither was willing to accept the consequences of imprisonment or execution. Their mission was to save their country, not sacrifice themselves in impractical gestures. And what better way was there to identify themselves with a democratic Hungary than by sharing the fate of its ordinary citizens? Catherine had come to know the plight of the unprivileged through her hospital work; now Michael could take advantage of a similar opportunity on the front lines.

Michael joined a cavalry regiment in Budapest so he and Catherine could live together in the Karolyi Palace. Though forty years old with a history of bad health, he threw himself into his training. No obstacle

was so high or wide or deep that he couldn't overcome
it, and he refused to take advantage of any of the
privileges available to members of his class. He even
earned the respect of the younger officers who
outranked him. They had been looking forward to
bullying the "mad Francophile," but Michael managed
to win them over by quietly accepting whatever tasks
they assigned him. It also helped that he was a member
of Parliament. The soldiers believed that anything more
punishing than push-ups—which Michael welcomed as
good for him—and they could wind up in a trench.

While Michael trained to fight, Catherine faced
the more terrifying prospect of redecorating the nine
wings and seventy-two rooms of the Karolyi Palace. No
one had lived there since Louis Batthyani had been
arrested for serving as Louis Kossuth's Prime Minister.
Michael had to keep Catherine's courage up with
dozens of new coats and dresses every week until the
job was done. Conscience-striken, Catherine would
occasionally return the week's seventh or eighth dress
only to see it brought back to her with an assortment of
hats.

On weekends, the Karolyis kept open house for
officers and politicians. The evenings they devoted to
dancing at the National Casino or the Jockey Club.

The Karolyi and Andrassy families thought
their children were behaving frivolously even by
aristocratic standards, but Michael and Catherine knew
the time to be sad would come soon enough. Just how
soon became clear when word arrived that Ilona's
husband, Paul Esterhauzy, had been killed by a
Russian bullet in his first battle.

Michael finished his training in the spring of
1915, but the Minister of War couldn't decide where to
send the regiment. Every day the soldiers waited for
orders that never came. April passed. May passed.
Then June and part of July. And still no orders. All the

soldiers did was repeat the drills they had been taught during the winter while other regiments shipped out as soon as they completed their training.

Michael and Catherine didn't mind. They were expecting their first child in August. If they were lucky, Michael would be there. It never dawned on them that Catherine's Uncle Lazos had convinced the War Minister to keep Michael's regiment in Budapest until after the baby was born.

Michael was furious when he found out. If the soldiers learned of it, all his hard work at proving himself would be lost. He made plans to bring the matter up before Parliament.

Catherine told him not to be so ungrateful. And not just because of the baby or what the soldiers thought of him. Who knew how many lives Uncle Lazos had saved in the past few months? And who could measure how much those past few months would mean to those who would lose their husbands, brothers, fathers, and lovers in the months to come?

Catherine believed it was this fear of losing Michael that kept the Karolyi baby in her womb. She had often been able to delay a menstrual period until after a dance or bring one on before it was due if she wanted an excuse to get out of something. Something similar was occurring now. Only her doctors were concerned. Catherine had carried the baby for ten months.

Nature would only be delayed, however, not denied. When labor finally began, it continued for days. Wave after wave of pain for almost a week.

A baby girl with thick black hair was forced into the world.

Catherine began hemorrhaging. The doctors were so frightened they forgot to bind the baby's navel.

But the baby survived the doctors and Catherine survived the baby and Michael was there when she needed him most. He wanted to name the child "Eva." He and Catherine were going to create a new world. Eva would be its first citizen.

Catherine added "Victoria." There was no sense in being the first if you weren't also going to come out on top.

So it was: Eva Victoria.

Michael left soon after for the front, Catherine walked on crutches for the next six weeks, and Eva demanded milk every three hours for months. And when she wasn't drinking, she was crying.

Catherine felt like a trapped cow. Here Michael was proving himself worthy of his privileged position and all she could do was sleep, eat, nurse, and go to the bathroom. Had all their plans and work and dreams come down to this?

Yes. But Michael wasn't having an easy time of it either. Or rather, he was having too easy a time. Considerate Uncle Lazos had arranged a cushy job for him a safe distance from the Russian lines. Michael's half-brother, Joseph, was there and so was his sister's husband, Sigfried Pappenheim. Their indispensable belongings included: hot water bottles, Persian rugs, dozens of custom-made uniforms, a small army of cooks, valets, and chauffeurs, and a combined wardrobe of over eight-hundred suits. The only things missing were Aunt Geraldine and her *petit point* chairs.

Michael's job, as he saw it, was to amuse General Apor. They played bridge in the morning and polo in the afternoon. Evenings were reserved for reading, conversation, and hot chocolate. And because the general preferred fresh milk to tinned, he had his own cow.

When Michael discovered General Apor had enough aides to field two polo teams—more than twice the number permitted by Parliament—he requested a transfer to the trenches. The general had no choice but to comply. It was either give Michael what he wanted or be brought before Parliament and run the risk of losing his polo teams.

The Karolyi and Andrassy families did not give

way so easily, however. They had paid General Apor a lot money to make sure Michael didn't suffer the same fate as Paul Esterhauzy. Being a pacifist and a democrat were bad enough, but not caring about his own safety or the welfare of his new wife and child was beyond comprehension.

Nevertheless, the families did not abandon him. Uncle Lazos pulled a few more strings, and Michael soon discovered that life at the front wasn't much different than it had been in General Apor's villa. Even Catherine got to visit him along with two maids and an ailing dachshund whom she said she preferred to Eva Victoria.

Catherine found the trenches a great improvement over the nursery. There was no crib, she participated in the regiment's riding exercises, and the officers made her the center of their attention. When a group of them serenaded her one night with guitars, flutes, and violins, however, Michael decided it was time for Catherine to move on to her sister's hospital in Stanislas.

It was also time for Michael to begin his work as President of the opposition party. He wanted to know, for example, why the officers ate so well and the soldiers so poorly. The officers credited their chef, "Uncle Pesce," but Uncle Pesce credited his orders to curtail the soldiers' rations. This put Michael in an awkward position. To expose the officers' corruption could weaken the soldiers' morale, and the officers would feel he had betrayed them. A bullet in his back one night during a routine patrol would almost surely follow. But as a member of Parliament, Michael had a duty to report any irregularities. Underfed soldiers couldn't hold off the Russians forever. How many times had he seen the Hungarians gathering for an evening's rest in the local cafes. Still covered with the dirt and squalor of the trenches, they watched with envy and scorn as Michael and his spic-and-span officers paraded about with Catherine.

And Catherine hadn't helped. Wearing the latest Parisian fashions and smelling of *Houbigant*, she ordered food for her dog that no ordinary soldier could afford. This embarrassed Michael, but he didn't say anything. He knew Catherine felt unattractive after having Eva and needed attention to restore her confidence.

Worse than anything Catherine did, however, was the number of officers who found an urgent reason to return to Budapest whenever enemy shots were fired. The regiment's command, which could shrink from ninety officers to ten within forty-eight hours, was left to a few rich Jews who had bribed their way into the cavalry to improve their social positions. These were the most hated men in the army. One, a doctor named Gross, enraged the Magyar officers by volunteering first for every dangerous mission. "What insolence!" the officers complained. "A Jew presuming to be as brave as an Hungarian!"

Jews who showed fear, on the other hand, were shown no mercy. Michael told Catherine of a social climber who was so afraid of horses he couldn't mount one without a ladder he kept hidden under his saddle. When the other officers found out, they whipped the man's horse into such a frenzy the poor animal ran his pathetic rider through a cafe window.

Another would-be Magyar was made to eat his gramaphone records after he stood up and sang the national anthem at a drunken party.

But it was the Jews in the villages who got it worst. Especially if they happened to be women. Whenever a village was suspected of collaborating with the enemy, the captured scapegoats were almost invariably Jewish girls who had to allow themselves to be raped by Hungarian officers to prove their loyalty.

Michael never mentioned these things to Parliament. He reasoned that he couldn't do anybody any good if he was dead, and he believed—correctly—that Parliament would see the raped Jews as necessary morale-builders. The government was already shipping women captured in enemy villages to Hungarian camps for the same reason.

What Michael did write about—shoddy equipment, German strategy blunders, and practical reasons for peace—no paper would print. Most editors didn't trust him—he was, after all, the madman who had created the Battle of the Marne—and the publishers feared the government would shut them down for undermining the war effort.

Michael retaliated by buying the controlling shares in *Magyargrszag*. Circulation dropped every time one of his stories appeared, but at least now there was one newspaper in Hungary with an alternative view of the war. Just as important, Michael made sure copies of his articles reached the right people in Britain, France, and Russia. When the fighting finally ended, perhaps the victors would support his plans for a democratic government.

Whatever good Michael's articles may have done him outside of Hungary, they doomed every proposal he made in Parliament. His call for Hungary to remove its troops from German command was shouted down before he could finish reading it, and, when he countered with a proposal that German officers of Hungarian regiments be replaced with Hungarian officers, he was denounced as a traitor. Like the proverbial child, he was most appreciated when he kept quiet.

But Michael would not shut up. Not in Parliament and not in *Magyargrszag*. Catherine became concerned for his safety. Neither of them realized that he was actually playing right into the hands of Independents' real leader: Albert Apponyi. While Michael was stirring up trouble for the government, Uncle Albert concluded a secret pact with Uncle Duci. Together they promised Stephen Tisza unconditional support for the war if he would give them an advisory seat in his cabinet. Michael was told to go along or get out.

He got out.

Twenty others followed to form the Karolyi Party. Michael was the President and their aim was peace. The first time they openly challenged the government to state its war aims or remove Hungary from German control, however, Stephen Tisza ordered them all to the Russian front.

Michael reported instead to his villa at Parad. At least now the Allies could know that there was an anti-German party in Hungary that stood for a separate peace.

The press called the Karolyi Party "treacherous" and "subversive," but Michael felt the people—the ones who suffered most from the war—were tired of fighting. If they weren't, the coming months did little to raise their enthusiasm. Romania joined the fight against Hungary, Transylvania was overrun, the Russians broke through in the north, and German troops were sent to occupy whatever territory hadn't already fallen into enemy hands. Hungarian rule and Hapsburg sovereignty evaporated almost overnight. The dying empire and the dying Franz-Joseph were now controlled by the German General Staff. And what did these officers care if allowances to Hungarian families whose "heroes" were fighting in the trenches hadn't been paid in months? If it wasn't the families it was something else. The paper soles in the soldiers' shoes, the lack of thread in their buttons, the wrong number of holes in their belts. Anything to keep the Hungarians from doing what it took to win the war and make sure the Germans did their fighting for them.

Michael contacted Sigismund Kunfi. Kunfi had initially supported the war, but recent events and increased German control had changed his mind. Kunfi was more than just the only politician outside of the Karolyi Party to protest against the government's handling of the war, however. He had a vision that

Michael believed would damage Stephen Tisza as much from within Hungary as anything the Allies were capable of from without. Kunfi's vision was called "socialism."

And Michael was ripe for it.

So was Catherine. At Ilona's hospital in Stanislas, she saw first hand the effects of the war's improved weaponry and participated in Michael's discussions with Kunfi about the new international order for preventing war. But Catherine also felt the need to act, to test Kunfi's system of equitable cooperation among nations on a more immediate level.

The village of Parad became her laboratory. Typical of many in Hungary, the people of Parad still followed the ancient custom of tying the arms of male babies behind their backs for the first year of their lives. If the babies survived, they would be strong when they grew up. If they died, they never would have made it anyway.

Paradians also raised their children on dry beans soaked in vinegar. If the babies survived this, they could eat anything. Catherine tried to improve the babies' diet—or at least broaden it—by hiring a nurse to introduce all the latest baby foods to all the latest mothers. The nurse could then use the baby food as a way of introducing the most up-to-date techniques in first aid and child care.

The woman Catherine hired didn't last a week. All but a few of the mothers resented "Miss Know-It-All," the men flirted with her, and the grandmothers threatened to beat her if they caught her in their daughters' homes. The village priest—Parad had no doctor, infirmary, welfare center, or school—told Catherine her money would be better spent on stained-glass windows.

Catherine retaliated by inviting Parad's most stubborn mother to her villa. Once the woman saw how healthy Eva was, she'd change her mind and become an ally.

But the woman wasn't impressed. She had given birth to fourteen children, Catherine to only one. The Countess had a nurse, a nanny, and a special cook to raise her child for her. What could she possibly know? She was practically a child herself.

Catherine admitted the woman had a point. Awed and more than a little humbled, Catherine asked the woman where her children were now.

"Eleven died before they were six. It was God's will. The rest are all strong men with strong arms."

Catherine realized that trying to improve the people's condition on an individual basis or through charity was a waste of time and energy. What was needed was an institution. Something with some authority. Something that—like the Church or government—would force ignorant people to do what was good for them.

But this was an unlikely prospect. In Hungary, the Church and the government worked hand in hand to keep their subjects poor, backwards, and subservient.

"Precisely why a completely new order is so important," Sigismund Kunfi told Catherine and Michael. "Universal suffrage must come and the aristocracy must go. Imagine what would happen if the land of every estate was divided among the peasants who worked it. A new class of small, ambitious, independent landowners would create an Hungarian market for Hungarian industry. By relying on each other instead of on foreign capital, Hungarians would free themselves from political and military dependence as well."

This was heady stuff even for the Karolyis, but they decided to give it a try. Their "experiment" called for dividing the profits from their glass factory into four equal shares: 25% to the workers, 25% to establish a clinic, library, and sports club, 25% to the business, and 25% to the owners.

The plan was doomed from the start. On their first visit to the glass factory, the Karolyis discovered that 100% of the profits couldn't help these workers. Grey complexions, hollow chests, and stopped shoulders seemed to be requirements for the job. Ranging from seventeen to twenty years of age, most would die before they were thirty. Soldiers at the front had a higher rate of survival.

Michael and Catherine talked about turning a nearby castle into a convalescent home, but fate had other plans: Franz-Joseph died.

Hope filled the hearts of the pacifists. They knew that the new Emperor was his own man and recalled how he had acted after the death of Archduke Ferdinand. Franz-Joseph, who hated the assassinated heir, forbade any member of the royal family to attend the funeral. Charles not only went to the funeral, he told the press he disapproved of his granduncle's behavior. Here was a king with a mind of his own. And a heart. Surely he wouldn't remain insensitive to the tragedy taking place in the trenches.

But Charles also gave hope to the country's militants. They too remembered his behavior at Ferdinand's funeral and were confident their new Emperor would suppress the peace movement Franz-Joseph had refused to take seriously.

Charles' first act was to replace his uncle's advisors.

Score one for the pacifists.

His second was to invite Germany to make a joint peace offer.

Score another.

But Charles' invitation was only a ploy to block Woodrow Wilson's offer to mediate a truce.

Haymaker for the hawks.

Down but not out, the pacifists decided to support anyone who worked for peace. Charles was the first Hapsburg to even mention the word.

When Charles came to Budapest to be crowned—the Emperor of Austria was also the King of Hungary—militants and pacifists competed with each other for his attention. They were outshone, however, by everyone else. The people had grown tired of death. They wanted to celebrate their country's first coronation in more than fifty years.

Preparations were feverish. The court robes of aristocratic grandparents had to be taken out of mothballs, and all the palaces in Budapest reeked of camphor. Catherine's robe, which had been worn by Michael's grandmother when Franz-Joseph was crowned, was made of bright red velvet with gold embroidered into designs on the mantle, the puffed sleeves, and the train. At the time it was made, the smallest of the dress's designs cost more than 5,000 crowns.

Catherine's hair, though not as costly, was just as extravagant. Monsieur Toni began working on it at four in the morning. As Lady of the Court to the Queen—a great honor given in spite of the rumor that Michael planned to whistle at the coronation—Catherine was also privileged to be her hairdresser's final appointment. She had her own hairdresser, of course, but he wouldn't do for this occasion. By the time Monsieur Toni was through, Michael's best high-steppers stood ready to pull the family's centuries-old carriage through the streets of Budapest.

Crossing the suspension bridge that linked Buda with Pest, Catherine saw lights burning in the Royal Castle for the first time in her life. Franz-Joseph hadn't stayed there since the Hungarians rebelled against him in 1848. Keeping the palace dark was one of his ways of punishing them.

Everyone who saw the lights hoped their new sovereign would share with Budapest the balls, titles, and decorations of the Viennese court. The Hungarians, after all, were giving Charles their Holy Crown of St. Stephen. Whoever wore the crown was king and no king could rule without it.

Pope Sylvester gave the top part of the crown to

Stephen I in the year 1000. The bottom part was the gift of a Byzantine emperor. But the crown was more than a symbol of the country that linked East and West. The crown made the nobles a part of its own mystical body the same way the crown was part of Christ's Mystical Body. The three—court, crown, and Christ—were inseparable.

So was the aristocrats' land. Made holy by the Crown of St. Stephen, it couldn't be sold and had to be passed on from generation to generation.

The crown took on an added dimension when the newly-anointed king mounted his charger and galloped up a mound that had been built with soil from Hungary's sixty-three counties. Brandishing his sword in four directions, Charles IV of Hungary and Charles I of Austria vowed to vanquish his enemies in the north, south, east, and west.

Then it happened: the crown, which was too large for the Hapsburg's small head, slipped over Charles' ears and landed on his nose.

Thousands watched in helpless embarrassment as Charles struggled to control his horse, raise his crown, and hold on to his heavy scepter.

And that wasn't the worst of it.

The worst came when one of the nobles climbed to the top of the mound in his medieval robe and led Charles' horse back to the twentieth century.

The image stuck. Charles couldn't carry the weight of the monarchy. He wasn't equal to the responsibilities. The Empire was beyond his control. If Hungary was to survive, Charles would have to be led out of the war.

Two months later, Michael tried to do just that. The Germans were talking about a U-boat offensive that would wipe out English sea power and make the United States think twice about getting involved in the war. Michael argued that an English defeat of that size would only make America enter the fighting sooner.

"That's just how I feel," Charles replied. "That's

exactly what I've been saying all along."

Michael asked the Emperor if he approved of an anti-German party.

"The existence of such a party is very useful to me, especially as Austria-Hungary has no intention of becoming Germany's vassal."

Michael reminded Charles of a message he had sent through an advisor asking the Karolyi Party not to attack the German alliance.

"I know of no such message. You continue to do just what you're doing. If I'm going to bring the war to an end, I'm going to need all the resistance to Germany I can get."

This was plain-speaking, and Michael returned to Budapest confident that Charles appreciated the work of the Karolyi Party. Two weeks later, Uncle Duci and Uncle Albert announced their support for the pro-German coalition. Charles praised the agreement as a model for other rival factions. If the Forty-Eighters and Sixty-Seveners could put aside their differences and unite in favor of their country's most important undertaking, there was no reason for every other party not to.

Michael took this to include the Karolyi Party, but he couldn't be sure. One day Charles said Germany was Austria-Hungary's closest ally; the next day Germany was Austria-Hungary's greatest danger. One morning he announced the Empire's most important task was to maintain its independence, and that afternoon the papers carried a story about his appeal for loyalty to Berlin.

Which was policy and which was persona? Michael thought he knew when the War Ministry announced his membership in the Dutch Anti-War Council was treasonous. Charles said nothing about this. When the Immunity Committee determined that Michael couldn't be prosecuted because he was a member of Parliament, however, Charles wired Michael that his peace policies were vital to the nation. Then he

turned around and announced he was retaining
Stephen Tisza—the war's staunchest supporter—as
Prime Minister.

The truth was Charles had no policy and
several personae: he told whomever he was with
whatever they wanted to hear. One time three
Hungarian politicians met with him for half an hour
each on the same afternoon. Each left his meeting
thinking he'd been appointed Prime Minister.

Michael realized the Karolyi Party would have
to follow its own path to peace and equality.
Unfortunately, the path Michael envisioned was a little
too rough for many of his followers. Originally attracted
to Michael by his call to end Hungary's feudal society
and the war, they weren't willing to go as far as he
wanted to take them. Democracy was one thing;
socialism was another.

But Michael's followers had more than one
reason to resist him: he and Catherine had been seen
just a few too many times in the company of writers,
artists, and journalists. People the upper classes
considered "cranky" regardless of their talent.

The followers' resentment rose noticeably
higher when the Karolyis went to a party given by a
Jewish publisher. It peaked—at least for a while—when
Catherine reciprocated with an invitation to a ball at
the Karolyi Palace. Some of her guests called her a
"madcap" for inviting such "impossible people" and tried
to separate her "behavior" from Michael's "policies."

But the writers, artists, and journalists weren't
too keen on the Karolyis either. They didn't believe a
socialist who had money could possibly be sincere. The
Karolyi Palace, with its chandeliers, gilded ceilings,
glittering mirrors, and shiny parquet floors, was the
antithesis of socialism. So were the overly made-up
women gliding in the arms of extravagantly uniformed
men to the too-sweet tunes of Johann Strauss. These
people weren't workers; they were mannequins.

And the Karolyis weren't much better. Like all

the other wealthy landowners, they had tripled their income as a result of the war's rising wheat prices. If they really believed the existing social order was immoral and unjust, weren't they equally immoral and unjust to profit by it?

Michael didn't think so. He agreed that it was wrong to profit by injustice, but he argued that he was no St. Francis. To distribute all he had to the poor would only help a few people for a short period of time. He preferred to use his money and power to bring about a new economic order that would affect many people for many lifetimes.

Nor was Michael a socialist. At least not yet. If asked to describe himself, he would have said he was a liberal with proletarian sympathies. He didn't want to overthrow the government or even break with it. He still believed the ruling classes would give way to argument and reason. Unfortunately, as is often the case, anyone who wasn't a reactionary was a "red," and anyone who didn't believe in social-democracy was a "pig." If you weren't for something, you were automatically against it.

This absence of a middle ground is best understood in the different way the aristocrats and the common people viewed the war. While soldiers died in the trenches and their families tried to survive on government allowances that never arrived for rations that were rarely available, the ruling classes saw the war as a business. That was the only way it affected them. Or even interested them. War, with the exception of a few Paul Esterhauzys, was something carried on by "the other classes." To mention it was considered "bad form."

As news from the front grew worse and worse, however, even the wealthy landowners came to realize that business wouldn't be good forever. If the Russians broke through, they'd just take the wheat the Austrians and Germans were paying such high prices for. Where would the aristocrats be then?

Michael proposed a separate peace with Russia and the West before it was too late. The landowners, on the other hand, wanted to keep the money rolling in for as long as they could. They found it easier to have hope in the new U-boat offensive than admit they might be fighting a lost cause.

Catherine, meanwhile, was expecting her second child, but that didn't stop her from launching a campaign on behalf of the socialist Freidrich Adler. Mostly through letters written in bed, she tried to convince influential friends in Vienna that Adler's murdering the Austrian Prime Minister was an act of violence intended to stop violence. Adler had only wanted to save Austria before it self-destructed.

Adler's lawyers took a different approach: they claimed their client was temporarily insane. But Adler, who was as balanced, unemotional, and rational as they come, wouldn't let them get away with it. In his own defense, he said he had acted with neither hatred nor vengeance. The assassination was a protest against the war. It was as simple and as complex as that.

The Crown Prosecutor pointed out there was a big difference between political protest and political murder and that under no circumstances could murder escape punishment in any civilized community.

Adler agreed and went on to say that Austria was no longer a civilized community. If Adler was guilty of murder, so was the Emperor who continued to wage a war in which thousands of people died every day.

Catherine had Adler's defense printed in Michael's newspaper and distributed on broadsides in Vienna. The Austrians, who were ready for an argument on the morality of the war, responded with massive demonstrations.

The Andrassys then gave Catherine a dose of what it felt like to be a Karolyi. "Adler is a coward," Uncle Duci informed her. "A *real* man would have challenged the Prime Minister to a duel." Ella told Catherine that there was nothing special about Adler's

defense. "The style," she pointed out, "is quite ordinary."
But Catherine wasn't concerned with duels or literary merit. And neither were Adler's jurors. They gave the fiery socialist a life sentence.

Catherine went into labor the day she received the news about Adler's sentence. Thanks to the jurors she was only a few days late. Nevertheless, her doctors were worried. They knew they'd have to make an incision and Catherine was too far into her labor to apply an anaesthetic.

Catherine told them to go ahead and make the incision. Nothing could be worse than the pain she was already suffering.

Or so she thought. Her scream from the first cut caused someone on the street below to call the police.

"Courage," the mid-wife told her. "Think what a handsome little soldier he will be."

"He won't be a soldier!" Catherine yelled back. "I won't bring him into the world to be a soldier!"

The doctors tied her down.

"He won't be a soldier!" she continued hysterically. "He won't be a soldier!"

"Don't worry," one of the doctors comforted. "When he grows up, there won't be any more wars."

But Catherine wouldn't calm down and the doctors were forced to give her ether. Immediately she was transported to a world where time was non-existent and nothing seemed important. It was more than joy or happiness; it was relief. That was the only reality. Everything else was irrelevant.

Michael was holding her hand when she came to.

Catherine had given birth to a boy: Adam.

Those who stood to benefit from the Karolyi heir rejoiced, but Adam's material inheritance was of little importance to Michael and Catherine. They knew the system of entailed property wasn't going to last. Adam and Eva's heritage would be a new world that held its parents' short-sighted class in contempt and replaced its hypocritical religious values with intensely humanitarian ones.

Eager to play a role in creating this world, Catherine hired a wet-nurse to free her from having to feed Adam. Unfortunately, the woman didn't have enough milk for her own baby. Catherine wound up feeding both.

Catherine had suckled Eva because she had wanted to do what was best for the baby, but she hated every minute of it. She also resented her daughter for keeping her away from Parliament, the National Casino, and wherever else Michael was pushing his programs. Now she was saddled with two captors, each more demanding and cruel than Eva had ever been. They bit when they weren't satisfied, and the nurse's child—whom Catherine describes in her diary as "a wizen-faced, swarthy commoner"—made her want to vomit.

Not even the Russian Revolution cheered her up. Greeted as the herald of a new age by those who were tired of the fighting, it only increased Catherine's bitterness. Here was a first step toward peace and where was she? Tied to her punishment for being a woman.

But Michael wasn't too thrilled with the timing of the Revolution either. He had used the threat of an Allied offensive to pressure Parliament into considering a new franchise bill. If the Hungarians had to withdraw into their own territory, they'd need the peasants' help. Giving them the right to vote was one way of winning their loyalty. If Russia decided to drop out of the war, however, Hungary could reinforce its troops in the West without granting the peasants any rights which could threaten Pariliament after the fighting ended.

King Charles also pressed Parliament for concessions. If America entered the war and the Allies won, they might be more lenient on those who had instituted democratic reforms.

Stephen Tisza said he'd resign before making any changes.

Charles replaced him with the liberal, progressive, pro-peace Maurice Esterhauzy.

Parliament then responded with its own version of a liberal, progressive, pro-peace franchise law: people over the age of twenty-four who could read and write and soldiers awarded the Charles Cross for Bravery could now vote.

In feudal, backward, illiterate Hungary, that didn't create a whole lot of new voters.

So Michael used the rights he had given up in the franchise bill to win support for his long-overdue secret ballot.

Parliament passed this one too but limited its application to the large cities. Where the people were more conservative, where the government had more control, and where fewer voters elected more representatives, the people voted the way they always had: as they were told.

It could have been worse. As word of Vladimir Lenin's peace offer spread across Europe, Germany's militarist spirit stiffened. Now it was the Allies who stood to benefit from a separate peace.

Michael argued that peace benefited everyone. Especially Hungary. With Russia out of the war and over three million soldiers still defending the monarchy, Parliament was in a position of strength. "Sue for peace before America becomes involved and we'll escape from the war with minimal damage," Michael urged his colleagues. "The Allies are as tired of fighting as we are. They'll accept nominal concessions, and we'll save lives. Hungarian lives."

Stephen Tisza wanted to fight harder than ever. Without Russia it was just a matter of time before the Allies were on the ropes. "America didn't enter the war with Russia on her side," he told Parliament. "She surely wouldn't do so now."

But Michael held that America would enter the war because Russia had bowed out. "Uncle Sam has too much money tied up in the Entente cause to let it fail."

Tisza told Michael to stop being so faint-hearted. Russia had guaranteed the Central Powers' victory.

The rest of Parliament agreed. Not only had Lenin doomed the Allies, he had prevented the minorities from rebelling. A number of Croates, Slovaks, and Romanians had been fighting to liberate their co-nationals, but without Russia's help they were as good as dead. In overthrowing the Czar, the Bolsheviks had preserved Hungary's historic continuity. "Long live Lenin!" the aristocrats shouted in Parliament. "Long live the Bolshevik Revolution!"

V.
REVOLUTION

Michael was in Switzerland when he heard about the Russian Revolution. He had gone to attend a peace conference not so much because he believed peace could be brought about by pacifists but because he had been cut off from the West for three years. He needed information. He needed something to throw at Parliament besides the Battle of the Marne.

Michael also needed to let the neutral and Entente nations know there was an anti-government coalition in Hungary. The Karolyi Party had joined forces with Sigismund Kunfi's Social Democrats and Oskar Jaszi's Radical Party. Their platform included universal suffrage, secret balloting throughout the country, land reform, peace without change in territory, and the creation of a federation which would insure equal rights for all Hungarians.

The idea for a federation was Oskar Jaszi's. A sociology professor with a reputation as a political writer, Jaszi suggested an organization of five autonomous states with a Hapsburg presidency.

To say Jaszi's idea wasn't well-received in Parliament is an understatement. When Michael introduced the measure—neither the Radicals nor the

Social Democrats had a representative—the laughter was so loud and for so long he wasn't able to continue.

Then the press took over. Jaszi's "United States of the Danube" was presented as typical of the kind of thinking Hungarians could expect from a theorist with no practical experience. Editorials asked: How can a Serb or a Croat ever be the equal of a Magyar? Who could guarantee these people would be more loyal to the federation than to their neighboring nationals? What was Hungary going to get for all the land and power Jaszi planned to give away?

Jaszi's proposal was given more serious consideration at the peace conference in Berne but only because it could serve as a buffer zone against German expansion. Of greater interest to the delegates was Michael's suggestion that one of the neutral countries invite the warring countries to negotiate.

Hugh Wilson, the American Ambassador to Switzerland, reminded Michael that the United States had already offered to mediate a peace but the Central Powers had rejected it.

Michael pointed out that the United States was hardly a neutral country. Nor did he expect Germany to accept an invitation to negotiate no matter who it came from. A German refusal, however, would give Austria-Hungary its chance to act independently. Charles had already expressed his willingness to negotiate in a secret letter to the French government.

"And when his secret letter was turned over to the Germans by his very own messenger," Wilson added, "Charles whistled a different tune. He's closer now to Berlin than Franz-Joseph ever was."

Michael wondered at the American Ambassador's resistance. Weren't they both on the side of peace? "Just because Charles' letter was turned over to the Germans instead of to the French and he had to retract some of his statements doesn't mean Charles no longer wishes to negotiate," Michael explained.

The Ambassador said Charles had already

made his choice.

Michael asked the Ambassador to be reasonable.

"You be reasonable," Wilson told Michael. "Or at least logical. If Charles wanted peace, he wouldn't let Germany stand in his way."

Michael tried not to lose his temper. "The situation is different now. Within the past few months, three anti-German parties have gained influence in Hungary. Give Charles an opportunity to negotiate and these parties will apply the pressure necessary to bring him to the peace table. The Karolyis, Radicals, and Social Democrats have over a million members."

Wilson countered: "If a neutral country invited the warring nations to negotiate and none of the Central Powers showed up, the Entente would lose face."

"Since when has the fear of losing face become more important than the risk of winning peace?"

Wilson ignored the question. "Allied troops would wonder if something was wrong, if there was something they didn't know about. They'd question the convictions of their leaders and lose confidence in their mission."

Michael didn't know what to say.

Wilson finished for him: "It was a good try, Karolyi, but your hiding from us certain facts exposed your real intentions. You told us about Charles' letter to the French without mentioning that he had retracted his statements. Then you told us about the pressure your anti-German parties would heap on Charles while not letting us know that yours is the only one of the parties represented in Parliament. I ask you, *Count* Karolyi, how much pressure can a party with only twenty members apply?"

Michael felt the delegates' sympathy ebb. No matter what he said now, they would wonder what additional information he held from them.

That's when the news of the Russian Revolution hit.

Michael gave up any hope for a negotiated peace.

A review of recent events furthered his depression. Parliament had watered down his franchise bill, made a mockery of his secret ballot, and laughed Jaszi's proposal for a Danubian federation right off the floor. Now the Americans had blocked Austria-Hungary's way to a separate peace and the word from Budapest was that Charles had replaced the moderate, pro-peace Prime Minister Esterhauzy with the militant, pro-German Wekerle.

Catherine wrote that the situation wasn't as desperate as it seemed. At last the people of one country had taken a stand against war and oppression. Others would follow. The Central Powers would soon see they had no reason to rejoice. Even Uncle Duci, who believed the Revolution would help the German cause, agreed. "Lenin is the greatest calamity of the war," he told Catherine. "He is the beginning of the end of civilization as we know it."

Michael saw one measurement of the impact Lenin was having on the masses when he returned to Budapest. Hundreds of people had gathered at West Station to encourage him to keep trying. Banners proclaimed him "The Apostle of Peace."

Michael told them he didn't deserve the title. All his efforts in Parliament and in Berne had failed.

But the people wouldn't listen. "Long live Karolyi!" they shouted. "Peace, Votes, and Karolyi!"

How different this was from the sentiments that had greeted the war. Even Kunfi's Social Democrats had called it "The Holy Cause of the Nation." Now, three years later, over 600,000 Hungarian soldiers were dead, another 700,000 were wounded, and almost 800,000 had been taken prisoner. Calculating on a short war, Parliament had drafted skilled workers in order to prevent over-production. Today there was a labor shortage. Special commissions had gone into the trenches to find what was left of the

111

skilled workers and returned empty handed. And while industrial production went down, the demand for guns, ammunition, and barbed wire went up. Paper products replaced leather goods. By the time Michael returned from the peace conference, Hungary was operating at less than 70% of its pre-war level.

Except for wheat. Because the aristocrats made most of their money from the land, Parliament maintained wheat prices at the expense of everything else. To keep everything else functioning, however, Parliament also had to station police in the factories, ignore the recommendations of municipal councils, forbid certain political groups to meet, censor the press, impose long-term sentences on labor organizers, and ratify the use of concentration camps for "undesirable elements."

But what once might have been thought necessary was no longer acceptable. The rising class of workers and merchants wanted a share in the government's power. Parliament responded with a resounding Not Now! To share any of its power would only weaken the war effort. Perhaps after the fighting was over, accommodations could be made.

But the bourgeoisie refused to wait; slowdowns became common.

To get the workers back in line, the government set production standards, regulated pay, and sent garrisons into the cities. It then created a grievance committee to hear complaints from the trade unions. The purpose of gathering the information, however, was not to improve conditions. It was to determine the direction the unions were most likely to take and then work to undermine them.

The unions reacted by forming a coalition with Sigismund Kunfi's Social Democrats. Before the war, the two groups didn't have 100,000 members between them. By 1917, they had 700,000. Business clerks, city employees, railroad officials, civil servants, even engineers signed on as they saw their incomes drop to less than half of their pre-war levels.

The Social Deomocrats then formed a coalition with the Karolyi Party, to secure a voice in Parliament. Oskar Jaszi's Radical Party contributed to the coalition what it lacked in writers, poets, journalists, and students.

Prisoners returning from Russia also swelled the movement. Neither several weeks in quarantine nor the best efforts of the Catholic clergy could prevent them from setting up Bolshevik cells wherever they went.

Michael thought the greatest impact, however, was Woodrow Wilson's "Fourteen Points." That was the one thing that gave all these forces a single focus. By advocating disarmament, democracy, and international justice over revenge, territory, and historic continuity, the American President completely undermined the Central Powers' reasons for fighting. With one blow, he gained the sympathy of the masses and invested a new spirit in the struggle for human rights.

Wilson also claimed he had no desire to reduce or change Austria-Hungary in any way, but he wanted its people to have a say in determining their future. The message, as the Karolyis, Radicals, and Social Democrats read it, was clear: Charles could avoid war with America by initiating democratic reforms. No longer were equal rights limited to the pronouncements of cranks. Universal suffrage and land reform were now crucial to peace. Even Jaszi's vision of a United States of the Danube gained new life.

Charles, meanwhile, had come to the conclusion that if he didn't act soon he wouldn't have a country to reform. Over a million workers in Vienna and Budapest were demanding an immediate end to the war. Wildcat strikes broke out in the non-union factories, revolts had to be put down on military bases, and many recruits were refusing to fight. At least one regiment had to be shipped to the front in sealed boxcars.

Charles tried to reverse these movements by

advocating some of the reforms Wilson called for, but he met with stiff resistance from the landowners. They claimed Wilson was only competing with Lenin for converts. If Charles was smart, he'd do nothing. The Central Powers would either win the war and Prussianize Europe or lose it and force America to save everybody from communism.

By the time America declared war, however, democratic reforms were no longer enough. Wilson had sent word to the minorities living in Austria-Hungary that if they remained loyal to the Hapsburgs, they would suffer the same fate as the losers. If, on the other hand, they chose rebellion, liberty, and democracy, they would share in the spoils of the victors. Wilson encouraged them to form independent councils which the United States would then recognize as governments. The Czecho-Slovak National Council in Paris, for example, occupied an office in a building, but it was a full-fledged American ally. Once America won the war, all the council had to do was promise to outlaw Bolshevism and Wilson would hand over the country.

Catherine wanted the Karolyis, the Radicals, and the Social Democrats to form an Hungarian National Council with Michael as its president, but Michael wouldn't hear of it. History, after all, was proving him right. As news of German defeats filtered through the government's censors, the people's demands for peace had become increasingly more insistent. Parliament was sure to come to its senses soon.

Once again, however, Michael underestimated the density of the landowners' senses. While history was busy proving him right, a petition was circulated in Parliament to have him banned from the National Casino, and, as late as the summer of 1918, he was still the only deputy calling for compliance with Wilson's "Fourteen Points."

Catherine discovered just how unwilling some senses are to change when she picked up a telephone and overheard Uncle Duci trying to convince one of her cousins not to assassinate Michael. "He's already done irreparable damage to every cause he's been associated with," Uncle Duci explained. "To kill him would only turn a fool into a martyr."

When Catherine told her mother about the plot to kill Michael, Ella decided to organize a family picnic in Transylvania. If Michael was going to die, she wanted everyone to have chance to show him that there were no hard feelings, that, whatever his politics, he was still a member of the Andrassy family. Besides, the Andrassys hadn't all been on a picnic together since before Tivadar died.

Catherine couldn't get over how everything at the shooting box had changed. The steep hill that she and Caja used to roll down was now only a small slope. It barely reached her shoulder. The prison where her mother locked her up for being disobedient was nothing more than a guest house. While she had grown and changed so much in the past ten years, everything at Dubrin had shrunk and gotten old.

"Long live the Bolshevik Revolution!" Ella had hung the words over the Karolyis' bedroom. Michael and Catherine were so grateful they decided not to mention the war. Even Uncle Duci, who was still deeply attached to Catherine despite their differences, stopped reading the newspapers.

The party ended on September 29th. Catherine knew from the way the courier spurred his horse that something was wrong: British, French, and Serbian troops had overpowered Bulgaria. Within days they would team up with Romania to invade Transylvania, and the Romanians already living in Transylvania were sure to side with their co-nationals.

Uncle Duci, visibly shaken, withdrew to his study. At dinner that evening, he announced that he was retiring from politics. All hope for victory was gone;

the country had to sue for peace immediately. "Now it's your turn," he told Michael and Catherine. "You backed the right horse and must now be given your chance. We will support you in every way that we can."

Michael left for Budapest in the morning. Along the way, landowners sought him out to ask how they could hold on to the Romanian territory they had gained from the Peace of Bucharest in 1917.

Michael explained that the problem now was not how to hold on to Romanian territory but how to prevent Romania from taking Hungarian territory. Parliament had to renounce the Bucharest peace and make immediate concessions to the Romanian minority in Transylvania.

But the landowners didn't understand. Why should they have to give up something they already owned? Even if they had it for only a short while, it was *theirs*. God had put it in *their* hands. "Land is sacred," Count Belthen told Michael. "To ask me to give it up at this point is like asking me for my pants."

The mood at Dubrin echoed this sentiment. Catherine was now being treated as if Michael was personally responsible for the Bulgarian defeat. Uncle Duci told her that her beloved shooting box would soon belong to the Romanians.

"Then Michael will be satisfied," Ella added.

"Michael didn't start the war," Catherine reminded her parents. "Nor did he support the Kaiser until it was too late."

Uncle Duci said not to support Hungary in its time of need was dishonorable.

Ella then explained the real reason for all the trouble: "People like Michael and Catherine have a different definition of honor."

Michael received pretty much the same treatment in Budapest. An Allied demand for the immediate democratization of Austria-Hungary was tabled while Parliament debated whether to try him as a French spy.

Michael accused Parliament of trying just as hard to lose the peace as it had worked to lose the war.

A motion was made to strip him of his officer's rank.

Michael decided to do something *really* treasonous. Or at least close to it. Something that would get Parliament's mind off the fictions his enemies were creating about him and back on Hungary: open negotiations with the minorities. The more agreements he could reach, the more support he'd have for his coalition.

His first meeting was with Matthew Dula. Leader of the Slovak National Party, Dula demanded autonomy for the Slovaks, but he never mentioned independence. Leaders of the Romanian minority also made no mention of separation. And they had British, French, and Serbian troops backing them up. Talks with the Serbs followed similar lines: more autonomy, a looser connection with the Hapsburgs, but no separation from Hungary. In fact, only Croatia demanded complete independence, and only Fiume—Hungary's sole seaport—was a subject for debate. But even in these cases, Michael felt that a Karolyi government could solve the problem in Hungary's favor. The minorities trusted him, and he was the only member of Parliament willing to make concessions.

While Michael worked with Oskar Jaszi on the minority issue, Sigismund Kunfi's unionists worked on converting the soldiers and the peasants.

The soldiers were easy. Many of them had been prisoners of war during the Russian Revolution and returned to Hungary after Lenin took over. Ordered to the front, they spread the Bolshevik word. The problem the unionists faced with these soldiers was holding them back. They wanted too much too soon. And the few still loyal to the Hapsburgs didn't care. They were so beaten down by four years of fighting they just wanted to go home.

The peasants were tougher to convert, and part of the reason was the workers. They saw the peasants as the ones who took their jobs, kept their wages down, and then headed for the fields as soon as the planting and harvesting seasons began. Dull, conservative, and uneducated, the peasants' only aim in life was land: get all you can, hold on to what you have, and envy any that isn't yours.

The peasants weren't too keen on the workers either. They were from the city. City people were different from country people. You could admire them, but you were better off when you avoided them.

And Marxists were no exception. They acted as if they had all the answers to all the questions you didn't have enough sense to ask. And why would workers from the city suddenly be so interested in what happened to the peasants? Why were they suddenly so fired up about improving the conditions of the people they hated? Something had to be in it for them..

On October 11th, Charles summoned Michael to Vienna. He wanted to replace Primes Minister Wekerle, and Stephen Tisza had suggested he talk to Michael.

Michael told Charles he had to disassociate himself from Germany and face the Allies alone if he hoped to save the Empire. He also had to appoint leaders who would practice what he preached. This meant elevating people such as Sigismund Kunfi and Oskar Jaszi and assuming a lesser role for the Monarchy. It also meant freeing all political prisoners, including Friedrich Adler, and reaching radical agreements with the minorities: autonomy in some cases, independence in others. Then there were the questions of universal suffrage and land reform. The more Charles showed he was no longer controlled by those responsible for the war, the better off Austria-Hungary would be.

Michael wasn't offered the job, but Charles did

send agents to seek a separate peace with the Allies and, within a week of talking with Michael, invited the minorities in Austria to form national councils for the purpose of creating autonomous states.

Suddenly there was a wheat shortage. Every time Charles did something the landowners didn't like, there was a wheat shortage.

Angered by his not being asked to lead the Hungarian government and wanting to force Parliament to take some responsibility for the direction of the war, Michael announced that Charles' plan to divide the Hapsburg dynasty into autonomous states automatically made Hungary a free country. Parliament could now send its own representatives to negotiate with the Allies.

A member of the Karolyi Party then stood up and nominated Michael for the position. "Michael Karolyi is a friend of the Allies," he explained in his endorsement.

"Friend of the Allies!" a landowner jeered.

Michael claimed the Karolyi coalition was a friend of peace and democracy, but it was too late. The conservatives picked up their colleagues' cry. "Friend of the Allies!" they shouted. "Friend of the Allies!"

Wekerle suspended the session.

The next day, Stephen Tisza—still the symbol and paragon of the old order—rose to address Parliament. "I will not play with words," Tisza told the deputies. "Karolyi is right. We have lost the war."

The landowners were stunned. Many only now believed the truth because Tisza had told them. The rest finally accepted what they had denied for months.

But Tisza wasn't through. He renounced the Dual Monarchy, called on Parliament to remove Hungarian troops from German control, and petitioned for an independent foreign service.

Michael seconded Tisza's motion but claimed the former Prime Minister hadn't gone far enough. Except for the Germans, every minority group in

Austria had voted for independence. Parliament should declare Hungary's independence as well.

Uncle Duci, whose "retirement" from politics hadn't lasted twenty-four hours, urged Parliament to stay with the Monarchy until after a peace was concluded.

Michael argued that to stay with the Monarchy was to go down with the Monarchy.

A telegram interrupted the debate: the 79th Croation Infantry had mutinied against the Hungarian officers.

Uncle Duci didn't know what to say. Prime Minister Wekerle muttered something that no one understood. Stephen Tisza didn't understand anything that was said to him. The lost war, the abandoned monarchy, and now a mutiny. It was too much for any of them to handle all at once. Their minds simply couldn't adjust to the speed with which their lifelong convictions were being altered.

"Free the story!" a journalist shouted from the gallery. "Down with censorship!"

The Karolyi Party rose and cheered.

"Throw them out!" Tisza shouted. "Throw them all out!"

Thus ended the last meeting of Parliament under the old regime.

That night, Michael met with Kunfi and Jaszi at the Karolyi Palace. Werkle had resigned as Prime Minister. "The time to act independently is now," Jaszi told his colleagues. "The government no longer has any standing. We must form a National Council before Parliament can recover."

Michael agreed that Wekerle's government was finished, but he didn't want to create a National Council unless it was absolutely necessary. If they were patient, Charles was sure to ask them to form a new government."

Kunfi wanted to know what made Michael so sure.

"We're the only logical choice," Michael replied. "Who else can make peace with the Allies *and* save Hungary's land from the minorities?"

A telephone rang in the next room.

"That's probably Charles right now," Michael joked.

It was Uncle Duci. Charles had appointed him Foreign Minister. He wanted Michael to work with him on opening negotiations with the Entente.

"So much for logical choices," Kunfi commented.

"We've got to separate ourselves from this madness," Jaszi argued. "We've got to set up a National Council with its own foreign office. We've got to conclude our own, independent peace."

Kunfi agreed: "The longer we wait, the harder it's going to be."

But Michael still hesitated. Forming a National Council meant breaking his oath of allegiance to the Hapburgs. He wanted to take over the government legally. "We should accept Andrassy's appointment on the condition that the ruling classes assume all responsibility for the war. A new foreign minister representing a new, independent Hungary can take over after a peace has been concluded."

Kunfi and Jaszi agreed. Reluctantly. Catherine was ecstatic. Finally, the two men she loved most in the world were on the same side. Together they would work for the future of Hungary.

Someone should have told Uncle Duci. He was still working for Hungary's past. He told Michael at their first meeting that he "loathed" Wilson's "Fourteen Points," had "no intention" of signing a separate peace, and would "never" turn against the Germans.

Michael informed Uncle Duci that Germany had been pressing for a separate peace for weeks.

"What Germany does is no concern of mine," the new Foreign Minister replied. "I answer only to my conscience."

"And who answers the Hungarian people after your conscience has prejudiced their interests?"

"As long as I am true to myself, I don't have to answer to anyone."

Michael left his father-in-law's study. There was nothing more he could say.

But Catherine continued sitting with her mother behind Uncle Duci's curtain. She wanted to hear the reaction of her stepfather's advisors, and all Ella could do about it was frown. Anything more would reveal their hiding place and undermine the government's confidence in Uncle Duci.

Catherine couldn't remember being more pleased with herself. To score a victory over her mother and help Michael at the same time was beyond anything she had hoped for. Her spirits sagged, however, when Uncle Duci's advisors decided to adopt Michael's program as their own.

It was time to go. The National Council could not wait a moment longer.

Michael called a meeting at the Karolyi Palace. Jaszi was the first to arrive, then Kunfi, then a messenger from the King. Charles was at a secret villa just outside of Budapest; he needed to see Michael; it was urgent: the Soldiers' and Workers' Councils were preparing a *coup d'etat*.

Kunfi told Michael not to go. The *coup* was only a rumor to pressure Charles into seeking a separate peace.

Jaszi said that Michael could do nothing for the King. Charles had lost his chance when he formed a new government without any representatives from the coalition.

Catherine said it was 1848 all over again. The King would kill Michael just as Franz-Joseph had killed Louis Batthyani.

Michael said he wanted one more chance to take over the government legally.

Charles showed Michael a table littered with telegrams. All were addressed to Karolyi. Naval units and regiments on every front had abandoned their positions and were awaiting his orders. "How do you explain this?" the King wanted to know.

"As you have already read them," Michael answered. "You know exactly what they mean."

Michael expected Charles to be irritated, but he wasn't. He needed Michael's help. The minorities in Austria were declaring their independence with or without their King's approval. More than half the country was gone. If Michael didn't help, Charles would go down in history as the Hapsburg who had blown the Empire. Would he be willing to form a government with Julius Andrassy?

Michael explained the differences that separated him and Uncle Duci.

"He will soon see that yours are the only feasible solutions," Charles replied. "Already Wilson is demanding that Hungary give up Slovakia and Croatia. I imagine he'll give away Transylvania too before it's over."

Michael said he'd set up a National Council that would admit representatives from Andrassy's party, but he wouldn't form another coalition. "The Karolyi, Social Democratic, and Radical Parties express the will of the people," he told Charles. "We intend to exercise that will."

"But a National Council in Hungary is illegal. My manifesto only applies to Austria. You need the consent of Parliament."

"Parliament no longer represents the Hungarian people. In a fair election, not one of its deputies would retain his seat."

The next day, October 25th, 1918, Michael,

Kunfi, and Jaszi formally founded the National Council of Hungary. Its programs included independence from Austria, the immediate conclusion of a "hopeless war," and liberty for all political prisoners.

The Council also intended to preserve through democratic action the historic kingdom of St. Stephen. Each nationality would decide by secret ballot whether to be independent or part of a new "brotherly alliance of equal people who support a territorial integrity based on economic and geographic interests instead of national jealousies."

Copies of the Council's proclamation were posted all over the city and thousands of demonstrators filled the streets. Although organized by Kunfi and Jaszi, not all of the demonstrators could be controlled. One group of students—bored with marching around the university—headed for the Karolyi Palace. They wanted pictures of Michael to carry with them to the King's castle.

Michael said they shouldn't apply too much pressure too soon. "Let the landowners get used to the idea of a democracy before throwing it in their faces. If the King thinks a revolution is taking place, he'll call out the troops. Many innocent people will get hurt."

But Catherine convinced Michael to let the students go. They were only children; what harm could they do?

Michael said the military didn't distinguish between students and unionists. In fact, they preferred students. Students didn't fight back.

Nevertheless, Catherine prevailed. While a maid ran to get a flag from the attic, Catherine tossed from her bedroom balcony whatever posters she could find with Michael's picture on them.

An hour later, the students were back. Mounted police had surrounded them, beaten them with clubs, destroyed their posters, and taken their flag.

Catherine turned the children's nursery into a ward.

A group of soldiers asked to speak with Michael. They had seen the beatings and wanted to prepare the way for his takeover. Whom did they want him to kill first? Stephen Tisza or Julius Andrassy? All he had to do was say the word.

Michael said killing Tisza or Andrassy would only lead to more violence, but his anger with what had happened to the students undermined his words. The soldiers sensed that Michael was only saying what he *had* to say. The truth was that he would really welcome an assassination and take over.

Catherine overheard the conversation and telephoned Uncle Duci.

He wasn't home. He and Ella had left for the Foreign Minister's office in Vienna.

Catherine rushed to West Station. The train hadn't left, but the only people on the platform were her parents and an aide at one end and several soldiers walking toward them from the other. The Vienna Express was usually packed.

Ella got on the train when she saw her daughter run toward her. Uncle Duci explained that she was afraid she wouldn't be able to control her temper. When he heard about the plot on his life, he sent his aide to warn Tisza and alert the city's garrison. Any number of government officials could be in danger.

Catherine decided to chat with the soldiers until the train pulled out. They looked like the same ones Michael had spoken to at the Palace? Had she saved her parents' lives?

She'd never know.

The Council had planned a rally in front of Parliament for October 27th. Michael, the main speaker, would present the changes his government would make. Before he left his Palace, however, he received a call from the Director of the Hungarian Bank. He had come up with a way to solve the crisis and the King had already agreed to it: Michael would form a coalition government with representatives from all the parties. He would be the Prime Minister and Andrassy would stay on as Foreign Minister until a truce had been signed. Then a new ministry would be formed and Michael could staff it with whomever he chose. Michael was to come immediately with the director to meet with Charles at his secret villa .

Michael postponed the rally for twenty-four hours. At the villa in Godollo, he found Charles pacing in his field uniform before a map of infantry positions that no longer existed. Michael, who couldn't help but feel sorry for the disillusioned monarch, said he was prepared to form a government on the terms Charles had offered.

"And what terms are they?" Charles asked.

Michael repeated what the Director of the Hungarian Bank had told him.

"I agree to everything though I knew nothing about any terms before you told me." Then Charles added: "I've been warned that you want to set up a republic. Is this true?"

Michael said he wanted an independent, democratic Hungary that included a personal union with the King.

"Good," said the King. "Now, sit down and tell me your whole program. Start from the beginning. I want to know all about it."

Michael went through just about everything he had ever said to Charles. The only difference was that this time Charles didn't ask if every person Michael mentioned was a Jew.

"Yes, you are right," Charles said when Michael finished. "Andrassy already has my orders to denounce the alliance with Germany. I'll tell him to do whatever else you say."

Charles then asked Michael to go with him to Vienna. It was important to talk with the Austrian Prime Minister and Andrassy to make sure everyone understood where the new government was heading.

Michael, who already had a cabinet formed from the National Council, made arrangements for Charles to meet Kunfi and Jaszi that afternoon. He'd return to Godollo in the evening for dinner and Charles' response to his nominees. If Charles approved, Michael would go with him to Vienna.

At dinner, Charles behaved like a man who has just been relieved of a heavy burden. Though obviously exhausted, his spirits were high and he kept his guests entertained with stories about Franz-Joseph's personal habits. But he left the table without talking to his newly designated Prime Minister.

Michael waited until everyone except him and Count Janos Hadik were left. Neither knew that the other was waiting to meet with Charles. Nor did they know that Charles had asked them both to be Prime Minister.

Finally, the King sent for Michael.

Queen Zita intercepted him: "You will be able to help the King and the country, won't you?"

Michael said he would do everything in his power, but the situation was grave and demanded drastic action. "Even the Queen must be prepared to make tremendous sacrifices."

"But you will do everything you can, won't you?" she asked.

Michael promised her he would.

A bottle of port and a box of cigars had been set out in the King's study. Charles appeared in a smoking jacket. Yes, he said, he was very pleased with Kunfi and Jaszi. Were they Jewish? It didn't matter. Good minds and good hearts both. With Michael at the helm, Hungary would surely be saved. Perhaps one day the Austrian throne would be regained. Anything was possible with a man like Karolyi.

A telephone call interrupted the King's stream of confidence. It was Julius Andrassy. When Charles told him who was going to be Hungary's next Prime

Minister, Uncle Duci said the King could kiss his throne goodbye.

"You lost your throne because of people like Andrassy," Michael told Charles when the King repeated what Uncle Duci had said. "Your reforms got away from you and into the hands of the people. Once they seized the power you refused to share, they didn't need you any more. Now they don't even want you. If you haven't already lost all your power, I can guarantee you'll lose what's left if you don't follow my advice."

Charles said he would do whatever Michael said, but there was no conviction in his voice. On the train to Vienna that night, he didn't say anything at all.

Michael spent the next day waiting in his hotel room. Neither Charles nor the Austrian Prime Minister nor Andrassy called. And none of Michael's calls were returned. Suddenly, it dawned on him: Charles had lured him to Vienna to keep him from taking over the government.

Michael took the first train back to Budapest. In the dining car, he ran into Archduke Joseph. Charles had just appointed him *Homo Regius* of Hungary. There was no way Michael would be Prime Minister now.

But he might be something else. An enormous crowd had filled the platform and spilled over into the large square in front of West Station. Word had spread that Michael had been pushed aside as Prime Minister and Archduke Joseph had been named Dictator. "Down with the Archduke! Up with Karolyi!" the people shouted. "Down with the Dictator! Up with the Minister of the People!"

Michael spoke to the crowd while Archduke Joseph was led out a back way. People who claimed to represent the masses told Michael that since the King had not appointed him Prime Minister, they were going to make him the People's Prime Minster.

Michael thanked the representatives and ran

for the first carriage he saw. The last thing Hungary needed now was a premature revolution and the bloodshed that would surely follow. He had to get to the Council's headquarters. He had to find out what was going on and what Kunfi and Jaszi were doing about it. But the people, almost hysterical now, unhitched the carriage's horses and began pulling Michael themselves.

Michael jumped out at a passing car, but his supporters lifted him onto their shoulders. "I have to get to the Hotel Astoria," he told those passing him above the crowd. "Please put me in a cab."

The people broke into the *Marseillaise*.

When Michael finally made it to the Astoria, Oskar Jaszi told him that the journalists decided not to hand their manuscripts into the censors. "Our manifesto has appeared in every paper."

"We want Karolyi!" a crowd shouted outside the hotel.

Sigismund Kunfi went to the balcony. "The Viennese think they are playing cards with us," he told the people. "They don't know that a crown is at stake."

"We want Karolyi!"

Then it was Stephen Friedrich's turn. Friedrich had been with Michael on his tour of America and, in the Bordeaux prison, wrote the first drafts of a book he called *Karolyi, Prisoner in France*, but no one ever thought of him as much of leader until he stood before the crowed to shout "AC-TION! AC-TION! AC-TION!"

The press printed their stories about the demonstrations next to the news that Andrassy's terms for a separate peace in the name of the Monarchy had been refused. The Czechs declared that Andrassy had no right to speak in their name. So did the Yugoslavs. They wanted out of the Empire. Now!

The government bureaus were the next to abandon Charles. One after the other, postal workers, railway men, and civil servants joined the National Council. Merchants and manufacturers followed. Hundreds of Hungarian soldiers made their way from the train stations to the Hotel Astoria to offer their support. Many more went to their barracks, however, and Michael feared they'd been brought to Budapest to suppress any signs of revolution.

Kunfi decided to infiltrate these regiments with agitators. On the morning of October 29th, posters filled the walls of every barrack. The soldiers read they'd soon be ordered to shoot at unarmed citizens whose only crime was to demand bread, peace, and freedom. Join the National Council, the posters urged: "Your place is not on the side of an antiquated system but on ours."

Archduke Joseph reacted swiftly, but he didn't accomplish much. The troops he ordered to evacuate the city refused to budge, and the ones he ordered to raid the headquarters of the Soldiers' Council found it empty. His own telephone operator had betrayed him.

Joseph's next move was to have the soldiers who had disobeyed his orders sent to the front. When the Soldiers' Council heard that two companies were being held in sealed boxcars at South Station, they organized a demonstration. Ten thousand people surrounded the train.

"Disperse these people at once," an officer told the army separating the train from the crowd.

The guards didn't move.

The officer repeated his orders.

The people moved toward the soldiers.

"Fire!" the officer shouted.

The soldiers handed the people their guns.

The Revolution had begun.

In another part of Budapest, demonstrators marched on Archduke Joseph's palace. The city's police met them with a barricade at Andrassy Bridge but didn't stop them. The last demonstrator to pass through wasn't ten feet from the barricade, however, when the first shot rang out. Mounted police rushed onto the other side of the bridge with drawn sabers.

The Revolution had its first martyrs.

Michael suspended all negotiations with Archduke Joseph and declared a general strike. Catherine rushed to Vienna. Uncle Duci had to convince Charles to meet the National Council's demands before it was too late. Michael would not be able to hold back Kunfi and Jaszi much longer. This was the Monarchy's last chance to save itself.

Michael saw Catherine off at West Station and headed for police headquarters. General Albert Varkonyi, the City Commander, wanted to surrender his sword.

"That won't be necessary," Michael told him.

A large bang sounded.

Several others quickly followed.

The general's eyes brightened. "The troops are on their way to free us," he told the only aide not to betray him. "I can tell machine-gun fire a long way off."

Michael explained that the bangs the general heard were only doors slamming in a breeze.

Their numbers bolstered by the men who had arrested General Varkonyi rather than defend him, the Soldiers' Council took over every important building in Budapest. There was no resistance. Even the police who had attacked the crowd on Andrassy Bridge were now with the people.

Charles ordered General Lukachich to take Budapest. A strong supporter of the dynasty with a reputation for cruelty, Lukachich knew his Bosnian soldiers would need little prodding to fire at Magyars. Not only that but the Soldiers' Council seemed to be running ahead of its political leaders. Or at least down a different path. The Council didn't have enough soldiers to stop regular troops, and it couldn't recruit factory workers because of the general strike.

Michael saw the problem this way: if Catherine convinced Uncle Duci to convince Charles to rescind Lukachich's orders, the revolutionaries would win. If she failed, the Revolution would perish under Lukachich's sword.

Catherine arrived at the Ballhausplate Palace just as Ella and Uncle Duci sat down for breakfast in the Metternich study. Her grandfather had directed Austria-Hungary's fate for eighteen years from this room, and Uncle Duci was obviously at ease in it.

Ella seemed to possess it as her birthright. "The ceiling is ruined," she complained to Uncle Duci. "I don't know what we're going to do with that maid. You'd think we brought her here to destroy the place."

Catherine used this remark to introduce the reason why she had come, but Uncle Duci couldn't believe things were as bad as she said. If Archduke Joseph showed "some energy," everything would be all right. Besides, Julius had his own problems. The people of Vienna had demonstrated against him the day before, and a group of Prussian officers had been caught planning to assassinate him for betraying the German alliance. "The people have lost their heads completely," he told Catherine. "Czechoslovakia has denounced me and that madman Masaryk has gone and set up a republic. I suspect Michael is capable of the same folly."

Catherine said a republic could still be avoided if he convinced Charles to call off his troops and reach an agreement with the National Council.

Her argument fell on deaf ears. Uncle Duci's disregard for the masses was so ingrained he could not imagine that their demands ever had to be taken seriously.

Ella told Catherine to eat her egg before it got cold.

Then the telephone rang.

It was King Charles. He wanted Uncle Duci to tell him if he should hand over the fleet to the Yugoslavs.

132

"Hand it over?"

"The admiral says resistance is impossible."

"Then I guess there's nothing else to do."

A telegram arrived. "The Croat National Council has just proclaimed the independence of Croatia."

"You haven't touched your egg," Ella admonished Catherine.

Another telegram: "The Isonzo front has just collapsed. The commanding officer wants permission to surrender. His men are too exhausted to retreat."

Then the doorbell rang. Louis Windeschgraetz, Uncle Duci's chief advisor, and Catherine's cousin, Princess Marizza Lechenstein, were announced. "Good news!" Windeschgraetz shoouted as he swept into the room. "Everything is going well. The Germans will suppress any revolutions."

"What's happening in Budapest?" Princess Marizza asked Catherine.

"Seven people were killed in a demonstration on Andrassy Bridge."

"Only seven? Louis will have to speak to the city commander about that."

Uncle Duci showed Catherine to the door. "Tell Michael to be patient and calm the hysterical Jews," he whispered. "In a few days an armistice will be signed and he can take over. All I ask is enough time to deliver my own father's death blow."

Catherine embraced her stepfather and headed down the broad staircase. When she looked back, he was still watching her from the landing.

The wire she sent to Michael read: "Failed in Vienna. Uncle Duci determined to destroy the Empire on principle."

When Catherine reached the Karolyi Palace, she found machine guns starring at her from several windows of the ballroom and guards inside the front door. "The Bosnian troops under Lukachich are preparing to take the city," Michael told her.

Catherine led her husband into her bedroom and lit a fire. As rain fell softly on the pavement outside the window, they slid under a comforter on Catherine's bed. Neither had slept in over twenty-four hours. "Our children have been away for months," Michael said. "Do you miss them?"

"No."

"Do you mind that their nursery is still a ward?"

"No."

"You're worried about Lukachich, aren't you?"

"I'm worried about you."

"Don't. Whatever happens, everything has been worthwhile and nothing can stop what has already begun."

The doorbell rang. The editor of Michael's newspaper reported that King Charles had telephoned Lukachich. The Bosnians were marching on the Astoria Hotel.

Michael telephoned Archduke Joseph. He reminded him that national councils had been formed all over the Empire without bloodshed. He had to stop Lukachich from carrying out his orders.

Joseph said he would do what he could, but Charles had just appointed Count Hadik Prime Minister. He was running the country now.

Knowing the pro-German wouldn't need a reason to open fire, Michael and Catherine hurried through the rain and empty streets to the Astoria.

A volley of shots broke the silence.

"The attack has started," Michael told Catherine.

They started running. As they approached the Astoria, the firing grew more intense. A mass of people had jammed the hotel's revolving door while a group of laughing soldiers shot their rifles into the air. Ordered to the front, they had turned back at the station and headed for the Astoria. Their shots were shots of joy.

"Have you nothing better to do than make noise," Catherine scolded.

The soldiers recognized who had spoken and snapped to attention. "Long live peace, liberty, and Karolyi!" one of them announced.

The mood inside the hotel was less optimistic. "Our workers are on strike, and our soldiers have run from the rain," Oskar Jaszi told Michael. "We'll all hang at dawn."

Michael, Catherine, Kunfi, and Jaszi sat, smoked, and waited for the inevitable.

At three in the morning, Lukachich telephoned King Charles. He needed help. His orders for the Magyar troops to assemble had not been carried out, and he wasn't sure he could trust the Bosnians. They had been told if they supported the National Council now, the National Council would support them later. Lukachich wanted Germans.

An hour later, the telephone rang in the main office of the National Council. Archduke Joseph had a message from Prime Minister Hadik. He wanted to meet Michael. Secretly.

Everyone told Michael not to go. It was a trap. Surely he would die.

Michael said he had no choice. To stay at the Astoria was to wait for certain death. If the National Council had any chance, it was in talking to Hadik.

But Catherine wouldn't let Michael go without her.

"Don't be selfish," he told her. "One of us has to live for Adam and Eva."

Catherine returned to the Karolyi Palace. In front of the fire in her bedroom, she relived her life with Michael. Where would she be now if it hadn't been for him? What will she do now without him?

A single shot pierced her thoughts.

She rushed to the window.

The house across the street was jammed with people. Others danced in the street below. People were

placing chrysanthemums in each other's lapels.
"KAROLYI HAS WON!" they shouted. "LONG LIVE
THE FIRST HUNGARIAN REPUBLIC!"

VI. The New Era

October 31st, 1918. From the steps of Archduke
Joseph's palace, Michael looked over the city. The rain
had stopped and a bright, dazzling sun bounced off the
windows of the Karolyi Palace. Today, as in 1848, the
heart of the revolution was beating there.

It had been a long night—the death wait for
Lukachich's troops, the fear of assassination, saying
goodbye to Catherine for what could have been the last
time—but the dawn had brought forth Janos Hadik in
his pajamas. Unshaven and still sleepy, he didn't want
to be Prime Minister any longer. What he wanted was
to put on his robe and slippers, walk Michael to the
Archduke's palace, and resign.

Joseph accepted Hadik's resignation and
appointed Michael Prime Minister in the name of the
King. Nothing more was said. When Hadik got back
under the covers of his bed, he hadn't lost more than a
half an hour of sleep.

Michael wondered if he'd ever need sleep again.
People on the street shook his hand and congratulated
him. Chrysantimums, a symbol of the revolution since
soldiers began exchanging their ensigns for them, were
in everyone's lapels. Workers waving flags and singing
national songs drove recklessly through the streets. The
strain and suspense of war had finally ended. For the

first time in years, the people had a future they could look forward to.

And it really had been a *people's* revolution. At least in Budapest. It may have started out as the private venture of the Soldiers' Council, but the workers had galvanized it into a movement that brought Karolyi and the National Council to power almost without their realizing it. "The victory was quite easy," wrote one observer. "The citizen of Budapest, the soldier from Jozsefvaros, the sailor from Obuda, and the student from the Galileo Circle were the Brutus, Rospierre, and Trotsky of the Hungarian Revolution. They put an end to the war with a flip and shook off that odious monster as if it were nothing."

But not all the people celebrated. A lot more—the landless peasant, the young soldier crippled by a lost cause—waited. Their joy was a more skeptical and limited endorsement of the revolution. Yes, they were happy the fighting was over, but they worried about what would become of their defeat.

Michael was aware of their concern and welcomed the opportunity to satisfy their centuries-old craving for land, to give them a country they could *feel* was their own.

At City Hall, Michael resigned his presidency of the National Council and formed a new government. His cabinet included liberal, socialist, and radical representatives with Oskar Jaszi serving as Minister of the National Minorities.

Telegrams of support arrived from all over the country. Former enemies crowded the ante-chambers. Bishops, bank directors, society presidents, and members of Parliament lined up to swear allegiance to the man they had wanted stripped of his officer's rank, banned from the National Casino, and shot as a French spy. Even Stephen Tisza made it known that he considered backing Michael his patriotic duty.

Michael told Tisza he didn't think the people would respond favorably to his endorsement. Nor would there be a place for the old rulers in the new government. He suggested they retire to the country. When the political climate changed, they would be contacted. In the meantime, measures would be taken to ensure their safety.

When Michael returned to the Karolyi Palace, Catherine told him about the people celebrating their new republic. Except as an accusation in Parliament or a taunt from Uncle Duci, this was the first Michael had heard the word associated with him or his government. It made him wonder if the revolution was going on without him.

The telephone rang. A group of soldiers had brought General Lukachich to the Astoria Hotel. They couldn't protect him anymore. The people in the square wanted his head. What did Michael want the soldiers to do?

Michael said he'd come right over.

The telephone rang again. Soldiers were gathering outside Stephen Tisza's villa on Andrassy Avenue. They were armed and looked as if they might be plotting something. What did Michael want the police guarding Tisza to do?

Michael had been afraid of this. Like most of the people of Budapest, he had welcomed the return of the soldiers. But as train after train of them arrived from the front, he also became concerned for the public's safety. War didn't usually improve human nature and there was a good chance many of these soldiers would become dangerous.

Michael telephoned the City Commander, but every available police officer had already been assigned to protect an aristocrat. He then tried a garrison he knew was still loyal to the old regime. The officer who answered the phone told him: "The soldiers won't come out of their barracks until the King retracts his order to refrain from bloodshed."

Michael ordered half of his own guard to Tisza's villa and left for the Astoria. His colleagues had been doing their best to calm the crowd outside of the hotel, but they could not make themselves heard. The people were becoming impatient. They wanted to hang Lukachich for all the deserters he shot during the war.

And they wanted him *now*!

Michael stepped out on the balcony. Lukachich was quickly forgotten. The people had a new demand: a republic. "Long live Karolyi!" they shouted. "Long live the First Hungarian Republic!"

"A stone is rolling," an aide whispered to Michael. "Dare we stay it?"

"No," Michael replied. "The stronger the people's voice, the greater the aristocrats' fear; the greater the aristocrats' fear, the more powerful our government, and the more powerful our government, the better our chances for reform."

"Those responsible for the war have been eliminated from rule," Michael told the crowd. "The new government will respond to *your* will. The question is how far do you want us to go?"

The people answered: "We want a republic!"

When Lukachich had been disguised as a worker and taken out a back way, Michael turned the crowd over to Stephen Friedrich. He and the members of his new cabinet then walked to the Buda Palace where Archduke waited to swear them in. When they arrived, they heard the news: Stephen Tisza was dead. A group of soldiers had entered his villa and shot him. "Yes," Tisza said as he fell to the ground. "It had to happen this way."

Others thought so too. But to prevent a provocation, the new government didn't raise a black flag and the newspapers only printed a few lines on their final pages. Tisza, whom many considered personally responsible for the war, was dead. So was the regime he symbolized.

But Michael knew it would take more than the death of Stephen Tisza to purge Hungary of its guilt. Already there was trouble within the new government.

Stephen Friedrich had seen the end of the war and the downfall of the aristocrats as the solution to all the country's problems. In spite of all the talk about a new beginning, he wasn't prepared to take the "AC-TION!" he had called for. He wanted to consult with the ruling classes; the people weren't politically mature enough to vote; it wasn't a good idea to be too revolutionary too soon.

Sigismund Kunfi, on the other hand, couldn't move fast enough. His control of the soldiers and workers was based mostly on the promises he had made: universal suffrage, nationalization of the industries, and land reform. The time to fulfill these promises was at hand.

Oskar Jaszi was all for keeping Kunfi's promises, but he wondered if the government should wait until the factories were profitable again before taking them over. He was also against breaking up the large estates. "Giving the land to the peasants will only sow the seeds of capitalism," he told the Cabinet. "Better to turn the estates into collectives."

Michael tried to reach solutions that satisfied everyone, but so many new crises arose so quickly he rarely resolved any of them: Russian armies had crossed the frontier, minorities had seized coal mines in the north and south, freed criminals were terrorizing the peasants, and a whole town had been taken over by escaped lunatics.

And these were just the telegrams. By telephone he learned that Kunfi was already distancing himself from the new government by forming secret pacts with the Soldiers' and Workers' Councils, that the press was undermining Kunfi to score points with Karolyi, that Stephen Friedrich had killed Stephen Tisza in exchange for a government portfolio, and that Catherine had ordered Tisza killed to prevent a counter-revolution. Whether these reports were true or false didn't matter. The government wasn't united enough to stop them, and much of what it did seemed to confirm everybody's worst suspicions. Catherine, for example, admitted to the press that she had called Tisza's villa to see if the soldiers had arrived, and the other suspected murderer, Stephen Friedrich, was appointed Deputy Minister of Defense.

Michael wondered if it was better to just let history take its course. The peasants would take over the land, the workers would seize the factories, and no aristocrat would win an election. That would solve three big problems quickly and easily. But, as he had done in the past, Michael opted for legal rather than social justice. The result was that nobody got all they wanted and everybody was dissatisfied.

A sign of what was to come appeared before the government was a week old. A large crowd of soldiers and workers demonstrated under Michael's bedroom window. They wanted a republic.

Michael suspected Kunfi was behind the demonstration, but the day's editorials echoed the same sentiment: the Allies had insisted on democracies within the Austro-Hungarian Empire; until the Karolyi government separated itself from the Dual Monarchy, Hungary couldn't expect favorable treatment at the peace conference.

Michael knew Jaszi was behind the editorials, but at his next cabinet meeting he finally accepted what was obvious to everyone else. Wilson had refused to negotiate with either the Hohenzollerns in Germany or the Hapsburgs in Austria. That had led to the establishment of the German and Austrian republics and a declaration of succession states throughout the Empire. Only Hungary remained loyal.

The situation would have been comical if it hadn't been so sadly ironic. For months the opposition parties had attacked the ruling classes for their obstinate allegiance to something that no longer existed. No sooner had they formed their new government, however, than they proclaimed its loyalty to the same non-existent monarchy.

Michael admitted this wasn't the most effective way to establish credibility with the Entente. By swearing allegiance to Charles, he had restored that part of the kingdom that was still Hungary.

Kunfi said the new government had no choice now but to declare independence immediately. The people demanded a republic, Wilson insisted on a democracy, and any alliance with Charles damaged their chances for leniency.

All except Michael agreed. In spite of his revolutionary zeal and his realization that Hungary could not be the only state in the Empire to remain loyal to the King, he refused to break his oath.

The move toward a republic, meanwhile, had received support form an unlikely source: Archduke Joseph. Receiving Catherine at his palace, he asked, "When will the Republic be proclaimed? I don't think it wise to postpone it too long."

Joseph, of course, was speaking more on behalf of his own interests than any genuine concern for democracy. The disasters at Vittorio Veneto and along the Piave had virtually eliminated the Italian front. And with it went any protection for the Hapsburgs.

"Would your Highness consider the presidency?" Catherine asked the Archduke.

Joseph's answer was firm. "The Republic can have only one president: Michael Karolyi. He is the only man everyone trusts. Thank God we have him."

Even Catherine's most recalcitrant uncles accepted the inevitable. In a cleverly worded joint statement, they volunteered to give "all the land we don't need" to the peasants. They also claimed to have been good democrats as well as good aristocrats. By sleeping with peasant girls and populating the villages with their offspring, they had made sure the lands to be given away would stay in the Andrassy family.

King Charles offered further encouragement for a republic when he conducted a poll among the soldiers that had survived the war. Given the choice, a vast majority said they would vote for a democracy.

Nevertheless, Michael refused to break his oath.

Kunfi lost his patience. National Councils all over the Empire were voting to determine the kinds of governments they wanted while Hungary stagnated on a silly principle. "How can a democracy possibly be based on an oath to a King?" he asked Michael. "Since when does a government that has the support of its people need a royal sanction?"

Michael said he would resign rather than break his oath.

Kunfi told him his government would soon collapse if he didn't.

A Hapsburg ended the argument. Archduke Joseph, who had heard of the problem from Oskar Jaszi, volunteered to telephone Charles and ask him to relieve the government of its oath.

"You have to free them," Joseph told the King. "There's no other way."

Charles hesitated. Hungary was all he had left. Could he have some time to think it over?

"There is no time, your Majesty. If you do not free Michael from his oath, there will be a civil war. Many innocent people will die."

Charles told Joseph he'd call him back. He wanted to ask the Empress what she thought.

"The King doesn't fully understand the seriousness of the situation," Joseph told the Cabinet, "but I think he'll come around to our way of thinking. Will you proclaim the Republic today?"

Kunfi said they would.

Michael said a republic could only be established by an elected assembly.

The telephone rang. Archduke Joseph, listening to Charles' words, nodded approvingly. "He's cross with me," he told Michael when he got off the phone, "but he's been cross with me before."

Michael thanked the Archduke.

Kunfi said it was time to get down to business.

But there was one more problem. "Do you think," Joseph asked the Cabinet, "it would be a good idea for me to change my name to Alcsuti? The property I own in Hungary is in Alcsut."

Michael said the Archduke already had a good name.

November 2nd, 1918. The new government sat down to implement the pre-revolutionary program of the National Council. Its first concern was peace. The war had to be ended and an armistice reached with the Allies as soon as possible. The Chief of the Austro-Hungarian General Staff, Arthur Staussenburg, had been negotiating with the Italians since October 28th, but the Karolyi government now decided that representatives of the defunct monarchy could no longer negotiate in Hungary's behalf. When Michael sent a telegram to Padua telling Staussenburg his services were no longer needed, however, it didn't get through. The lines had been cut down by retreating armies.

The next day Staussenberg signed an armistice that the Italians considered binding on both Austria and Hungary. Included in the treaty was a proviso that any Allied power could enter any defeated country anytime it wanted.

Serbian troops immediately crossed the Save River with the idea of annexing Hungarian territory. Backed by the French general, Franchet D'Esperey, they demanded the surrender and withdrawal of all Hungarian troops along the Danube.

Michael refused on the grounds that the armistice applied only to countries bordering Italy or fronts where Italian troops were stationed. He then sent emmisaries to Esperey. If he could negoitate a separate peace with the French, he might save some of Hungary's territory.

A poll showed that the people agreed. They

were confident that Michael's well-known affection for the French and his early oppositon to the war would save them.

Oskar Jaszi was less optimistic. He compared the delegation that went to Belgrade with the burghers of Calais. A few weeks earlier, something might have been done. Now it was too late. Hungary had remained Germany's ally too long. If the Italians had refused to negotiate separately with the Hungarians, why should the French? On the other hand, if there was one chance in a hundred of being treated less severely it lay with Michael.

The delegation, with Michael at its head, approached Belgrade with a tremendous sense of guilt. They saw the shells of buildings their armies had bombed four years earlier and wouldn't have been surprised if the people threw stones at them.

On the evening of November 7th, they met Esperey in a private house. He wore a self-designed, light blue uniform that sagged with the medals he carried on his chest. When Michael introduced himself, Esperey placed his right hand in an opening in his coat. It was not a good sign. As each member of the Hungarian delegation was introduced, Esperey wrinkled his nose or rolled his eyes. He even went so far as to ask the President of the Soldiers' Council how he had come to sink so low.

Michael opened the negotiations by asking Esperey if he or General Diaz in Padua was entitled to sign the armistice with Hungary.

Esperey said the French didn't allow Italians to sign so much as a parking ticket for them.

Michael then explained that the war was the responsibility of an old regime that had silenced its opposition and allied itself with Germany. That opposition, which represented the true will of the Hungarian people, was now in power.

"Not 'Hungarian,'" the general corrected. "Magyar."

146

Michael knew what this meant. Esperey planned to separate the Magyars from the minorities. He would see himself as the liberator of the oppressed, and the Magyars would have to pay for the sins of the landowners. Michael said he had come to negotiate for the benefit of *all* Hungarians. His goals were peace, democracy, universal suffrage, and land reform.

Esperey nodded his approval.

"If Hungary is to be occupied by foreign troops," Michael continued, "we request that they be French, English, Italian, or American. Serb, Czech, and Romanian soldiers are more likely to seize territory and abuse the people they'd been directly in conflict with."

Esperey dismissed these notions with a wave of his hand.

Michael then explained that his government needed the general's support if it was to succeed in making peace with the minorities.

Esperey laughed at the idea. Then his face turned grim. "You have marched with Germany and her lust for power and now you will be punished with her," he told the delegates. "You will pay for suppressing the minorities, you will pay for attacking Serbia, and you will pay for all the things your press said about France."

"Not *our* press," Jaszi corrected. "The landowners' press."

Esperey acted as if he heard nothing. "You are too late. Two weeks ago, it might have been possible, but now that I am in Belgrade I hold the Czechs, Romanians, Slovaks in the palm of my hand. One word from me and they will annihilate you."

Michael tried for one last favor. "Winter is coming on. Our people have no fuel. Could you influence the Czechs and Poles to release the coal sent to us by Germany?"

"What did the Hungarians use before there was coal?"

"In the days before trains and factories, wood

was sufficient," Jaszi answered.

"And what industry does Hungary possess?"

Jaszi mentioned, among others, the country's mills.

"Then why don't you simply grind your wheat with windmills?"

Jaszi felt as if he was talking with a twentieth-century version of Marie-Antionette. "This man shows an ignorance that would embarrass any Breton village *dominie*," he whispered to Michael.

Esprey then asked the delegates to follow him into his private study. He had written an armistice that made the Padua treaty seem like a blessing. Hungary had to withdraw its troops behind a line that gave the Allies a direct route into Russia as well as Berlin. The new government also had to demobilize all but a small number of its troops and allow the Entente to occupy any part of the country it considered strategically important. The victors also had the right to take over any areas of disturbance.

There were no lines to read between. Giving the Allies direct access to Germany and Russia didn't leave much Hungary. And what was left would be occupied by Czechs, Serbs, Romanians, and Slovaks as soon as they incited the minorities to riot.

Michael pointed out that with its troops demobilized Hungary wouldn't be able to suppress any disturbance or resist any invasion. Would Esperey agree to recognize the country's present boundaries and protect them from attack by the surrounding nationals?

No. Michael either signed the treaty or watched the nationals divide Hungary among themselves.

The government had little choice. Hungary's twelve divisions were no match for the Allies' forty-nine and the country was suffering from a shortage of food, coal, and war materials.

"I'm not about to give away Hungary," Michael told the general.

Esperey pointed out that to resist was to commit national suicide.

Michael didn't care. Echoing one of Uncle Duci's favorite maxims, he said, "Better to die in honor than live in dishonor."

Esperey said he would allow Hungary's new government to administer the whole country until after the final treaty was signed in Versailles.

"That won't keep neighboring nationals from creating excuses to invade the country," Michael replied. "My ministers have opposed the war since it began. Many times over the past four years we've demonstrated our loyalty to the Allies. If you can't show a little compassion in return, my government will resign, civil war will break out, and you will be personally responsible."

Esperey countered that he couldn't be responsible for what happened if Michael *didn't* sign the armistice.

Jaszi explained that as representatives of a republic, the delegates could sign nothing without approval from the National Council. This wasn't true, of course—the National Council was only a coalition of parties that had opposed the war—but Jaszi hoped a delay would give Esperey some time to think about how his superiors would react if he failed to negotiate a peace.

And it worked.

At least for a while. When the Serbian and Czech newspapers heard that the delegation had left Belgrade without signing the treaty, they claimed Esperey had been duped. The *Narodni Listy* wrote that the French were not sophisticated enough to deal with Hungarians.

The Hungarian newspapers had the opposite reaction. They accused the new government of hurrying off to Belgrade in a panic, of trying to conclude its own armistice for reasons of prestige, and of foolishly not sticking to the more lenient terms of the treaty signed in Padua.

Michael telephoned George Clemenceau. Was the Belgrade treaty an example of the way France treated her friends? Why weren't the French encouraging the Hungarian people to support their new government? Did Clemenceau not see the bloodshed that would result from such short-sighted policies? Were Wilson's principles only catch words?

Clemenceau said that Esperey's treaty was purely military and temporary. France needed to gain control of Hungary's water and railway routes for the quick transportation of troops to Berlin. The Entente might also need easy access to Russia if the counter-revolution there failed. By showing his loyalty to the French now, Michael could win favorable consideration when the final treaty was drawn up at Versailles.

Michael sent his Minister of War to Belgrade to sign the treaty. With the Serbian army occupying Ujvidek and the Czechs ready to seize the northern districts, any further delay would only give Hungary's other neighbors an excuse to seize whatever land they wanted. By signing the treaty, Michael hoped not only to strengthen his position in the final peace negotiations, as Clemenceau had suggested, but blame the French for any invasion by the neighboring states.

The Hungarian people, however, didn't trust the French. Nor the Serbs, nor the Croats, nor anyone else they had been fighting. Nor did they believe the treaty was purely military and temporary. Whatever they gave up now would be lost forever.

The former ruling classes capitalized on the people's fear to reconstruct a base of power for themselves. They insisted on representation in the new government and secretly sent feelers to Paris to see if the French were willing to topple Karolyi in exchange for whatever they needed to mount an invasion of Soviet Russia.

To keep the people's support, Michael tried to institute internal reforms and secure the abdication of

Charles who, at least theoretically, was still King of
Hungary.

The aristocrats also pressed the King to step
down. When they arrived at Schonbrunn on November
13th, but Charles thought they had come to offer their
support. Tears filled his eyes when they told him the
interests of the country demanded his resignation. "Is
this the thanks I get for limiting all my reforms to
Austria?" he asked. Then, in a change of mood, Charles
told the aristocrats that if they didn't support him,
Karolyi would. "Karolyi and I have always agreed on
what is best for Hungary."

The aristocrats replied that Karolyi was
controlled by the peasants, the workers, and the Jews.

Charles admitted he never had much affection
for the Jews. "But the peasants and workers are on my
side," he exclaimed. "I'm their friend! Don't you think
they would help me regain my throne if I asked them
to?"

"Perhaps someday," replied Baron Julius
Wlassics, the head of the landowners' delegation, "but
not today. Unless you abdicate you will place your
subjects in a difficult situation. Perhaps a future
government with a majority of aristocrats might ask
you back. It's best for Hungary now that you give up
your crown."

Charles asked for time to think it over. It
wouldn't take long. Just a few minutes by himself in the
woods behind the palace.

The Hungarians left the room.

Suddenly a shot rang out. Was this Charles'
answer?

The aristocrats ran into the woods.

More shots. An assassin?

Charles was shooting at trees. It was his way of
collecting his thoughts, calming his nerves, and making
decisions. He told the breathless aristocrats he would
abdicate. Then, falling into Wlassic's arms, he sobbed
violently and without control.

November 16th, 1918. Michael announced the founding of the First Hungarian Republic. A "Bill of Rights" published on the same day said that all males over the age of twenty-one and women over twenty-four could vote and hold public office. Elections for a new Parliament would be held early in 1919. Another law introduced an eight-hour workday and a forty-eight-hour week. Taxes would no longer be the burden of the poor. An inheritance tax was established and excise taxes on oil, sugar, and wheat were reduced. When the country got back on its feet, they would be eliminated.

The people responded enthusiastically to these bills, but their creator Pal Szende wasn't named Minister of Finance because Sigismund Kunfi thought Jews in the Cabinet would work against the government's image. With White Russian refugees blaming the Czar's fall on the Jews, Winston Churchill warning the West of an international Jewish-Bolshevik conspiracy, and the United States protecting itself from communism with some well-publicized Jewish witch-hunts, people associated Jews with revolution.

Michael agreed, but to keep Jews from participating in the republic would be equally as damaging. They were the only social group besides the discredited aristocrats capable of running a government. He decided to enlist Jews for important roles but not name them for any top positions.

The aristocrats used these obvious tactics to portray Michael as a Bolshevik puppet. Their campaign was so effective that French diplomats began referring to Budapest as "Jewdapest." Other diplomats questioned the credentials of non-Jews and Michael's integrity received an enormous setback when it was discovered that one of Tisza's suspected murderers was serving as his Deputy Minister of War. That Stephen Friedrich had led Michael to believe the War Minister had appointed him and convinced the War Minister that he had been Michael's choice didn't do much for the government's credibility either.

The situation worsened when the government failed to nationalize the factories and the minorities found independence more attractive than autonomy. And as for land reform, sixty estates had been seized and their land distributed to the peasants that worked them, but it was the peasants who had seized the estates, not the government.

Following the peasants' lead, the Republic nationalized all estates over five hundred acres. Former owners were compensated on the basis of 1913 property values and the land was distributed among landless peasants, unemployed laborers, and war veterans. They could either lease the land or buy it with a fifty-year mortgage at five percent interest.

Because she was expecting their third child, Catherine didn't attend the ceremony in which Michael gave away his lands to the peasants, but her diary reveals how glad he was to be rid of his inheritance. All his life he had felt guilty for possessing so much when so many had so little. He told Catherine how the peasants had come from the various parts of his Kapolna estate to stand in the rain and stare at their former master in wonder and suspicion. Was it possible that the land they had worked for generations was really theirs? Had their centuries-old dream come true? Or was it a trick?

The Catholic Church, which was still supported by the aristocrats, interpreted the land reform bill as a veiled attempt to win popularity for the Republic, but Michael played down any recognition he received from it. "Giving away the land," he told Catherine, "was no great sacrifice because I never had to work for it. I never developed a sense of property. If anything, I hated my estate for constantly reminding me it had been given to the Karolyis as a reward for helping the Hapsburgs crush the Rakoczi Rebellion."

Unfortunately for Michael, few aristocrats shared his attitude toward the land. His half-brother Joseph was the first to condemn the bill and call for a dissolution of the Republic. Other landowners spoke out when they saw Michael meant what he said about freedom of speech. Through their agent, the Catholic Church, the aristocrats reminded the peasants that it was a sin to want more than God wanted them to have. Knowing the Lord helps those who help themselves, however, the aristocrats also established a network of ex-military officers to organize illegal armies.

The government broke up these counter-revolutionary forces wherever they were discovered, and the peasants were skeptical of the Church because of the role it had played in supporting the war, but the Republic couldn't seem to please enough people enough of the time to prevent something from damaging almost every program it tried to put into practice.

Part of the problem was the government itself. When united by the common cause of ending the war, Michael's coalition was a success. But building a new regime based on as many different opinions of what that regime should be was a different matter. The socialists couldn't carry out all their programs because they didn't have a majority. On the other hand, their control of the trade unions made them powerful enough to block any legislation they disagreed with. The radicals couldn't create a People's Army because the socialists didn't trust the peasantry from which it would be recruited, and the socialists couldn't enact any welfare programs because the Karolyis didn't want the Allies to suspect them of Bolshevism. The result was a government whose policies were formed by negation.

Only Stephen Szabo was content. As Deputy of the Landless Peasants, he twice threatened to resign: when the car he expected wasn't delivered on time and later when it wasn't the model he had ordered. After that, there was no further trouble from him.

Difficulties among the other ministers increased, however, as different strata in the city's population demonstrated in front of the government's offices. Soldiers who had spent time in the trenches and now considered themselves a privileged class were the most demanding. The workers were next with doctors, lawyers, teachers, students, and shopkeepers uniting to form their own special group.

Catherine, as President of the Red Cross, represented the poor and disabled. Confined by her pregnancy and perhaps not thinking as clearly as she might have otherwise, she initiated a bill that allowed no person to have more than five suits. Representatives of the aristocracy managed to defeat the bill on the grounds that it couldn't be enforced, but they also gave Catherine an appellation she'd carry for the rest of her life: "The Red Countess."

Pressure on the new government increased when word got out that the French, who saw themselves as liberators as well as victors, wouldn't interfere if their Eastern European allies wanted to take over any Hungarian territory where co-nationals resided.

Michael protested, but the French mission in Budapest refused to forward Michael's complaint to Paris until the motives of the invading armies could be proven.

When Michael sent emissaries to the other Allied missions, the result was the same. The aristocrats had already won their allegiance in ways the new government couldn't compete with. The aristocrats spoke foreign languages, entertained lavishly, surrounded themselves with attractive women, and offered the best food, wine, and music in Budapest. The socialists and radicals, on the other hand, spoke only Hungarian and knew nothing of international protocol. They found themselves fighting an unbeatable combination of ignorance—the foreigners' of them as well as their own of the foreigners—and snobbery. As a result, the Entente missions turned down most of Michael's requests and forwarded most of the landowners' to Versailles. Once Michael had been successfully portrayed as a Bolshevik pawn and a

friend of the Jews, the aristocrats founded the League
for the Integrity of Hungary. Its slogan was: "No! No!
Never! Never!"

Then fell the news that the reactionary Count
Arco had murdered the Bavarian Prime Minister, Kurt
Eisner. Conservatives touted the assassination as the
will of the people and dragged out the liberals' old
arguments in defense of Friedrich Adler to prove there
was no difference between Arco's murder and Adler's
killing the Austrian Prime Minister in 1916.

Catherine had campaigned for a life sentence
for Adler and Michael had made his release a condition
for becoming Prime Minister. Both were embarrassed
now by their own arguments, but Catherine's
discomfort turned into an almost irrational fear when
she realized that Michael could also be killed. She had
nightmares, carried a pistol, and even went so far as to
convince herself that the child she was carrying would
be emotionally damaged by the constant tension in her
body.

Michael, for his part, became increasingly more
tolerant. As the leader of the opposition party, he had
been a fighter whose passion and violent indignation
had frequently frightened Catherine but, as Prime
Minister, he displayed the kind of generosity and
magnanimity he must have hoped the Allies would
favor Hungary with. Hard and uncompromising during
the struggle, he now refused to limit his adversaries'
civil rights regardless of how unfair or damaging they
were to the new government.

Kunfi reproached Michael for not being
practical, Jaszi claimed there were more effective ways
to be popular, and Catherine accused him of failing to
learn the lessons of Kossuth, but Michael said his
position didn't have so much to do with ideals, praise,
and stupidity as it did with consistency. "If you're going
to fight for civil rights," he told his ministers, "you have
to respect them."

That was all Bela Kun needed to hear. He had been fighting for civil rights since he was a boy, but his mission in Budapest was to bring down the Karolyi government. Following a strategy he had worked out with Vladimir Lenin in Moscow, Kun planned to undermine Michael's domestic programs, discredit his foreign policy, and convince the Hungarian people to reject democracy in favor of communism. It was no small task, but Michael's liberal views, the aristocrats' resurgence, and the Allies' shabby treatment of the new government gave him more than a little hope.

Bela Kun also had a some good reasons to grind axes. Most of these started with his father, a drunkard who couldn't hold a job, couldn't stop drinking, and couldn't keep his fists under control. As a result, Bela developed a finely tuned hatred for authority at a very early age. Kun's mother, on the other hand, was so anxious to contribute every penny she could find to her son's education she had to stay inside in the winter because she didn't have any warm clothes. Between school and bedtime, she filled Bela's head with folk ballads about Transylvania and its greatest hero, Louis Kossuth. These ballads distracted Bela from his cruel father, the frequent visits of creditors, and whatever else may have been bothering him, but they also gave him some pretty clear ideas of right and wrong, a deep sense of patriotism, and a strong belief in the necessity of action.

These ideals took on a more universal application when Bela was introduced at school to the lyric works of Sandor Petofi. "The storming rage of Petofi's soul," Bela wrote in a prize-winning essay, "turned against the privileged classes and confronted them with revolutionary abandon. He knew the country could not be saved unless it used the most extreme means available. There is no room for prudence in revolutions whose success is always decided by boldness and raw courage. Petofi hated even the thought of cowardice."

157

A gymnasium degree in pre-World War I
Hungary generally entitled its holder to a safe job with
the government, but Bela was denied this route because
of his heritage. That he didn't observe any of its laws or
customs and clearly identified with its obsessive urge to
assimilate with the Hungarian bourgeoisie made no
difference: Bela Kun was a Jew.

Ironically, Bela didn't feel this to be an unjust
limitation and prepared to enter one of the "free
professions": medicine, law, journalism, or the arts.
Though not as secure as a government position, they
were open to anyone who had been "Magyarized," and
Bela, like most lower-middle-class Jews, could out-
Magyar most Magyars.

He entered the University of Kolozsvar Law
School but left after one semester to work part-time in a
Workers' Insurance Bureau. He also wrote without pay
for a community newspaper, joined a club for radical
thinkers founded by Oskar Jaszi, and taught evening
classes in history and politics to local workers.

It was an engaging life. Kun helped the
workers, rubbed elbows with the intelligentsia, and
developed his skills as a writer. He discovered he had a
sharp eye for detail and was quicker than most at
grasping the social and political implications of a story.
His early articles promoted people like Karolyi, Jaszi,
and Kunfi but, when the coalition sacrificed its radical
ideals to gain a stronger voice in the mainstream, Bela
switched his focus to the local clergy and the city's
inefficient bureaucracy.

The effect was almost immediate. Freed from
the large chorus of politicians ranting about national
issues, Bela found himself alone on the local stage.
People learned to recognize his name and value his
insights; other papers sought his stories and gave them
better play; he began wearing wide-brimmed hats and
silk scarves; he rose from cub reporter to editor; he was
only twenty years old.

Still, he never gained full acceptance with the

politicians, journalists, and literati who frequented the
New York Cafe. They saw him as vain in a rustic sort of
way, aggressive in a Jewish sort of way, and determined
in a childish sort of way to destroy the reputation of
whatever authority figures he could get his pen on. Nor
did they appreciate his chivalrous defense of a woman
whose honor had been jeopardized by a rival reporter. It
made all the other reporters look bad.

Kun's journalist days ended when he punched
the editor of a competing newspaper for unfairly
criticizing Sigismund Kunfi. His own newspaper fired
him and no paper, not even the Social Democrats'
Nepszava would take him on.

Back in his position as a clerk in the Workers'
Insurance Bureau, Bela met Iren Gal. They fell in love
and wanted to marry, but Iren's father objected. The
salary of a junior clerk at a socialist organization
offered little security and no promise. Iren was told to
forget Bela Kun.

Those acquainted with Bela expected him to
rebel against this most authoritative of authority
figures, but those who knew him best weren't surprised
when Bela decided to establish himself as just the kind
of middle-class citizen Iren's father would approve of.
Within three years, he worked his way up to deputy
managing director of the insurance bureau and became
a founder and director of the Kolozsvar Workers'
Cooperative Society. He also recouped his losses among
the intelligentsia and was elected as a delegate to the
1913 Congress of the Hungarian Social Democratic
Party. Here was a man both the reformists and the
bourgeoisie could admire.

Following his marriage to Iren, Bela became
managing director of the insurance bureau and was on
his way to settling down in a nest of office work, trade-
union lectures, and Sunday visits to the Gals when
World War I broke out. He joined a reserve officers'
training school at Galicia. There he formed a study
circle to discuss the works of Marx, Engels, and Bebel.

Neither he nor any of his fellow cadets had heard of Lenin.

When the Russians broke through Galicia in 1916, Bela was captured and sent to a prisoner of war camp in Tomsk. His study group, almost miraculously, continued intact. By that fall, they were advocating socialist ideas through groups of their own and soon became leaders in a movement that spread to all the prison camps in Russia. They contacted Bolsheviks on the outside, wrote articles for the Tomsk *Sibirskii Rabochii* and *Pravda* and dreamed of the day they would destroy the old order in Hungary.

Their plan had five steps: they would incite the war-weary Hungarians to protest their condition, the government would order the military to suppress any dissents, soldiers sympathetic to the masses would refuse to fight, organized workers would overthrow the powerless government ,and a proletarian dictatorship would take over. Bela and his comrades would then divide and control the country pretty much the same way they ran the prison camps.

When Lenin freed all of Russia's prisoners in 1917, the Hungarian Bolsheviks took advantage of their notoriety to work their way up in the Communist Party. Lenin noticed their ability to inform, organize, and agitate. After they distinguished themselves fighting in an Allied-supported attack by Czechoslovakia, the Soviet leader created an Hungarian Section of the Communist Party and named Bela Kun to head it.

Working closely with Lenin, whom he saw as the kind of man he wished his father had been, Bela vowed to make Hungary the first country outside of Russia to embrace communism. It wouldn't take long. The Hungarian's national pride, their disappointment with the Entente, the deteriorating conditions at home, and the bourgeoisie governments' tolerance of criticism were already working in his favor. All he had to do was complain loud enough and long enough. The people would do the rest.

VII.
ⲦⲎⲈ ⲈⲚⲆ ⲞⲢ ⲦⲎⲈ
ⲂⲈⲄⲒⲚⲚⲒⲚⲄ

Not many Hungarians noticed the small group
of Bolsheviks that got off the train the morning of
November 16th, 1918, but the Bolsheviks noticed the
people's guarded optimism. Yes, the war was over; yes,
the Hapsburgs had been overthrown; yes, Michael
Karolyi had just been sworn in as Prime Minister of the
First Hungarian Republic, but no, the new government
had not received the support it hoped for. Romanian,
Croatian, Serbian, Slovene, and Czecho-Slovak
National Councils had already declared their
independence and weren't going to jeopardize their
freedom by allowing the Allies to develop any sympathy
for the new Republic. Michael was portrayed to the
West as either an aristocrat or a Bolshevik, and
everything he did was interpreted one way or the other.
When his Cabinet didn't include representatives from
the old regime, the minority leaders pointed our how
similar his tactics were to Lenin's. When he named
Oskar Jaszi Minister of the Nationalities and ordered
him to conduct a plebiscite, the minorities accused him
of ignoring their wishes. If Michael was tolerant of

other people's criticism, he was soft on communism; if he broke up counter-revolutionary cells of soldiers, he wasn't any better than the aristocrats who preceded him.

The initial reaction of the United States and Great Britain was not to interfere, but French occupying forces overestimated the Bolshevik threat. Heavily influenced by the minorities' leaders, they feared all Eastern Europe was on the verge of a revolution. The question was where the revolution would take them: to communism or capitalism.

France wanted to grant the nationalities their independence and install democratic governments that would keep Bolshevism in Russia, but President Wilson favored Michael's program to let the nationalities decide for themselves how they wanted to be ruled. The Allies had won the war, supported the independent councils, and treated the oppressed minorities as co-victors. All Lenin had to offer was an untested ideology. Wilson knew which way the people would vote.

What he didn't know was how hard it would be to get his message through to Michael. Because the United States had no embassy in Hungary, Wilson sent his call for a plebiscite through the American Committee on Public Information in Switzerland. The Committee's Director Whitehouse translated the message into four languages, but, because of the deteriorating conditions in Austria-Hungary, she had no place to send it. So Whitehouse called on Michael's recently arrived representative in Switzerland: Roza Bedy-Schwimmer.

A leading feminist in Hungary, Bedy-Schwimmer had made a name for herself as the newspaper correspondent who warned Lloyd George what would happen if Austria declared war on Serbia after Archduke Ferdinand was assassinated. The British Prime Minister didn't take her warning seriously; later he admitted she was the only person he had met who recognized the situation's international consequences.

Bedy-Schwimmer also knew President Wilson. In 1914, she persuaded him to call for immediate negotiations among the warring nations. Her reputation as a pacifist widened a year later when she convinced Henry Ford to help finance a Peace Ship that would carry international celebrities all over Europe to speak against the war.

Whitehouse first met Bedy-Schwimmer at the American Women's Suffrage Convention in 1914 and supported her call to convince President Wilson to establish a peace committee of neutral nations. Although Wilson never officially endorsed Bedy-Schwimmer's proposal, he used many of her ideas in his plan for the League of Nations.

Michael could think of no better person to represent the Hungarian Republic than this extraordinary woman. Bedy-Schwimmer knew all the people with whom Michael hoped to make the most lasting alliances, and her reputation as a pacifist was beyond reproach. Whitehouse not only immediately entrusted her with Wilson's message, she swore her in as an agent of the Committee on Public Information and gave her an official pass as well.

The new government interpreted this as a great triumph, and Michael immediately ordered couriers to spread Wilson's appeal for a plebiscite to all the national councils. What Michael didn't know, however, was that the idea to contact Bedy-Schwimmer had been Whitehouse's, not Wilson's. Thinking the American President had chosen him as a personal representative to the seceding minorities, Michael assured his Cabinet that Wilson's message was a prelude to preferential treatment. The Cabinet, which had previously rejected Bedy-Schwimmer's nomination for Representative to the Allies, now elected her to the Executive Committee. When she went back to Berne, her train compartment had more flowers than it could hold.

The day Bedy-Schwimmer left, Michael received

an appeal from Vladimir Lenin: Wilson's overtures for peace were part of a plot to distract people from the war the Allies planned against Soviet Russia. French troops had already landed in Odessa and the Americans controlled Vladivostok. The only way to stop them was through an international proletarian rebellion. Lenin asked that his message be distributed among the people. "You have taken an important step on the road of revolution in Hungary," he told Michael. "Now continue fearlessly toward a victory for people everywhere."

Michael suppressed the message. He didn't want to jeopardize the relationship Bedy-Schwimmer had just established with President Wilson.

Big mistake. An alert revolutionary had copied Lenin's message when it arrived at the government's receiving station. When it didn't appear in any newspapers, thousands of copies were printed and dropped from airplanes the day Michael declared Hungary a "People's Republic." The headline on each leaflet read: "The Government Has Kept This Message a Secret From the People."

The Workers' Council was the first to demand an explanation.

Michael told them his reason.

Not good enough. In a republic, the people have the right to choose their own destiny.

Michael argued that no peasant would accept Bolshevism and a proletarian revolution would only lead to Allied intervention.

"No fear can justify deceit," Sigismund Kunfi replied. It was his first public attack on Michael.

Oskar Jaszi wanted to know why, if Wilson wanted a close relationship with Hungary, he didn't come out and say so the way Lenin had done.

Michael didn't know.

When Lenin's call for a communist revolution appeared in the November 20th edition of *Nepszava*, the Czecho-Slovak National Council used it to justify its recent seizure of Hungarian land. Edward Benes, the Council's chief spokesman, claimed his people were fighting as much against Bolshevism as for their own freedom. The two were inseparable. If no Czecho-Slovak state existed, he said, one would have to be created to stop communism in Hungary from spreading to Austria, Germany, and the West.

Michael issued orders to drive the Czecho-Slovaks back into their own territory.

Benes appealed to the French for help. France had recognized the Czecho-Slovak Council as an ally during the war; was France now going to sit back and allow Allied territory to be occupied by the enemy?

The French Foreign Minister, Stephen Pichon, ordered Michael to withdraw his troops.

Michael pointed out that it was Hungarian territory that had been invaded. If anyone should withdraw, it was the Czecho-Slovaks.

Pichon ignored Michael's protest and distracted others from it as well by telling his ministers to create a crisis over Hungary's naming a woman ambassador. In all the Allied countries, French diplomats spread the word that Bedy-Schwimmer's presence in Switzerland was designed to divert Allied attention from Hungary's repression of the minorities.

The Serbs and Croats applauded France's insight. The Romanians took it one step further: they invaded Transylvania.

Michael sent Oskar Jaszi to negotiate, but what could he do? Offer the Romanian minorities the autonomy and authority the Romanian army had just seized for them?

Jaszi threatened the Romanians with the very reason they had invaded Transylvania: Bolshevism. "Don't exaggerate the importance of your success," he told the Romanian National Council. "Peace in this region is not going to be made by either the Romanians or the French but by a council of workers and soldiers from the European Soviet Republic. Already the

Hungarian government has approved Kristian Rakouski's nomination to represent the Russian Soviet Republic in Budapest. Rakouski knows better than anyone the situation of the Romanians in Hungary."

This made the Romanians think twice. Russia, after all, was a lot closer to them than France. If the Hungarians switched their alliances, Romania would be trapped between two powerful countries. The National Council decided to let Hungary continue running Transylvania for the time being.

Michael's accepting Rakouski as the new Soviet Ambassador was the Social Democrats' price for not having been told about Lenin's letter. As unwise as it may have been to receive a diplomat from a country no Western power would recognize, however, Michael could have followed Jaszi's lead and used Lenin's interest in Hungary to pressure the Allies into a more favorable treatment of the new republic. Instead, he based all his policies on what he thought was the special relationship he had with Woodrow Wilson.

This misperception increased in importance as the situation in Hungary grew worse. On November 19th, after returning from his unsuccessful meeting with General Esperey in Belgrade, Michael appealed to President Wilson to prevent an invasion by the Serbian army. He also asked Wilson to persuade the Czechs to lift their coal blockade. With soldiers threatening to overrun every border, industry facing collapse in the cities, and people everywhere announcing their arbitrary demands for higher wages, the Republic founded on Wilsonian principles wasn't going to last.

This sounded serious enough for Wilson to reconsider his policy of non-interference, but he also thought it best to discuss the problem with the French before making any decisions. They were the occupying force in the region and knew first-hand the accuracy of Michael's claims.

The French Ambassador, under orders from Paris, told Wilson that the minorities in Hungary had been America's allies during the war and should be treated as such. Karolyi and his government were nothing more than Bolsheviks, the proof of which lay in their accepting a Soviet Ambassador and appointing a woman representative in Switzerland.

Wilson then asked Pleasants Stovalls, the American Ambassador in Switzerland, what he thought. Stovalls said he disapproved of Bedy-Schwimmer for several reasons: she was woman and women had no place in politics (they were too emotional), she had no credentials as a negotiator, she was of the Jewish-Bolshevik mold, and she offended the Swiss with her liberal views. The capital initials in her last name told you all you needed to know about Bedy-Schwimmer.

When these reasons failed to carry much weight with Wilson, the American press gave him a few more. Influenced by planned leaks from the French Embassy, a *New York Times* editorial called Bedy-Schwimmer a "mistress of middle and low diplomacy: an expert in the secret and public, open and shut." She was the kind of diplomat who "appealed to writers of a certain school of fiction." Her pacifism pertained only to the "losers," her Ford Peace Ship was a "swindle," and her "preference for backroom politics was exceeded only by Tallyrand's." The art of diplomacy, the *Times* concluded, was "likely to learn much from this feminine incursion."

Michael was shocked when Stovalls informed him of America's displeasure with Bedy-Schwimmer. His Cabinet had warned him she would be a controversial appointment, but he had continued to promote her not only for her work with Wilson, Ford, and Lloyd George but for her connections with the Labor Movement in England as well. No matter who won the upcoming elections there, Bedy-Schwimmer knew the person in charge. How could he have misjudged the impression she would make? What other way could he have possibly interpreted America's trusting her to distribute Wilson's message among the national councils? How many more setbacks could the Republic withstand?

Michael sent Michael Esterhazy, a former parliamentarian with the old Independence Party, to Berne to see if the other Allied countries shared America's views. Esterhazy reported the situation was worse than Michael feared. Not only had the United States refused to accept Bedy-Schwimmer's credentials as a diplomat, the Swiss government had begun proceedings to have the first woman ambassador in modern European history deported as an "undesirable element." Esterhazy suggested a more conservative approach in the Republic's dealings with the West.

Which was just what the old regime needed to hear. The loss of their land, the collapse of the economy, the rise of the Jews, and the failure of the government to negotiate a favorable peace were all Michael's fault. If the landowners didn't keep up their pressure at the Allied missions, there wasn't going to be any Hungary. Just that tiny little region, "Magyarie," the French were always talking about.

Bela Kun also called for the restoration of Hungary—both in spirit and in square miles—but he wanted its preservation secured by a proletarian dictatorship that promised to make the division of land into nations meaningless: "There are no Frenchmen, Englishmen, Hungarians, or Romanians," he announced in the first issue of the Hungarian communist newspaper on December 7th, "only French proletarians and French bourgeoisie; Hungarian, Romanian, and English proletarians and Hungarian, Romanian, and English bourgeoisie." The bourgeoisie leadership in Hungary had to be replaced by proletarians who would enroll the people in an international union of workers.

The wide gap separating the conservatives and communists also divided the parties of the Republic. While the Radicals and Social Democrats had been leaning more toward the left since Michael had failed to reach a favorable agreement with the French at Belgrade, the Karolyi and Peasant Parties had begun gravitating in the opposite direction after Jaszi failed to enlist the minorities' support for his Danubian Federation. Michael was left in the middle of a power vacuum created by former parliamentarians with no following and leftists who had a popular base but little political experience. Instead of uniting the two groups or forging ahead with policies of his own, however, Michael became paralyzed. He concluded that capitalism was an unfair and unworkable system but held on to the principle of private property. On the other hand, he voiced support for the social, economic, and political ideals of Jaszi and Kunfi but refused to enact any measures that the Entente might mistake for Bolshevism. The result was a catastrophic state of ineffectiveness. Nothing was thoroughly prepared for and every crisis was met with a knee-jerk reaction.

A critical but by no means untypical example of this is the government's decision to replace Roza Bedy-Schwimmer with Michael Esterhazy. Esterhazy was chosen because he was a man, because he was an aristocrat, because he had political experience, because he once belonged to the old Independence Party, and because his mother was a British peeress. Unfortunately for the Republic, Esterhazy's first loyalties were still to his class. Most of the reports he sent to Michael were written after consulting with Julius Andrassy and other conservative expatriots in Berne.

But Esterhazy wasn't content to misinform just Michael. He wrote to the members of the Republic's Cabinet as well. Marton Louaszy, the Minister of Education, was the first to resign, and his first stop after clearing out his desk was the French military commander, Colonel Ferdinand Vix. Louaszy told Vix he would help overthrow Karolyi and lead the kind of government France would approve of.

Knowing the fall of the Republic would only put

the reactionaries and Bolsheviks in better positions to assume more power, Vix refused Louaszy's help.

Nevertheless, the damage had been done: Louaszy's resignation weakened the Karolyi Party and made the Social Democrats wonder if they were on a sinking ship. Half of them wanted to abandon the Republic, while the other half wanted to overthrow it and form an all-socialist government.

Michael decided to resign. He refused to lead a government so many people had no confidence in.

This threw the Cabinet into a panic. Michael may not have had the unified support of his ministers, but none of them felt they could accomplish much without him. Even the renegade Louaszy preferred Michael to any alternative other than himself.

Sigismund Kunfi said what the Republic needed was a new coalition. For any one party to rule—either by default or takeover—would mean the end of the government. The next Cabinet would either have to yield to the masses and the kinds of reforms that would lead to an Allied intervention, or it would have to continue the same moderate policies that were already alienating the people and strengthening the counter-revolution. Kunfi's solution was to increase the Social Democrats' influence by two seats, thereby creating a Cabinet that not only reflected more accurately the will of the people but broke the deadlock that limited the government's ability to make decisions.

The Karolyi Party, or rather the left wing that had remained loyal to Michael, argued that the socialists' claim of widespread popular support was an illusion. The only people they controlled were the workers. The peasants hated the socialists and most of the soldiers had either gone home or gone over to the communists.

Kunfi pointed out that, since most of the ex-soldiers were workers, the Social Democrats hadn't lost as many members as the Karolyis liked to believe. They had just changed uniforms. The communists still held a faction within the Social Democratic Party, and, as for the peasants, they . . . well, they still hated everybody. No government would have their support. On the other hand, no government was possible without the trade unions.

Faced with the realization that it was their political experience which had been the illusion and not the socialists' popular following, the Karolyi Party capitulated. All its members had been Parliamentarians before 1918 and, their progressive ideas notwithstanding, they were still very much a part of the old Hungary. Belonging to either the aristocrat or gentry class, they discovered they had more in common with people like Julius Andrassy and Stephen Tisza that with their socialist and radical colleagues.

Nevertheless, they still had a leader who was willing to wrestle with the chaos of the new age. The problem was what to do with him. To accept Michael's resignation would further weaken the government; to reject it meant admitting the Republic wasn't strong enough to carry on without him.

The Cabinet decided to promote Michael from Prime Minister to President. That would negate the Louaszy vote of no confidence, enhance the Republic's democratic image, and strengthen the government's resistance to attack by counter-revolutionaries.

It did none of these. The reactionaries attacked the compromise for having gone too far to the left, and the communists criticized the Cabinet for betraying Marx. Bela Kun accused the Cabinet of having made the same mistake twice in keeping Michael as its leader. The aristocrat in democratic clothing had almost singlehandedly alienated everyone from the Allies to the minorities to the members of his own party and, at the same time, failed to improve any of the conditions he inherited from the war. Only a proletarian dictatorship could save Hungary. Kun demanded the Republic create a dual authority with communists holding half the power and all other parties sharing the second half.

The Karolyi Party wrote Kun's proposal off as mere insolence, but the Social Democrats decided to act. Up to this point, they had either defended the government's policies or tried to placate the communists with promises and pleas for patience; now they voted to kick the Bolsheviks out of the labor unions.

Kun accused Sigismund Kunfi of betraying the proletariat.

Kunfi threatened to re-establish the old regime's censorship laws.

Michael wouldn't hear of it. Kun had as much right to express his opinion as Kunfi.

But Michael had another reason for not wanting to restrict the communists. Representatives from the Russian Red Cross in Budapest had recently been arrested under pressure from the French mission and charged with plotting to undermine the Karolyi government. General Vix then ordered the prisoners transferred to France. By the time Michael learned about what had happened, the press had accused Vix of being a dictator, the Soviet Red Cross had threatened to expel the Hungarian Red Cross, and Lenin had suspended the repatriation of 100,000 Hungarian prisoners of war.

Michael pleaded with the French to release the Russians, but they saw in Lenin's reaction an unexpected bonus: 100,000 Hungarians in Soviet camps meant 100,000 fewer communists in Budapest. Lenin's holding the Hungarians hostage also gave the Allies another reason for invading Soviet Russia as well as an excuse not to repatriate any Russian prisoners of war. It was better for the Entente to let them rot in European camps than fight counter-revolutionaries in Latvia.

Kun took to the streets.

Kunfi infiltrated the Bolsheviks' demonstration with agents who purposely provoked the police.

Six officers died in the ensuing riot.

Michael called an emergency meeting of the Cabinet. The Chief of Police stated his case: communist cells had been gathering arms for a revolution; Michael had decided any further arrests would only damage the Republic's image; now it was too late.

Under pressure from Kunfi, indictments were brought against forty-eight Bolshevik leaders.

But the police didn't trust Karolyi to prosecute political prisoners and took the law into their own hands. Kun wound up senseless in a hospital. The Chief of Police then appeared at his bedside with a reporter to prove that the beating had not been officially sanctioned.

Kun begged for protection.

Before the Chief of Police could respond, a group of plainclothesmen burst in and began battering the Bolshevik with rifle butts.

The reporter's account of this story generated a great outpouring of sympathy for the communists.

Michael called another emergency Cabinet meeting. He had warned the police about the importance of the government's image. Yesterday, they were the sympathetic victims of a Bolshevik-inspired riot; today they were the perpetrators of a heinous crime. From now on, Bela Kun was to be treated as a head of state and the arrested communists given all the deference due political prisoners.

But this wasn't the end of it. Kun sent a report to Lenin, who ordered forty-eight Hungarian prisoners of war held hostage. Whatever happened to Kun and his followers, the same thing would happen to the Hungarians.

Michael immediately released twenty-nine Bolsheviks and dropped the murder charges against the rest. He also instructed everyone in his government to say nothing critical of Soviet Russia until he had a chance to rethink his strictly pro-West policy. That policy, to put it bluntly, wasn't paying off. The Allies hadn't prevented the surrounding countries from seizing Hungarian land and they had done nothing to pressure Czecho-Slovaks to release their coal supplies. British and American investigators visiting Hungary had agreed with Michael that the best way to stop communism was with food and jobs, but British and American diplomats in Paris continued to defer to the French, who held that economic aid only served to revive the Entente's defeated enemies. When Michael complained that the Allied blockade of goods was doing more to spread Bolshevism than anything Lenin or Trotsky had done, the French accused him of being soft on communism. And when the French finally did do something good—such as expose Michael Esterhazy's plan to execute a *coup* for the Magyar aristocrats—they planned their announcement to undermine the Republic's credibility abroad.

Then, at 10 o'clock on the morning of March 20th, Michael received the blow that would topple Eastern Europe's first democratic government. Colonel Vix and members from each of the Allied missions arrived with an ultimatum from the Peace Conference in Paris. Michael had twenty-four hours to begin evacuating thousands of square miles of Hungarian territory. The Allies, who feared the Republic would resist the recent Romanian invasion of Transylvania, decided to give Romania whatever land it wanted and provide a neutral zone between the two countries that Romania could use in retreat if the planned invasion of Soviet Russia suffered a setback.

Michael asked the delegates if all of Hungary would eventually become a French colony administered by Romanians and Czecho-Slovaks.

Colonel Vix suggested Michael summon his ministers of state and war.

The Hungarian War Minister, Vilmos Bohm, claimed the ultimatum violated the Belgrade Treaty—he didn't know the French had secretly promised the land to Romania in 1915—and argued that Communist Party membership would jump from 2,000 to 200,000 as soon as the ultimatum was announced. Hungary would fight rather than give up three-fifths of its territory.

Vix wasn't impressed. He knew when the Karolyi government had tried to recruit 70,000 soldiers to repel the Czecho-Slovak invasion in northern Hungary it could barely enlist 5,000. The last thing the Hungarians wanted was more fighting.

Michael pointed out that if the Hungarians pulled back as far as the Entente wanted, the Romanians and Czecho-Slovaks would join forces to take over the Ruthenian zone. The Ruthenians had already decided by plebiscite to remain loyal to Hungary. Why weren't the other minorities not going to be given a similar opportunity to choose their alliances?

Vix said the Ruthenians were a special case. Mostly Jews who had been trying to Magyarize themselves for years, they were the only minority to remain loyal to Hungary. Where the will of the people was obvious, no formal plebiscite was necessary.

When the Allied delegation left, Michael called his Cabinet to its daily emergeny meeting. The situation was desperate. The government had no choice but to commit political suicide. To accept or reject the ultimatum meant not only the fall of the government but the economic and military destruction of the country as well. The only face-saving path was to resign and hand over complete power to the socialists.

But the socialists were not so sure they wanted the power now. Not unless they could enlist the support of the communists. Their popularity seemed to double with every day that their leaders spent in jail. Just that morning a Bolshevik-inspired printers' strike had shut down every paper in Budapest, several thousand ironworkers announced they were joining the Communist Party, and rumor had it that an army of middle-class shopkeepers was preparing to storm the prison that held Bela Kun.

Knowing what would happen when word of the ultimatum reached the streets, Sigismund Kunfi left the Cabinet meeting to rush with his followers to Kun's bedside. So quickly did the socialists enter the room, Kun thought he was being attacked again. Then he thought he was being tricked. Several times the socialists had to repeat the government's predicament before Kun realized all his demands had been met: the socialist and communist parties would be united, the dictatorship of the proletariat announced, and an alliance with Soviet Russia proclaimed.

Michael didn't know about Kunfi's joining forces with Kun when he met with his Cabinet the next day. Nor did he know when he volunteered to stay on as President until the situation stabilized that Kunfi and Kun had already decided they didn't want him. The Cabinet voted to reject the ultimatum, announce the formation of an all-socialist government under Michael, and release the news of both to the press.

The response was overwhelming. Demonstrations took place on all the major thoroughfares, rifles were distributed from behind shop counters, 30,000 members of the metallurgical union voted to join the Bolsheviks, representatives from Budapest's biggest factories demanded an alliance with Lenin, and soldiers inspired by recent reports of Soviet victories against the White Army in Russia began positioning cannon on the hills above Pest.

That night, Bela Kun and the communist prisoners were released. The Workers' Council, which only weeks before had ejected them from its meeting, now gave them a standing ovation. Kun called for the establishment of an Hungarian Soviet Republic. "From now on," he said, "Hungarians have to look to the East for the justice that has been denied them in the West."

In the royal palace in Buda, meanwhile, Michael's secretary rushed into the President's office with a letter that had to be signed immediately.

Michael read his own resignation. "Where did

you get this?" he asked.

"It's all been arranged," the secretary explained. "The Dictatorship of the Republic requires that you resign."

Michael refused. The idea of him stepping down now was absurd. Whoever had written the letter was in a state of hysteria and panic. Didn't the Bolsheviks realize that he was the only thing standing between them an Allied invasion?

The secretary left the room. Michael could hear him talking on the phone at his desk. When he returned, he said the resignation had already gone to the press.

"Well ring them up and tell them to break the type if they have to," Michael ordered. "I'm not resigning."

The secretary didn't have to call. The papers were being distributed as they talked, and posters proclaiming Michael's resignation had already been plastered all over Budapest.

Michael wrote a denial.

"No one will publish it," his secretary warned.

What else could he do?

"Plenty," Catherine later told him. "To begin with, you could rally the soldiers outside of Budapest. They're still loyal to you, and the peasants prefer you to anyone else. Surely they will fight rather than see their land turned into collectives."

"What you're suggesting would lead to civil war," Michael replied. "Even if we won, there would be blood spilled, and we'd never know when a reaction might come."

The next morning, March 22nd, the streets of Budapest filled with people. Unlike those who had celebrated the end of the war and cautiously looked forward to Michael's saving the peace, these demonstrators were united by the Allies' ultimatum. "No! No! Not That!" they shouted. "No! No! Not Ever!"

The communists and socialists also celebrated,

but the speed and range of their announcements measure the anxiety with which they faced the future. One manifesto asked the workers of England, France, Italy, and America not to permit military intervention in Hungary. A second announcement declared Hungary's ideological unity with Lenin and appealed for a Soviet military alliance. A third communique called on the Hungarian people to strengthen the proletarian dictatorship against the Romanian and Czecho-Slovak invasions.

There was one group in Hungary, however, for whom Michael's fall and the Bolsheviks' rise was a complete victory: the aristocrats. They knew the Allies would never tolerate a communist state so close to Western Europe. It was only a matter of time before the Entente intervened and restored the former ruling classes to power. With tears in their eyes, they fell into each other's arms. Michael hadn't been able to enact a single program and neither would Bela Kun.

But Kun, unlike Michael, wasn't out to please everyone. Especially the Allies. His first acts were to refuse the ultimatum and order the army increased to a size greater than any of the peace treaties permitted.

The Allies immediately sent a new negotiator to Budapest. The lines which the Hungarian Red Army now had to honor were modified to the country's advantage, the neutral zone between Hungary and Romania was abolished, a substantial loan was granted the Bolsheviks, and Hungary was invited to send its own representatives to the Peace Conference in Paris. Within one week, the Allies gave Bela Kun everything they had refused Michael for five months.

VIII.
LEFT TO RIGHT

Michael couldn't believe the favorable conditions the Entente had offered Bela Kun. Nor could he believe it when Kun rejected them. He wanted more. Much more.

But General Christiaan Smuts, the Allied negotiator, couldn't give Kun the land and money he demanded without consulting his superiors in Paris. There, under strong pressure from the French to see Kun as a friend and accomplice of Lenin, the Allies decided to cut off Hungary from the West. They realized they had helped drive the country into Bolshevism by bribing the Romanians, Czecho-Slovaks, and Serbs with Hungarian land, and they realized they had hampered Michael's efforts to work with the Allies, but they couldn't just sit back and allow Kun & Co. to take over. So they armed Hungary's neighbors against the spread of Bolshevism and equipped Hungary's aristocrats for a counter revolution.

When the Czechs discovered that the Allies couldn't afford to let them fail, they launched new attacks from the north. The Romanians also took advantage of the situation by crossing the Tisza River.

But the people in Budapest didn't seem to care. They were too busy dancing in the streets. Walls were plastered with propaganda, windows were covered with red bunting, and rumors spread that Trotsky's Red Army was crossing the Galician frontier. It was only a matter of time before the Russians cut off the invaders, linked up with the Hungarian Soviets, and freed the country from its Allied tyrants.

The people also celebrated the communists' new domestic programs. Actors were now state employees and two-thirds of all tickets had to be reserved for workers at reduced prices. Special free performances were set aside for the Soldiers' Council and the trade unions. "From now on," the government announced, "the arts will no longer be for the special enjoyment of the idle rich. Culture is the just due of the working people."

Children were among the first to benefit from the nationalization. Everyone under fourteen had to report for a free medical examination, dentists had to devote two hours a day to free care for school children, and every child had to be taken to the public baths twice a week. Pre-schoolers were referred to wealthy families who had to set aside their Saturdays and provide without compensation all the heat, light, towels, soap, and water the children needed to bathe. For many children, this was their first time in water.

The Bolsheviks next allocated money for families who took in city children for the summer. While the students vacationed, their curriculum was completely overhauled. Hungarian and world literature replaced Greek and Latin, rational discussion substituted for corporal punishment, "satisfactory" and "unsatisfactory" took the place of grades, and works that glorified war were exchanged for stories about peace, brotherly love, and equality.

History experienced the most radical reorientation. Students now learned about wage-labor, capitalist production, and imperialist competition. Instead of God, King, and Hungary, they studied the role of the proletariat and international revolution.

History, like art, was no longer the culture of privileged individuals.

The medium for many of these new messages was posters. In fact, posters became a highly respected art form during the Bolsheviks' rule. Alcohol and prostitution were their most popular subjects, and both were the fault of capitalism. Hungarians learned that temperance was their most powerful weapon against the dangerous wine industry and fourteen to sixteen-year-old girls had to beware of the special fascination bourgeois men had for them.

Teachers also had to be re-educated. The *Communist Manifesto, The Civil War in France, Utopian and Scientific Socialism*, and *The Program of the Communists* became required reading. Anyone failing their Marxist competency tests had to attend special seminars. And just to make sure the teachers remembered their lessons, state-appointed students reported any lapses of memory in the classroom.

Few of these changes went over very well with the teachers. Nor was the government's attempt to restrict the influence of the Catholic Church very successful. More than half the schools in Hungary were parochial; their teachers weren't about to exchange vows and habits for state licenses.

The new society also eliminated all but occupational titles. Anyone who employed someone for profit or lived off of income not derived from work couldn't vote. And people who worked, wanted to work but couldn't find a job, or were unable to work became rulers. They couldn't be fired and the state would always take care of them.

If only it had worked out that way! Hungarians discovered they were no longer slaves to piece work, but they didn't produce as much either. Dead wood hardened and the government had to create economically wasteful jobs. Then the Treasury discovered that the money it printed to pay these new employees was only good in the cities.

Michael had created this problem when he ordered the printing of new "Republic" money. Because this money had no printing on one side, it was called "white money." The old regime's bank notes became "blue money," and the Bolsheviks' new notes became "new white money." No one liked the old white money because it looked like it was worth less than it said and a date gave the impression that it was no good after June 30th, 1919. This made the blue money more valuable and the new white money suspect. As a result, the peasants would only sell their food for blue money, while all the workers had to spend was new white money.

The government tried to bypass the problem of money by sending trains of "city goods"—clothes, furniture, utensils—to the country in exchange for milk, eggs, cheese, fruit, and vegetables. But only the peasants with land had any food to exchange. This intensified the landless peasants' distrust of the Bolsheviks even more. Once again, everyone was profiting but them. Once again, the government had changed names but everything else was the same.

No policy caused as much trouble, however, as Kun's decision to nationalize all the private homes and apartments. Owners now had to pay rent to a housing commission that allotted three rooms as the maximum living space for each family. They also had to turn over any superfluous furniture. Owners who neglected to report a room—foyers, closets, offices, and servants' quarters didn't count—or hid "extra" furniture could be sentenced to ten years in prison and have their homes given to another family.

Government agents entered people's houses to make long lists of everything from beds to jam pots. This alienated the housewives, many of whom bought new jam pots so they wouldn't have to worry about breaking the state's. And what they couldn't afford to buy, they stole.

The aristocrats also stole. One of Michael's

cousins claimed the new laws prevented him from
returning a fur coat he had borrowed, and one of
Catherine's relatives took her motorcycle. "If we must
have communism," he reasoned, "we might as well
profit by it."

Ironically, the aristocrats fared better under
Kun than they did under Michael. The Republic's Land
Distribution Bill was revoked, the estates were turned
into collectives, and their owners were asked to stay on
as "managers." The land's new owners saw their name
change too—from peasant to "agricultural laborer"—but
their status remained the same. Their new old bosses,
on the other hand, could meet openly under the guise of
"collective leaders" and plot to change all the names
back to the way they were before 1918.

The words that stayed the same appeared in
new contexts. In an attempt to present communism as
the logical extension of Christianity, sayings such as "It
is easier for a camel to pass through the eye of a needle
than for a rich man to enter the kingdom of heaven"
and "What does it profit a man if he gain the whole
world and suffer the loss of his soul?" became Bolshevik
doctrine. Property was now a sin that had to be
renounced, but violence was a sin that had to be
committed for the redemption of mankind. As one of
Catherine's departing secretaries told her, "Christ took
upon himself the sin of mankind and died for the love of
man. We love man with the same self-sacrificing love as
Christ. That's why we're willing to make people suffer
and die. We're expiating the sins of violence before we
commit them."

Their personal and professional staffs reduced
by the new levels of awareness, Michael and Catherine
moved to a small villa overlooking Budapest. But that
wasn't their only reason: the aristocrats blamed the
Karolyis for the Bolshevik takeover and talked openly
of revenge. The communists, on the other hand,
concluded that Michael was a spy for the West and
planned to kill him at the first sign of a counter-

revolution. If the Karolyis could hold on long enough for Catherine to have their third child—again she was in her tenth month—a villa outside of the city would give them a better chance to escape.

The Karolyis' fears abated somewhat when Kun ordered three soldiers to guard the villa and asked Michael to go to Vienna with a message for the Allies. Kun would mediate any differences between them and Soviet Russia if the Allies promised not to intervene in Hungarian affairs. This seemed like a reasonable proposal to Michael, but the Allies were still too shaken by the Bolshevik takeover to know how to respond. The United States didn't understand why a supposedly loyal country would defect to communism, France held the Hungarians were never loyal to anyone but themselves, and England concluded that few countries needed a social revolution as desperately as Hungary. The problem was it had chosen the wrong kind.

Catherine, meanwhile, went into labor. Because the wartime narcotic she was given was defective, however, she also went into a coma. Then, with the sudden shock of what seemed like an electric current, she woke up to find herself surrounded by doctors. The doctors faded and the next time she opened her eyes a priest was rubbing her forehead with his thumb. Someone else was praying. Then came a weariness that was both comforting and frightening at the same time. She tried not to give in to it, but the sensation was stronger than her will. It felt good not to fight it, to let it take her where it wanted. When she opened her eyes again, Michael was standing over her. Catherine had given birth to a girl: Judith.

Much of the next few months was spent recuperating on the gentle slope of lawn that stretched out from under Catherine's window. At dusk, she and Michael would contemplate the winding strip of Danube below them, listen to the muffled sounds of Budapest, and wonder. The people were no longer celebrating. Their wages had been raised, but the Allies' blockade had sent prices skyrocketing. When the peasants refused the city workers' money, the city workers held up supplies marked for the divisions of peasant soldiers fighting against the Czech and Romanian invaders. The government tried to keep up morale by sending the soldiers' wives to the front but, when the wives told the soldiers the landed peasants were hoarding food and blue money, morale sank even lower. Nevertheless, the soldiers fought bravely for their homes and families. The Czechs were driven out of the territory they had occupied and the Romanians were pushed back to the Tisza River.

The impact of these victories was blunted in Budapest, however, by the shortage of food and fuel. The people were more concerned with themselves. Every day, the newspapers reported charges of larceny, influence peddling, nepotism, favoritism, and outright theft. Doctors would send every worker referred to them to spas for eight-week cures, office workers swindled their way to higher paying positions, and so many housewives shoplifted so much merchandise they were suspected of having been influenced by counter-revolutionaries.

Liberal aristocrats began following their conservative cousins into exile, and many of them, including Michael's uncle Albert Apponyi, went by way of the Karolyis' villa. It was the safest place in town. Who would suspect that anyone would be crazy enough to hide out at the home of people who had made enemies of the aristocrats *and* the communists? Disguised as maids, servants, and cooks and wrapped in everything from furs to carpets, the aristocrats arrived, stayed until their papers were put in order, and left.

Michael and Catherine knew their turn had come when the railway workers went on strike to prevent supplies from reaching the front and the French turned over Hungary's second largest city to a group of aristocrats headed by Michael's cousin. Defeat

was in the air. The Red Army had failed to penetrate
the White Army's lines in the Ukraine, the Allies were
funding counter-revolutionaries in Szeged, and an army
of angry peasants was lining up to institute another
four hundred years of illiteracy, superstition, and
ignorance. Communism, for all its ideals, had tried to
do too much too soon with too little.

The last time Michael saw Bela Kun he was
lying on a couch. Lack of time, a shortage of funds,
repeated failures to execute his plans, and the West's
strangling quarantine had all done him in. Michael
suggested turning the government over to the socialists,
but Kun was incoherent. His government's end and the
reactionaries' takeover were in sight.

On July 4th, Michael and Catherine left their
children with Michael's sister and headed for the
Austrian border. The Czechoslovakian President Tomas
Masaryk had agreed to grant the Karolyis asylum in
exchange for Michael's advice on dealing with the
aristocrats once they overthrew the Bolsheviks.

But Michael wasn't sure he wanted to help
Masaryk. His coal embargo, invasion of Hungary, and
efforts to discredit Michael as a communist had all
contributed to the Republic's downfall. Even now,
Michael and Catherine had to go to Prague by way of
Vienna because of Masaryk's invasion of northern
Hungary. Almost any other country would have been
preferable.

The problem was no other country would accept
the Karolyis. The West saw them as communists and
the East saw them as spies. Their only choice was
Masaryk or death at the hands of the avenging
landowners.

At Savanyukut, a small town on the Austrian
border, the Karolyis got their first taste of the life in
store for them: the farmer paid to smuggle them out of
the country wouldn't let them stay in his house for fear
of arousing suspicion. The man suggested a nearby
field, but Catherine had read enough romantic novels to

insist on a haystack behind the barn. It never dawned on her that what she imagined as a yellow cloud would turn out to be dusty and prickly. And who could lose themselves in expatriate love with a pigsty nearby? In the morning, they discovered their chauffeur had run off with Catherine's cosmetic bag.

Now it was Michael's turn to be disillusioned. The man had been his aide-de-camp during the war; his father had been Michael's personal valet since Michael was fifteen years old. They were the most trusted members of the household staff. The father had accompanied Michael on all his trips to Paris, London, and America, and Michael had entrusted him with the family's jewels the day he and Catherine left Budapest. The son, apparently, wanted more. Watching the care Catherine had given her cosmetic bag, he thought it must have contained valuables.

Then their patriotic farmer announced his fee had doubled. "I can disguise your wife as a peasant," he told Michael. "But you will be detected immediately for what you are."

"And what is that?" Michael asked.

"A Jew, of course."

So Michael paid the Jewish rate to ride in a potato cart to the Lajta River. From there, he and Catherine set off under a pouring rain into Austria. Because strangers were regarded with suspicion, however, no one would serve them food or give them shelter. The Karolyis, in turn, became skittish about asking. By nightfall, they were hungry, wet, chilled, exhausted, and just told for the sixth consecutive town to move on.

Catherine refused to take another step. Her feet swollen with blisters, tears streaming down her cheeks, she threw herself in front of the next cart to come by. The man had no choice but to find a place for them.

The couple's spirits improved the next day when they boarded a train for Melk. Oskar Jaszi was there with two Czechoslovakian passports in the name of

Koplen. Jaszi told the Karolyis that word of their fleeing the country had made all the papers. Reactionaries from the Austrian Jockey Club had sworn to see the couple hanged for treason.

This didn't scare Michael. Had the socialists or Bolsheviks wanted him, he might have been concerned, but he knew how much the aristocrats preferred talk to action.

Catherine knew better. The aristocrats killed people the same way they did everything else: they paid someone to do it for them. Every night in Melk, she went to bed with the door barricaded and a loaded revolver in her hand.

Catherine planned to make up for the lost sleep on the train to Prague, but they were barely out of the station when a porter from the Bristol Hotel in Vienna recognized Michael.

"And when I think of how many times I overtipped him," Michael complained as the police led him and Catherine down a gauntlet of smiling passengers. In an empty mail car, the police went through the couple's suitcases. They knew from the papers that the Karolyis had stolen great sums of money from the Hungarian government. If they found the money, they could divide part of it among themselves, return the rest for a reward, and win a promotion. Unfortuantely for the police, there was no money. All they could do now was turn Michael and Catherine over to guards at the Czechoslovakian border.

The Czechs charged the Karolyis with using false passports.

Michael explained that the passports had been given to them by President Masyrk to insure their safe passage through Austria.

The police thought this a "likely story" and took their turn at the couple's suitcases. By the time the Karolyis got to Prague, news of their arrest had spread throughout the city. A crowd had gathered at the arrival platform: "Down with the Bolsheviks!" the people shouted. "Down with the Karolyis!"

The Chief of Police was more accommodating. He had reserved a suite of rooms reserved in a hotel and ordered a dinner of *Wiener-schnitzel*. If Michael and Catherine needed anything else, they were to call him on his personal number.

The next morning, apologies poured in like invaders into Hungary. Everyone from President Masaryk to the hotel manager had something to be sorry for. A wealthy countess offered them rooms in her palace, and the crowds that gathered now shouted their support for the exiled couple. Michael and Catherine thought their troubles had finally ended.

They were just beginning. Tossing his hat over a low bust in a restaurant that night, Michael sat down with Catherine to celebrate their good fortune. Within minutes, the police were at their table. Michael was under arrest for insulting Woodrow Wilson.

Papers in Austria and Hungary reported that Michael had met President Masaryk in a restaurant and knocked his hat off.

But stories about hats weren't Michael's top priority. He wanted to convince President Masaryk to adopt his plan for a union of Eastern European states.

The son of a coachman, Tomas Masaryk first made a name for himself as the professor who disproved the widely accepted theory that the Czech literary language had remained virtually unchanged since the thirteenth century. Straightforward, seemingly idealistic, and completely free of affectation, he convinced the Allies in Paris that the West needed a Czechoslovakia to stop the spread of Bolshevism and that he was the best man for the job. Just as good at convincing Michael that he was against annexing

Hungarian land without the consent of the people in these territories, Masaryk claimed the Allies had pressured him to invade Csalokoz and Komarom. "Naturally I will return the lands to Hungary," he told Michael. "But not to the Bolsheviks and not to the reactionaries."

This left only Michael, who had reason to hope the Republic might be restored. Unlike the French, who had discredited themselves by letting the Bolsheviks take over, the British and Americans wanted to save Hungary from foreign domination. They demanded Kun's resignation and insisted on a government representing all parties. Only then would they lift their blockade and provide economic help.

When the Hungarian Chief of Staff heard the Allies' conditions, he offered to mobilize the army and personally overthrow Kun.

The Allies were shocked by the sudden switch in loyalty, but they weren't about to strengthen Kun's government by exposing his Chief of Staff. So they cut off negotiations with the Bolsheviks altogether.

Kun reminded the Allies of their promise to save Hungary from the Romanians. When he got no answer, he decided to attack. But his Chief of Staff, hoping to remain in the Allies' favor, shared Hungary's battle plans with the Allied negotiators. The negotiators consulted with several Austrian generals, and the generals passed the information on to the reactionaries forming a conservative government in Szeged. The reactionaries then told the French and Romanians who had placed the Romanian nationals in power. The Hungarian Red Army was almost completely annihilated.

Kun had no choice but to flee Budapest. Promised asylum by the Austrian government, he was arrested the minute he stepped off the train in Vienna. Hungarian emigres all over Europe began packing their bags.

Calls for Michael's head appeared in papers

from Budapest to Berne, and a percentage of the money he supposedly stole was offered as a reward.

No place was safe and no person could be trusted. When Masaryk uncovered two separate plots to kill the Karolyis in the same restaurant on the same night, Michael and Catherine started carrying revolvers. Neither would hesitate to shoot, but neither thought that day would come as soon as it did. Or in the way that it did. Six suspicious-looking men walked up to them as they left a late-night restaurant. In all her terrible fantasies of this moment, Catherine never imagined that she and Michael would be outnumbered. It was always them against a hired agent. Quietly, she cocked the pistol in her pocket.

Michael placed a cigarette in his mouth and began searching for a match. Catherine jabbed him in the ribs. How could he not see what was happening?

The men surrounded the couple.

Michael asked one of them for a match. Confidently, he bent forward to steady his assassin's hand. Perhaps it is better to go this way, Catherine thought. He'll never know what hit him.

Michael blew a stream of smoke into the air and shook the man's hand.

The assassin moved on.

"Didn't you notice how hostile they were?" Catherine asked afterwards.

"Of course I did, but what chance did we have? That's why I asked the leader to light my cigarette. Once we made contact, I hoped he wouldn't be able to shoot."

Catherine decided staying with a countess or even in a hotel was too risky and found a room in the home of a Czech working-class family. The woman, a communist cell leader, was Catherine's ideal. Up at the crack of dawn, she fed her family, got her children off to school, went to work in a factory, came home, made dinner, helped her son with his schoolwork, took notes on her husband's complaints about his job, got everybody off to bed, and left for workers' meetings. The problem was she hated Catherine. Michael she would call "comrade," but his wife never rated more than a "Mrs. Karolyi."

"Why don't you call me 'comrade?'" Catherine demanded to know.

"Because," the woman replied, "you are not a 'comrade.' You are only a 'lady.'"

Catherine ran from the room and threw herself on her bed. Great chocking sobs accompanied the tears that ran down her face.

"Don't worry," Michael comforted when he caught up to her. "You're no lady."

It was one of their few light moments. The reactionary government in Szeged had tried to kidnap Adam, Eva, and Judith and hold them ransom for their parents. Michael's sister, Elizabeth, and Aunt Geraldine were forced to bring the children to Prague. They also brought the news that one of Michael's most devoted followers, a man the Karolyis had chosen to carry their letters to Budapest, had been running them by the Chief of Police.

Michael wondered when the betrayals would end. What had he done to his most trusted servants and supporters that they could turn on him so easily? There seemed to be no more pressure on them than that of their own advancement.

Then came the news that the Romanians had taken Budapest only to leave eleven days later with all the treasures they could carry. On August 14th, the French-supported reactionary army under Admiral Miklos Horthy took their place. Pogroms against the workers and intellectuals began the next day. Michael was accused of having stolen millions from the National Bank, his former Cabinet members testified that he was an Allied spy, and the new government announced it was seizing his entire fortune. Anyone who even so

192

much as wrote a letter to the Karolyis would be arrested.

Now it was Catherine's turn to be disillusioned. That no single voice rose to defend Michael in a country to which he had devoted his entire career was almost more than she could bear. That the reactionaries had agreed to allow their hereditary enemy, the Romanians, to plunder Budapest so they could present themselves as liberators would have been funny if it hadn't been so sad.

A reign of "White Terror" ravaged the countryside. Suspected Bolsheviks were pulled from trains, offices, and homes to be imprisoned, tortured, and shot. "In days like these," Catherine writes in her diary, "faith in love, friendship, truth, courage, patriotism, and loyalty changes with the weather. The only way to maintain some confidence in human nature is to convince yourself that the people who have betrayed you are the victims of an epidemic and are no more responsible for their actions than someone suffering from a fever. You can't blame a person who's delirious. The germ of fear has altered his soul, or rather dug out qualities which were dormant, thus upsetting his ethical balance. People are capable of actions and neglects which never would have been committed in a normal state. Had this great upheaval not taken place, they would have remained decent, fair, and kind. I try to convince myself that at the time I knew and loved them, these people were their real selves."

Michael told Catherine of the time some soldiers at the front voted to execute an officer who had been especially cruel to them. One of the younger soldiers, a socialist or a communist, tired to prevent the murder by appealing to his comrades' new-found egalitarianism. The officer threw himself on his knees in front of the soldier. He said he now understood the crimes he had committed and wanted to atone for them. The soldier then dropped to his knees, and the two embraced with the uplifting feeling that murder had been avoided and a new recruit was ready to struggle against class oppression. No sooner did the officer return to his headquarters than he ordered the soldiers executed. Including the one who had saved his life. Their crime, he later told Michael, was not their ideological beliefs but his own humiliation. How could he ever trust them to obey commands after they had seen him on his knees?

The aristocrats acted the same way once they returned to power. Before the war, most of the resentment toward them had come from former parliamentarians, intellectuals, and middle-class Jews. The lower classes, unlike their counterparts in France in 1789 or Russia in 1917, had few urges for revenge. Stephen Tisza was the ancient regime's only high-ranking casualty. Even Bela Kun, according to Michael, could not overcome his humble origins. He was flattered whenever aristocrats came to visit him and rarely refused them anything. Against members of the lower classes, however, Kun advocated ruthless terror, cruel reprisal, and cutthroat vengeance. Of the 234 deaths attributed to his "Red Terror," only five were aristocrats and none were politicians. The return of the reactionaries, on the other hand, marked the beginning of a "White Terror" that confirms the truth in Michael's analogy of the Hungarian general. The editor of more than one opposition newspaper was found floating down the Danube, wives of communist leaders were raped by officers and then turned over to reactionary troops, Jews were dragged into the streets and hanged from nearby trees, and hundreds of peasants and workers—their executioners jokingly referring to them as fuel—were thrown alive into burning furnaces. Led by Admiral Nicholas Horthy, the last commander of the Austro-Hungarian fleet, an army of 25,000 reactionaries murdered more than 5,000 people and threw over 70,000 more into concentration camps.

A member of the landed gentry, Horthy's first sea experiences were on sailing ships. He later joined the Austro-Hungarian navy as an officer and served as Emperor Franz-Joseph's aide-de-camp from 1909 to 1914. During the war, he distinguished himself in the Adriatic but was forced to surrender his fleet to Yugoslavia in 1918.

Julius Karolyi, Michael's cousin and head of the reactionary government in Szeged, and Count Stephen Bethlen, the leader of a group of expatriates in Vienna, contacted Horthy shortly after he returned to his farm in Kenderes. Would he head an army to save Hungary from the Bolsheviks? Would he end the Red Terror and restore St. Stephen's Holy Crown? Would he liberate his Christian brothers from the Jewish plague? Eight of the eleven *people's* commissars and nearly all of their local representatives were Christ-killers!

Horthy didn't need convincing. He needed money, arms, men, and the Entente's approval. With help from the French, indifference from the Americans, and a British interest in social reforms that fell short of Bolshevism, he got them all.

The Allies approved of Horthy because he was neither an aristocrat nor a worker. Thus, they concluded he had no vested interests. As a Protestant, he was in a good position to ease tension between the Catholics and the Jews. His work with Franz-Joseph gave him a link to the past, and his choice by the Szeged government marked him as a man of the future. Furthermore, he looked distinguished, led an impeccable family life, and his viewpoints were universally conservative.

Taking Budapest after the Romanians had softened any resistance he might have encountered, Horthy usurped Karolyi and Bethlen's position as leaders of the counter revolutionary government and named himself Regent of Hungary. Until a king was found, he would appoint all the country's ministers, convene and dissolve its Parliament, and initiate its

laws. His person was "invoilable" and his title "Serene
Highness" was about as close to "Your Majesty" as you
can get. In short, Horthy introduced a system that later
became known under its Italian name: *fascism*. The
difference between Horthy and Il Duce, Der Fuhrer, and
El Caudillo, however, was that there was not even the
pretense of equality or justice under his Serene
Highness. Worship of the nation and punishment for
nonconformity became the country's most popular
sentiments. Secret societies, often government-backed,
sprung up all over Hungary. The Awakening
Hungarians and the Association of National Defense
alerted people to the Jewish conspiracy. The Scientific
Race-Protecting Society, organized on the pattern of the
early Hungarian tribes, and the Society of the Double
Cross pledged to take back the lands Hungary had lost
to Serbia, Romania, and Czechoslovakia. In 1919,
twenty-two "patriotic" organizations were founded; by
1920, there were over a hundred. Every one of them
vowed either to kidnap or kill the Karolyis.

The repeated and increasingly heated
announcements of their end forced Michael and
Catherine to move to Reichenau, a small village about
as far north of Hungary as anyone can go without
leaving Czechoslovakia. If they were going to die, at
least they'd see their killers coming and have a better
chance of defending themselves.

They also discovered what it was like to mix
with people who had nothing to gain from them.
Favored, flattered, and fawned over since they were
children, the Karolyis had come to believe they were
accepted or rejected for *what* rather than *who* they
were. It was not, Michael concluded, an elevating
experience. Most decent people kept away. Only one
person, a young Marxist with no stake in the town,
would talk to them. And the Karolyis were the only
ones in Reichenau who would exchange ideas with him.
Can the bourgeoisie be held in check without a
dictatorship? Can a dictatorship rule without terror?

Is it possible to change anything without destroying something?

Michael's answer to all of these questions was "NO!" Before the war, he believed a planned economy could be achieved democratically; now he knew socialism and capitalism were incompatible. The only way to insure a revolution's success was through a dictatorship that rewarded its supporters and wiped out any opposition. Had he ruthlessly crushed the aristocrats, the Bolsheviks would have had no case.

Catherine tried to convince Michael not to allow his disappointment to weaken his democratic beliefs, but his disillusion with humanity was too great. The Republic lacked strength in the time of crisis, the Bolsheviks proved reforms were impossible in a society that didn't value them, and the reactionaries were demonstrating that power was more important than truth, justice, or loyalty. Every day Michael was accused of some new atrocity. A scapegoat for the socialists and communists who stayed in Hungary as well as a target for the aristocrats, Michael saw his best friends join the chorus of condemnation. Not even his personal life was spared. One newspaper reported that the young woman travelling with him was not his wife. Catherine, a good Catholic from the Andrassy family, had left the revolution to live with her parents.

Still, it wasn't all bad. Michael and Catherine enjoyed the novelty of shovelling snow and skied when the sun was strongest. In the evenings, they read aloud to each other from Kropotkin and Dostoyevsky. Catherine thought about studying medicine in a German-speaking university, and Michael played with the idea of becoming a skilled worker. He even went so far as to buy a copy of *The Electrician's Manual*.

The Karolyis faith in humanity was restored somewhat when, their money melting away and the cost of fuel rising, a group of socialist miners from nearby Kladno volunteered to work an extra hour each day to provide the couple with coal. Michael and

Catherine would have accepted for the children's sake—Judith suffered from rickets—but President Masaryk informed them that they had become a liability. With Russian troops pulling out of Poland and the threat of a Soviet invasion eliminated, Michael was no longer needed to negotiate with Lenin. Moreover, his continued presence in Czechoslovakia made the Allies nervous.

Where there is no room for disillusionment, there is no room for disappointment either. At least the Karolyis hadn't found a home, placed their children in school, or made any friends. Leaving Czechoslovakia was easy.

The problem was where to go. Michael suggested the Soviet Union. He could mediate for Lenin with the West. Catherine preferred Italy. The weather was better, it would be easier to smuggle jewels through the Italian mail, and, if there was ever a time in their lives when they needed a steady diet of pasta, it was now.

"How long to you think we will have to stay away from Hungary?" Michael asked her.

"Three months."

"I predict a year."

They were gone twenty-seven.

1X.
EXILE

Florence contrasted sharply with Czechoslovakia. The Karolyis took sunny walks on the Lungarno, ate in gay trattorias where no one cared what Michael did with his hat, drank aperitifs on balconies in Fiesole, and slept in a pensione that housed a colony of Russian expatriates. Still carrying the glamor of the Imperial Court, the Mouraviefs, Narishkins, and Olsoufiefs knew it was just a matter of time before they returned to the white nights of St. Petersburg. While Michael helped them count the days, he also counted the money his sister Elizabeth sent him from the sale of his personal belongings. The Horthy government had decided to seize "only" his factory and estates.

With the money from his Renaissance art collection, Michael leased the Villa Primavera in Fiesole, hired a nurse and a maid, and engaged a secretary from Hungary to help him with his memoirs. Catherine signed up for acting classes. In the evenings, the Karolyis sat on their balcony and, as they had done in Budapest, listened to the sounds of the city below.

The Fascists had just begun to assert themselves. Led in Florence by the young Marchese Imperiali, they fought with communists in the streets,

RICHARD ANDERSEN

burned down the Trade Union building, and forced
socialists to swallow castor oil in the central piazza.
Every day there was a new atrocity.

The Karolyis tried not to get involved. They had
their children to consider, and Michael wanted to see
his memoirs published before their money ran out.
Neither had much confidence in Catherine's acting
ability. At one audition she cried when she had been
told to laugh and laughed when she had been told to
cry. Only her attempt to act terrified was convincing.

Two days after moving into Villa Primavera "for
good," the Karolyis noticed a young boy climbing the
stone wall beneath their patio. He pointed to the road
that led up the gate. A small army of Carabinieri were
waving their arms and pointing in as many directions
as there were Carabinieri. After a few minutes of
objecting to every order given by their commander, each
Carabiniero headed off in a different direction. The boy
dropped down from the wall and the Karolyis went back
to their reading. Fifteen minutes later, Catherine heard
what sounded like a slap in the face. "*Silencio!*"
someone hissed from behind a bush. Suddenly, three
Carabineri appeared. Each was holding a pistol.
"There's no use resisting," a voice called from the
garden. "You're completely surrounded."

Other Carabinieri then sprang from their
hiding places to search the villa. Books, letters, and
manuscripts soon competed for space on the floor with
dishes, silverware, and linen. Everyone in the house
was under arrest.

Michael and Catherine were handcuffed and,
with bayonets pointed at their chests, driven in an open
car through the center of Florence as trophies.
Everyone else rode behind them in a covered truck. At
the police station, the couple was locked in a cell while
the children, their Italian nurse, Catherine's Russian
maid, and Michael's Hungarian secretary were placed
in a room with no furniture and a stone floor. The
Carabinieri called this group "the proletariat." Any

time they wanted to go to the bathroom, they went with a bayonet held to their backs.

Michael demanded to know why they had been arrested.

The police gave him a copy of the local newspaper. On the front page was a story about a conversation he had several days earlier with the daughter of General Turr. Turr had been Louis Kossuth's partner in the Revolution of 1848 and, after Kossuth's government was overthrown, became an Italian citizen. Michael thought Senora Turr might have some information to enrich his memoirs, but they wound up talking more about his fear of the reactionary movement in Western Europe than anything else.

The newspaper printed every word Michael said and a good many that he didn't. Even his innocent remarks were presented in a way to discredit him. Senora Turr, it turned out, had been hired by the Horthy regime to undermine Michael's credibility in Italy.

"I see no reason for any charge in these stories," Michael told the Chief of Police.

"There are no charges," the officer replied. "The people of Florence merely want you expelled. You are no longer welcome here."

The officer then pointed to another story: a riot had occurred the previous night; Michael was suspected of using Bolshevik funds to incite it.

"How could I possibly have done this without the Carabinieri knowing abut it? You've been following me since the day we arrived."

"Read on."

A known communist owned the Villa Primavera and the brother of the children's nurse belonged to a trade union. "A communist landlord?" Michael asked. "It seems a contradiction in terms."

"Just more of the same old hypocrisy," the officer told Michael. "We also know the person impersonating your wife is spying on Russian refugees.

How do you plead?"
   "Not guilty."
   "Then how do you explain *this*?" the officer
asked as he shoved a copy of *Das Kapital* under
Michael's nose. The book had been confiscated from the
Karolyis' library.
   Michael admitted he read books.
   "To what country do you wish to be deported?"
   "Any except Austria or Hungary."
   They were sent to Austria.
   But the Austrians at Tarvis refused to accept
the Karolyis. They had no entry visas. The Italians then
refused to take them back for the same reason. That's
when Catherine discovered that all her jewels and
several volumes of her diaries were missing.
   Michael telephoned the Italian Ministry of
Justice.
   The person who answered his call told him not
to insult the honesty of the Carabinieri. Then the
Minister got on the phone and told him his library had
been confiscated to pay for the damages he caused in
the Tuscan riots.
   Nevertheless, the Karolyis had something to be
grateful for. The Carabinieri missed the one piece of
paper they would have liked to have gotten their hands
on: General Stromfeld's plans to overthrow the Horthy
regime and reinstate the Republic. Had the plans been
discovered, hundreds of Hungarians would have been
added to the White Terror's death list.
   Oskar Jaszi, meanwhile, had come up with a
country willing to accept the Karolyis: Yugoslavia.

   A long way from lush Austria and sunny
Tuscany, the barren shores, crooked cactuses, crippled
olive trees, and harsh, scorching heat of Split made
Michael and Catherine feel the full weight of their
banishment for the first time. They might just as well
have been on Mars. There were no books to read, no

cafes to sit in, not even someone to talk to about the
things that interested them. Just passive, overloaded
donkeys, suspicious farmers, and rocks, rocks, rocks. So
many rocks that, rather than try to clear their fields of
them, the Yugoslavs just piled them in lines within easy
tossing distance of where they'd been found. The result
was what looked like a huge chessboard. All the lines
on the board were rock piles, and no square could have
been more than ten feet wide. In the middle of one
space was an olive tree, in the middle of another a
lemon tree, a few potatoes or broccoli plants in a third,
and so on.

The Schiller Hotel, which the Karolyis chose
because they hoped the name implied a certain
standard, had been taken over by insects. Roaches
reigned in the kitchen, scorpions settled in the Karolyis'
shoes, and flies drowned in their coffee. To escape from
the hotel and the heat, Michael and Catherine took
their children to the beach. There they came in contact
with fishermen who, despite their traditional animosity
toward Hungarians, were proud that the couple who
had fought for liberty and justice had settled among
them. Every morning a bottle of milk still warm from
the cow and few fish waited outside the door of their
hotel room. Sacks of potatoes, lettuce, and broccoli also
appeared from time to time. One day, Michael picked up
his sandals at a cobbler's in the center of town. "No
money from you," the man told Michael. "You helped
the poor when you were rich; now that your are poor,
we will help you."

The Karolyi children, whose health had never
been good, thrived in Yugoslavia. The fish, food, sun,
and daily swimming removed all traces of any past
ailments, and little Judith discovered for the first time
the joy of sleeping without a plaster bed.

Not all of Catherine's experiences were positive,
however. Like all the women in the village, she was
expected to wash and cook. Washing she didn't mind.
Scrubbing stairs and cleaning sheets in the municipal

troughs were part of the new adventure she knew was only temporary. Cooking was another story. Whether lighting a match or boiling water, she somehow always managed to burn herself. Her fish and vegetables, on the other hand, were almost always undercooked. Michael and the children created a game in which Catherine would be rewarded with a meal in Split for every edible dinner she made at home, but nothing helped. They all wound up eating in town anyway.

Only one event interrupted this routine: the arrival of an American fleet. Split's prettiest women put on their best clothes and paraded on the docks for sailors who, because the lowest ranking of them made more money than a Yogoslavian minister, could pick and choose.

Michael and Catherine were appalled. Although they had been a party to suppression in their own country, this was the first time they actually felt the demoralizing prostitution that the "haves" can foster in the "have nots." Women whom they admired and respected were abasing themselves for a few American dollars. The men and the boys, meanwhile, waited on the docks to dive for whatever pieces of meat the Americans threw overboard.

Michael and Catherine decided it was time to move on. There was work to be done, and they weren't going to accomplish any of it in Split.

But Dubrovnik was only slightly better. Known as the City of the Seven Flags because it kept a flag prepared for any of the seven countries most likely to re-conquer it, this traditional home for losers was now a colony for White Russian emigres.

Michael and Catherine first made friends with the politicians. Of these, Count Homiakov had the biggest influence on their lives. A former President of the Duma who failed to outlaw the custom of shaking hands on the grounds that it was unhealthy, Homiakov convinced the Karolyis to go in with him on a nightclub. He already owned half the shares and was willing to split his half with Michael and Catherine.

Gratefully, the Karolyis sunk all their resources into the Stella Bar. When a French *diseuse* was hired to sing, Russians lined up at the door. They drank gallons of champagne, danced until dawn, forgot about their past, and paid with vouchers. They were all shareholders too. Within weeks, the Karolyis' investment dried up. Then came the news: Michael and Catherine had underwritten the White Russians' stock.

King Charles, meanwhile, had invested in Hungarian stock and come up just as short. After the aristocrats had taken control, he made several attempts to regain the crown that Regent Horthy was holding for him. The first effort was by train. Hidden behind tinted glasses and painted eyebrows, Charles traveled in a third-class compartment through the vast empire that had once been his. It was Holy Saturday. The Kingdom of Hungary, which had died three years before, would be resurrected on Easter Sunday.

Only no one told Horthy.

"My Admiral!" Charles exclaimed when they embraced in the study of the Imperial Residence.

Horthy said nothing. He never suspected that someday the King would actually want for his throne back.

Charles announced we was awarding his "loyal deputy" the highest of all Hapsburg decorations: the Order of Maria Theresa.

Again Horthy was silent.

"Are you not pleased?" the King asked.

"Not under the circumstances, Majesty."

Charles didn't understand.

"The neighboring countries aren't satisfied with occupying two-thirds of our land," Horthy explained. "If you take back your throne now, you will give them the excuse they need to overrun us completely. We wouldn't stand a chance; the Allies have made them more powerful than us; you must wait until the time is right."

This wasn't the reception Charles had envisioned, but he wanted to avoid bloodshed. Besides, some Hungary later was better than no Hungary at all.

Queen Zita was furious. Charles had decided to give up his crown on the advice of an admiral? Charles was the King! He didn't need Horthy's opinion any more than Hungary needed a regent. The next time he planned to take back his kingdom, she'd make sure he got it.

The next time came several months later. The Andrassys were celebrating a baptism in Denesfa when a plane circled over the chateau and landed in a nearby field. The men who rushed to the spot were so surprised at seeing the royal couple climb out of the cockpit they forgot to kneel. Queen Zita knew she hadn't arrived a moment too soon.

Charles interpreted the baptism as a sign from God: the Monarchy was about to be reborn. He decided to form a new government immediately. Uncle Duci was appointed Foreign Minister; his first task was to restore Austria-Hungary on the basis of his father's historic compromise.

Uncle Duci had some reservations about the compromise's chances for success, but he couldn't bring himself to say anything that would dampen Charles' enthusiasm. Instructions were sent to Budapest to prepare the throne.

Horthy wired Charles to return to Switzerland. His arrival in Hungary would alert the minority states that had become independent. If they decided to invade, Hungary would cease to exist. Charles had to forget about his crown for the sake of his kingdom.

Zita wired Horthy they were coming.

Charles requisitioned a train near Denesfa, and everyone with portfolios in the new government climbed aboard.

The ride was the longest of Uncle Duci's life.

Charles insisted on celebrating Mass at every station, and every Mass gave Horthy more time to prepare. The King told Uncle Duci all the preparations in the world wouldn't save Horthy. God was on the Hapsburgs' side. In His name, Charles was cleansing the nation of its original sin and resurrecting the Holy Crown of St. Stephen.

But God chose not to help the Hapsburgs. At Budaors, a detachment of soldiers opened fire on the train. Several people were killed, and Charles quickly surrendered. "No crown," he declared "is as sacred as the soul of any single Hungarian."

Imprisoned in the Esterhauzy mansion at Tata, Uncle Duci pondered the irony of his situation. His father had been sentenced to hang for fighting against the Hapsburgs in 1848 and fled into exile only to return and crown Franz-Joseph King of Hungary. His son, on the other hand, was now waiting trial for trying to restore the Hapsburgs while his daughter lived in exile for having helped dethrone them. Where would it all end?

In Moderna. The British struck a deal with Horthy to confine the royal couple to the island if the Regent would release everyone else on their promise to support his government.

With Charles and Zita now out of the picture—Charles died a year later—Hungarian expatriates on the Austrian border began dispersing towards the West. Michael and Catherine too became aware that their exile was going to last longer than either of them had expected. The struggle of the Left seemed hopeless: the Allies backed Horthy and the Hungarians accepted their fate.

Two years on the Dalmation coast had done much for the Karolyis' complexions, but the time had come for Michael and Catherine to think of their children's education. England was the best place for that. Only Michael didn't think England would admit them after accepting the Hapsburgs. Neither would France, which supported Horthy, nor the United States, which was conducting a communist purge of its own.

But England was worth the try. If the British would issue them a transit visa to get to Canada, the Karolyis could get to London. Once there, they'd find a way to stay.

Horthy guessed what Michael was up to as soon as he learned of the Karolyis' request and asked the British government to extradite the couple for embezzlement and murder. The Hungarian Embassy also supplied the Home Office with false information on the Karolyis' illegal activities in Czechoslovakia, Italy, and Yugoslavia.

Michael didn't think he had a chance.

But the English surprised Michael. Hungary's portrayal of Catherine as an ex-actress who had taken part in sadistic orgies with Bela Kun's Cabinet seemed unlikely to them. Nor did they put much weight on Hungary's charge that Michael had distributed Soviet funds to communist cells in Czechoslovakia and Italy. If the Karolyis had money to burn, they wouldn't have wound up in Yugoslavia. The British not only granted the Karolyis their visas, they praised them as noble fighters in a lost cause.

No sooner did Michael and Catherine arrive in London, however, than Michael came down with dysentery. The sudden shift from sun to rain was blamed, and, the next morning, Catherine applied for permanent visas.

Now it was Parliament's turn to hear the same arguments as the Home Office. Only this time the Hungarian government produced a witness to testify that Catherine was a lesbian. The Karolyis' supporters, led by Ramsey MacDonald, focused on Great Britain's traditional respect for unpopular opinions. "Tolerance for the eccentric and unorthodox protects England from radicals and reactionaries alike," the head of the Labor

Movement pointed out. "It's what enables the country to accept people with such opposing views as the Hapsburgs and the Karolyis. In fact, accepting the Hapsburgs almost necessitates accepting the Karolyis."

Parliament agreed.

This called for a celebration. A fish celebration! With so little in the Adriatic, the Karolyis had been overwhelmed by all they found in London. Most of it was beyond their means, but today was special: they had defeated Horthy and would not be banished to Canada.

Catherine ran to the nearest market with sixpence in her purse. She could afford a small fish cut into four tiny pieces or a long, shiny eel that would be more than enough for everyone. She pointed to the eel as if to ask "Is it good?" but the fishmonger, who had no time for questions or indecision, cut the eel in three and wrapped it in a newspaper. Two blocks from the store, the package jumped and Catherine watched in horror as each part of the eel wiggled along the sidewalk in a different direction. She captured the pieces and held on to them long enough for Michael to boil some water, but nobody ate them and no Karolyi could ever look at an eel again.

Winning in Parliament and losing in the kitchen established a pattern in the Karolyis' lives that stayed with them throughout their first year in London. On the important issues affecting them, Michael and Catherine encountered an objectivity and sense of fairness in the British people that was unlike any they had ever known. The couple's everyday lives, however, were struggles to survive in a world that had only recently become familiar to them. Before leaving Hungary, for example, they had never even dressed themselves. Now, with Michael's sister able to send them less and less, they had to learn to do things most people took for granted.

Michael had been to England before, but the two rooms he and Catherine rented in the boarding house on Stephens Road was a long way from tea at the Savoy or fox hunts at Blenheim. For Catherine, who had travelled only to Austria and Italy before being exiled, London was a place where "lovely" days meant it didn't rain, men didn't look at women, waiters couldn't be summoned no matter how long you waited, hostesses ate with their hats on, a farmer could be fined for killing an ox in front of its mate, and a woman's sharing her bed with a man didn't prove they were lovers.

And how, Catherine wondered, would she ever be able to cope with the subtleties and intricacies of English middle-class life? Her mother-in-law had advised them to settle in England when she visited them in Czechoslovakia: "There you can find congenial company and educated people who will discuss ideas with you without becoming upset." Then she added: "You can't frequent *only* the lower classes, you know."

Yugoslavia had proven Aunt Geraldine right on that one, but the Karolyis were the wrong kind of aristocrats to win many friends in England. Refugees of the right—Czarist Russians mostly—enjoyed the sympathy of the bourgeois because they were what the bourgeois wanted to be, and wealthy Americans were known to take a prince or a count home as a souvenir to be shown off at parties. But leftist refugees had no connections and no snob appeal. They usually spoke only one language, lacked the means to start over in new professions, and were often viewed with suspicion. Michael and Catherine found themselves in the middle of these two groups. Their titles and name were welcome among the aristocrats but not their politics. And where their political ideas were shared, their pedigree discredited them. Nevertheless, there was always someone to befriend them whenever they needed help.

Among the Karolyis first friends was St. Loe Strachey, the editor of *The Spectator*. Strachey paid

Catherine the first money she ever earned: five pounds for a story on feudalism in Hungary.

Another early acquaintance, H.G. Wells, quickly recognized the Karolyis as partners in the struggle against tyranny and often invited Michael to give lectures with him. These appearances brought Michael his first earned income, but there weren't enough appearances or enough money in them to support one person let alone five.

Nor did Michael and Catherine have much luck finding jobs. Neither had any practical experience and many Britains believed hiring former enemies was unpatriotic. The Karolyis were turned down as prospective store clerks, lift-operators, and unskilled laborers. They couldn't even wait on tables. For a while, they hung on to the hope that Elizabeth would sell some works from Michael's collection of Hogarth and Lawrence, but it turned out Michael had purchased the masterpieces of their pupils.

Moving to a cheaper boarding house—the last landlady having called their children "undisciplined continentals" for spraying her boarders with a fire house—Michael and Catherine learned what it was like to be sellers instead of buyers. Almost daily, they watched the amiable faces of salespeople change their expression when, after looking at a few items for sale, Catherine asked if the store would be interested in buying an eighteenth-century fan or Michael offered the silver cigarette case he had in his pocket. What Catherine lost in sales, however, she soon made up for in experience. One shop owner was so impressed by Catherine's persuasiveness, she hired her to buy in Paris the kind of hats a countess would wear and sell them in London.

Catherine had never been to Paris, but she did have a contact there: the Karolyis' family lawyer was President of the Republic. Perhaps he knew of a black

marketeer who would pay top money for a string of
pearls. It was the only thing she and Michael had left to
sell.

Poincare said he knew a minister in Germany
who dealt with a marketeer who might help. The man
was on his way to Paris. Could Cartherine stay a week
longer?

Catherine decided the hats could wait. If she
could find a job—any job—she could rent a room until
the pearls were sold.

Maison de Molyneux had advertised for a
woman to model evening gowns. Catherine was hired
on the spot. She couldn't remember when she last felt
so excited. This was the first time anybody had ever
wanted her because of *who* rather than *what* she was.
She couldn't wait to begin her new adventure. She
couldn't wait to enter a way of life she had never
known.

Catherine quickly discovered, however, that
models were only another kind of what, and working for
Maison de Molyneux was more of a way of life and less
of an adventure than she had thought. The twenty-five
francs she made at the end of her first week couldn't
pay for her food let alone her rent, and most of her time
on the job was spent in a poorly heated dressing room
where she listened for hours to her co-workers'
depressing stories of their cheerless lives. All their
problems had to with money. Or how to get it. None of
them could live on twenty-five francs a week but, when
they complained to their boss, Madame Rosine, they
were told there was more than one way for a pretty
woman to earn money in Paris. Many of them wound up
posing nude and turning tricks every time their needy
boyfriends wanted a *"bifteck."* Because of their middle-
class backgrounds, however, the women felt guilty for
what they were doing. They went to confession on
Saturday to ask forgiveness for their sins and to Mass
on Sunday to ask God to make them married and
respectable.

Catherine wasn't working long when Madame Rosine gave her some lingerie to model.

Catherine refused. She had been hired to show evening dresses, not underpants.

The other models gathered round. Perhaps something would come of this for them. They had heard Catherine was a Russian princess.

"You were hired to wear what I tell you to wear," Madame Rosine informed Catherine.

Catherine held her ground.

"There are many models." Madame Rosine explained. "But there is only one Maison de Molyneux. Don't bother asking for a reference."

Catherine was out the door before she fully realized what had happened. What made her think she was indispensable to the evening gown collection?

That night she met Herr Tuhrman. Over dinner at the Hotel Meurice, she took every opportunity to dangle her pearls in front of him, but the marketeer's mind seemed to be everywhere else: where Catherine was staying in Paris, the condition of their neighborhood in London, how they could afford a maid who cooked when they couldn't afford to eat.

Catherine wondered if she had made a mistake. Short, squat, and bald, Herr Tuhrman was nothing like she imagined a black marketeer to be.

After dinner, they took a cab to Catherine's hotel. As Catherine reached for the door handle, Herr Tuhrman brought up the subject of the pearls.

Catherine told him how much she wanted for them.

"And I have no doubt they are worth every franc, Countess, but I shall have to show them to my jeweller in Berlin. Can you lend them to me? I'll see you in a week at the Hotel Meurice. Same time as tonight. *"Einverstanden?"*

What else could she do? Refuse? Ask for a receipt? Painfully, she unwound the pearls and placed all three hundred and seventy of them in Herr

Tuhrman's hands.

The first of seven sleepless nights followed. How well did Poincare know the minister in Germany? How well did the minister know Turhman? Could he be trusted? Would she ever hear from him again? And what would she do if she didn't? She didn't even know where he lived and, when she called the Meurice the next morning, he had already checked out. Had he taken her family's future with him?

And what would Michael say? Coming to Paris to get the letters he needed to refute Horthy's charges of treason was the first time he had ever let her do something for him. She had secured the testimony, but she hadn't told him about the modeling job. She wanted to prove that she could not only take care of herself, she could return to London with more money than she had left with. If Herr Tuhrman didn't show up at the Meurice, her family wouldn't survive the winter.

Pale and anxious, Catherine watched the hands of the Meurice's clock move past six. It was not a good sign. Who ever heard of a German being late?

Then she saw him. She tried waving her hand as if their meeting was the most natural thing in the world, but the truth was she had all she could do not to embrace him.

Tuhrman handed her a check. The top price! More than Catherine had asked for.

The next morning, Catherine cashed Tuhrman's check and returned to the hotel for her bags. There was a note from Poincare in her mailbox: "Forget about Tuhrman. Can't be trusted."

Michael and Catherine used the money from the pearls to move into a flat and send their children to school. Accustomed to the carefree life they enjoyed in Yugoslavia, Adam, Eva, and Judith had a difficult time adjusting to London. They ran the wrong way on escalators, put shoe polish on the receivers of telephones, played under the table at restaurants, and spoke only German. Catherine convinced them that German wasn't going to endear them to many English people so soon after the war, but she couldn't convince them to speak any other language. The children became completely dumb for months. A school where they could learn English manners as well as the English language seemed to be the best answer.

But Adam, Eva, and Judith weren't the only Karolyis who had trouble adjusting to London. Michael and Catherine got on the wrong side of more than one concierge by forgetting that breakfast wasn't served after nine, no tea could be brought to their rooms, and no beds were made after ten. Moving into their flat overlooking St. George's Square was as much a relief to them as sending the children away to school. The living room may have been dark and damp from not getting any light, but it overlooked a grey stone church and a cluster of chestnut trees. And though the dining room and kitchen were in the basement—Catherine now knew why the French called the English "Troglodytes"—the gas stove and home deliveries seemed like luxuries compared to their fly-ridden lives in Split and Dubrovnik.

Bad times continued to plague them, however. When Catherine showed her employer the hats she had purchased in Paris, she was told someone who could make decisions faster had been hired in her place. The cost of the hats, which Catherine was free to keep, had been taken out of her salary.

Michael got the better end of a bargain when he sold his Burberry for thirty shillings, but he sold the coat too close to home. Whenever he walked to the underground, the shop owner would yell at him for selling a coat with no belt.

Then the Karolyis' maid got caught stealing from the local grocer. She told the police that Catherine never gave her the money she needed to prepare the meals the Karolyis expected. If she hadn't stolen as much as she did, she would have been fired.

Michael and Catherine's friend, H.G. Wells, also had trouble with the police. Why, they wanted to know, would a complete stranger put on nothing but a raincoat, ring his bell in the middle of the night, throw herself on his "reputation as a humorist" and, then, when he went off to make some tea, cut her wrists and bleed all over his newly upholstered sofa?

It was through Wells' subsequent retirement to the country that the Karolyis met Sidney Webb and Bertrand Russell. But the founder of Fabian thought and its most popular theorist were a different kind of socialist than the kind Michael and Catherine knew. They couldn't see any reason, for example, why Britain should give up India. Or even grant it dominion status. Nor did they think revolutions necessarily insured progress. The French Revolution, for all its violence and bloodshed, did not accomplish anything that couldn't have taken place through evolution. And yet, Webb and Russell ardently supported the Russian Revolution. The Soviet Union, they claimed, was "socialism adopted to Asia."

Other leftists disappointed the Karolyis in other ways. Friedrich Adler, who had murdered the Austrian Prime Minister in 1916 was now Secretary of the Second International in London. Catherine had campaigned to have his death sentence changed to life imprisonment, and Michael had made Adler's release a condition for his forming a new government under the Hapsburgs. Both looked forward to meeting the revolutionary hero.

What they discovered was an empty shell. They couldn't imagine the shy, timid little professor with watery eyes and awkward gestures actually killed someone.

Michael thought the months Adler spent in the condemned cell must have drained him of his passion.

Disappointment led to disgust, however, when Adler refused to sign a petition to commute the death sentences of several communists on trial in Hungary. Michael told him, "The Friedrich Adler of today would have refused to sign the petition for the Friedrich Adler of 1916."

Michael also had a falling out with Ramsey MacDonald, the man primarily responsible for the Karolyis' permanent resident status. At a luncheon party in his honor at Claridge's, Michael blasted the Laborites for their kid-glove approach to Hungarian politics. He then accused his host of fighting for the wrong side in England's class war.

Catherine scolded Michael for being unfair. "Just because you have an opportunity to vent your feelings after four years of silence and frustration is no reason to embarrass friends or make new enemies. Haven't you learned the power and receptivity of understatement in this country?"

Michael had, but he claimed he just wasn't able to hold himself back.

"It might be time to learn. I don't relish the idea of living in Canada or Australia."

Michael apologized to Ramsey MacDonald, but he was still so pumped up about the truth of what he'd said that he got into a fight with Oskar Jaszi. Jaszi had created the plan for a Danubian Federation and secured visas for the Karolyis to live in Czechoslovakia and Yugoslavia. If it hadn't been for Oskar, Michael would be living in a prison in Budapest instead of a flat overlooking St. George's Square. Neither this nor their deep affection for each other, however, could keep Michael from criticizing Oskar's political views the next time he came to London.

Jaszi had become increasingly opposed to the Soviet system. So had Michael, but he found himself mouthing many of Webb's and Russell's arguments in favor of it. He insisted that socialism as the West knew it would not bring about a socialist state. He also maintained that European socialists needed the Soviet Union's backing even if they disagreed with its methods.

Jaszi claimed the future of socialism in Europe was no reason to accept repression in Russia now.

While Michael and Oskar argued in Newbury Park—Catherine was tired of their fighting in the house—the doorbell rang. Half asleep and not pleased with having a day to herself interrupted, she looked out to see a thin old lady in black. It was her mother. How often had Catherine imagined what this day would be like. Unyielding, aggressive, and self-righteous, Ella reminded Catherine of the Andrassys' abandoning Michael.

But there was none of that now. Ella simply wasn't the same person who had asked Catherine why anyone would start a revolution for Michael's sake. You could see it in her eyes. She wasn't even the same person who let her children watch her order her wardrobe for the upcoming season. Frail and vulnerable, she had wanted to surprise Catherine; she didn't want to give her daughter time to think of all the terrible things that had pased between them.

And it worked. Catherine could feel only pity and affection as she took her mother into her arms. Ella told Catherine how much she regretted the conflict with Michael; he had always been her favorite son-in-law. What Ella didn't mention was the letter she had received from Michael. He had read an interview in which Ella had praised Queen Zita's staunchness in adversity and her loyalty to King Charles. "Is it only in a queen that loyalty to a husband and courage in the face of hardships are praiseworthy?" he had asked Ella. "Are they not praiseworthy in your own daughter as well?"

Ella's visit was short but, in the time they spent together, Catherine learned to balance her hurt with a respect and admiration she had never given her mother. That she forsook her daughter was understandable when Catherine considered the passionate wholeness of her nature. It wasn't any different than Catherine's. The two of them were simply incapable of compromise.

The day Ella left London, a verdict arrived from Budapest: Michael was found guilty of overthrowing the Hapsburgs. He had been sentenced to die and his land was to be given to the soldiers who had defeated King Charles at the "Battle of Budaors."

The next day, an agent contacted him with an offer. Hungary had applied for a loan from the League of Nations. If Michael promised not to call attention to his case by requesting an appeal, arrangements would be made to exploit his property. He would receive a share of the profits for the rest of his life.

Michael told the agent the land was no longer his.

"Horthy is willing to give it back to you. Your sister can live on it and you can also reap its benefits. All you have to do is keep your mouth shut."

Michael turned the agent down.

"The longer you refuse to cooperate," the agent warned, "the longer you deprive your family of their rightful benefits. Just because God appointed you Hungary's gadfly is no reason for them to suffer. God didn't appoint them."

Michael still refused. "Just because the Horthyites confiscated my property doesn't mean it's theirs."

Michael's lawyers appealed his case on the grounds that the Horthy government had also overthrown Hungary's legal rulers and that, under the Versailles Treaty, people couldn't be prosecuted for their friendship with the Entente.

The judges ruled against him. Overthrowing the Hapsburgs had nothing to do with the Allies.

The irony was not lost on Michael. Nor was it lost on R.J. Caldwell. A wealthy American whose hobbies included history and worthy causes, Caldwell came to see Michael shortly after the Karolyis arrived in London. He had just come from Prague, he had spoken with Masaryk and Benes, he had heard about Michael's plan for a Danubian Federation, and he had worked out solutions to all the problems on the train from Czechoslovakia.

Then he saw the condition of the rooms the Karolyis had rented.

"You don't seem to live under very comfortable circumstances," he told Michael as he wrote out a check for a thousand dollars.

Michael was so insulted he tore the check into pieces.

Caldwell, thinking the amount had been too small, promptly wrote another check for five thousand dollars.

The look on Michael's face sent Caldwell heading for the door.

Nevertheless, a letter arrived the next day. Although urgent business had called him home and their next visit would have to be postponed, the Karolyis could rely on R.J. Caldwell. He'd start looking for a governess position for Catherine as soon as he reached New York.

The next time the Karolyis heard from Caldwell was his response to Catherine's article on feudalism in Hungary. He had shown it to some of his friends, and he was now in a position to offer Catherine a six-month, expense-paid lecture tour of the United States.

But Catherine didn't want to go. Michael had just lost his case in Budapest and felt guilty for depriving his family of the money that could have been earned from the exploitation of his property. Then, on Franz-Joseph's birthday, he fell and broke his thigh while teaching Adam how to ride a bicycle. Before the thigh could heal, he became seriously addicted to pain killers. Nevertheless, he encouraged Catherine to make the tour.

Catherine left on a grey October morning. Michael was still on crutches, but he insisted on seeing her off. All the way to the quay, Catherine kept hoping for an accident that would keep her from getting on the ship. "Tell me to stay," she begged.

"You cannot miss this opportunity just because I've broken my leg," Michael replied.

Embracing on the tender that took them to the George Washington, Catherine imagined how happy Michael would be when he heard that she had gotten off the ship in Cherbourg. Then, almost before she knew it, the gangway was raised, the band started playing, and the tender began growing smaller. A man standing next to her pointed to the tall, gaunt figure towering above everyone else. "Look at that chap on crutches," he observed. "He won't live another week."

X.
ON THE ROAD

"I shall get off at Cherbourg," Catherine promised herself as the gap widened between her and the tender that carried Michael to shore. "How could I not see how sick he is!"

But the family needed money and Catherine knew how disappointed Michael would be if she failed their cause or herself. "You have the style and the talent," he had told her. "Each speech will be easier than the one before, but you must have courage. Nothing would please our enemies more than for you to give up before you've started."

The Karolyis had two major foes in the United States: Stanwood Mencken, the President of the American Defense League, and Catherine's cousin, Laszlo Szechenyi, the Hungarian Ambassador. While Szechenyi spread the word in Washington that the Karolyis were "bloodthirsty Bolsheviks" who had been kicked out of Italy because of Catherine's decadent character, Mencken insisted the State Department keep "the Red Countess" on Ellis Island. "She is a menace to the security of the United States," he wrote in an editorial for the *New York Times*.

R.J. Caldwell was worried. He wanted Catherine's arrival to cause a stir, but he knew people wouldn't pay to hear anything anti-American. Several members of the reception committee had already resigned over the publicity and Catherine's life had been threatened. Fifty police officers waited at the pier where the George Washington docked. There was also a large crowd of Hungarians wearing carnations that Caldwell was sure the press would interpret as a "red" demonstration.

The police decided to keep Catherine on board "for her own safety." When the demonstrators left, so could she.

Caldwell begged her not to admit she was a socialist. "Try to state your opinions without labeling them," he told her.

When the Hungarians got tired and went home, a procession of journalists and photographers were shown to Catherine's stateroom. It didn't take long for her to win them over. One headline announced "Red Catherine Not Even Pink," and an editorial in the *New York World* claimed that it was Mencken who was the public nuisance.

The next day, Caldwell took Catherine to a department store on Fifth Avenue. She could choose whatever clothes she wanted in exchange for permission to use her name and picture in advertisements. "This is how tours are done here," he explained.

Then it was off to the Press Club for an interview.

"Is it true that you corresponded with Lenin?" a reporter asked her.

"I didn't have the honor," Catherine replied.

The audience applauded and Catherine realized that most of the spectators were on her side. At the Foreign Relations Club, the audience shouted down a Horthyite who accused Catherine of plotting to murder her parents.

It was just like Michael said it would be. "Don't lose your courage," he had told her as she boarded the

George Washington. "Demosthenes didn't become a
great orator in a day."

     In his letters, Michael became less supportive
and more nostalgic: "Looking into the red cinders in my
small grate, I see all our past in its smallest details.
The pictures on the wall, the yellow lampshade in the
corner of the next room with the stairs leading down
and the table being laid for us on the landing. We were
Seigneurs then. Eva was with us already, unseen, only
perceptible to me in the changed expression of your
eyes. The little 'English' girl who will soon be a big one,
and a mother herself. These moments are so sweet to
me that I cannot part with them."
     Catherine's letters focused on the present: "I am
in a perpetual rush. Imagine me in a room where I am
dictating to two typists, both banging away on their
typewriters. A sculptor is modeling me, my secretary is
talking on the telephone, and journalists are waiting for
an interview. If ever I was nervous at home, I had no
right to be, for it is only now that it could be justified."
     Catherine enjoyed her first big success on the
Karolyis' tenth wedding anniversary. Over a thousand
people packed a small church in Jersey City. Catherine
was so moved, she spoke without her notes for over an
hour. When she was through, even the police wanted to
shake her hand. Tears ran down Caldwell's cheeks. "But
the greatest joy," Catherine wrote Michael, "is to speak
about you and feel as if I am working for you. It is to
you alone that I owe my success. It is you who have
made me what I am."
     This was the kind of news Michael had longed
to hear. "I feel a hundred times, a thousand times
happier about your triumphs that I ever felt about
mine. Not only are you helping our Cause, but, after all
the years of suffering, want, and humiliation that you
endured on account of me and which you accepted with
ease, you are now getting your well-deserved reward.

Now you know what you are worth. You achieved what you did not because you are my wife but in spite of it."

As Catherine's successes mounted and her popularity increased, people began inviting her places. She had lunch with Eleanor Roosevelt and even got to sit through a Harvard-Yale game. "It's the most important event of the season," she wrote Michael after the 1924 edition of The Game. "In pelting rain, 7,000 men and women sat for two hours, soaked to the bone. We too sat in the open. Water ran out of our clothes without dampening the excitement or enthusiasm. No great ideal could ever move the masses to such passion!"

It moved Catherine to catch a cold, however, and, by the time she reached Cleveland, her lungs were congested. In Chicago she came down with a fever. Chicago also brought her first public setback. "My talk at the Casino did not go well," she wrote Michael on December 2nd. "The Germans here have turned the people against us."

By December 6th, Catherine was confined to a bed. "Don't worry," she wrote Michael from a hotel in Columbus, Ohio. "I shall be well by the time you receive this letter. You know I have the health of a horse. Also, the confinement has given me time to revise my newspaper stories."

Since arriving in New York, Catherine had written several stories for newspapers in the cities she planned to visit. The stories, which were designed to raise sympathy for the Republic's fall and the Karolyis' impoverished life, were featured on the days she would speak. The one that appeared in the December 7th edition of the *Columbus Dispatch* is typical in its appeal to sensation and the degrees to which it strays from Catherine's other accounts of her experiences. The hayloft she and Michael slept in the night they fled Hungary, for example, is now a pigsty. The Carabinieri who arrested the Karolyis at their villa in Fiesole are now a company of cavalry with drawn swords, and the ride to Florence takes place not in an open car but in a donkey cart with people spitting on them.

Then there are the stories for which there is no other record. Like the time Michael and Catherine lived in exile with one of the Republic's former ministers. They were walking with their host in his garden when a stranger stepped out from behind a tree and shot the Karolyis' loyal friend. The assassin then turned his revolver on himself and fell at Catherine's feet.

Although the Karolyis had many reasons for not reporting this incident at the time—exposing their whereabouts to other assassins, for example, or discouraging other expatriates from helping them—there is no reason why this terrible moment shouldn't have been mentioned in their memoirs or letters.

Catherine's pearls show up in the *Dispatch* story, only the number of them has grown from 370 to 480, and we learn for the first time how they were smuggled out of Hungary:

With all the rest of our property confiscated, I intended to make this necklace the foundation of our future fortune.

Michael was aghast at first. Then he suggested that we send the pearls to friends in Vienna.

"That will take time, and I am afraid of these assassins," I demured. "We shall smuggle them across the river tonight and hide them in the sand. When we escape to Austria tomorrow, we shall have been searched on this side of the frontier. Picking up the pearls on the opposite bank will be an easy matter."

Of course, if we took a boat we would be watched and searched before embarking.

So we decided to swim!

We reached the opposite shore safely.

There we saw not merely one line of sentries, but several stretching back for what seemed like miles.

One of them approached us. I dropped down

and stretched myself out on the sand as if fatigued. As motionlessly as possible, I burrowed a hole in the sand with the hand that held the priceless necklace.It was too bulky to hide and, to my anxious eyes, it looked as if the moonbeams were maliciously picking out each pearl.

Michael explained that we were bathing for pleasure, that I had become slightly tired after our swim, and that we were going home after a few minutes.

The sentry was chatty. He told us that they were having a good deal of trouble with members of the old nobility trying to smuggle jewels out of Hungary. He instanced one banker who had escaped by dressing as a fat old peasant woman. More than a million dollars had gone with him.

"How foolish to try to smuggle anything," I shrugged, as I rose and re-entered the water.

Whether the sentry was suspicious or whether we had been watched on the Hungarian side, I do not know, but from the moment of our return we were under constant surveilance.

As we were unable to return for the pearls, a friend was obliged to go after them and take them to our contacts in Vienna just as my husband had suggested in the first place.

I quote this story at length because, like the story of the assassin in the minister's garden, it seems too important to have been left out of the Karolyis' memoirs or letters. As noble as her cause was, Catherine may have been willing to exaggerate fact for the sake of truth.

And what about those pearls? Were they the Karolyis' sole source of income? No. Michael received royalties from his memoirs, *Against the World*, which were published in 1923, and not all of his property had been confiscated by the Horthy government. The entailed land was given to Joseph Karolyi who used much of it to generate income for his exiled half-brother. The Karolyis' problem was not so much their lack of money but what they did with it. Unwise investments—a plan to introduce double-decker buses to the London suburbs was typical—kept anything from accumulating. The result was that enough money arrived from Hungary to keep three children in boarding schools and a cook in their kitchen, but the Karolyis always hovered on the brink of poverty because they never knew how long the support from Hungary would continue. Or where they would generate income once it stopped. Money became more important than their health. By the time Catherine completed her tour in New York, she had developed typhoid fever and was admitted to the Post Graduate Hospital.

Michael used the $1,000 Catherine had sent him from the tour to book passage on the first ship to New York, but the American Embassy in London refused to issue him a visa. He appealed to the United States Senate on the grounds that his wife's life was in danger. The Senate voted to uphold the decision of its Embassy but, because Catherine was not expected to live more than a few weeks, to allow Michael to visit her on the condition that he not give any speeches, grant any interviews, or write any articles.

He wouldn't have to. Michael's attempts to see Catherine before she died covered the front pages of newspapers all over the country. Americans interpreted the Karolyis' plight as a love story, were shocked by the government's insensitivity, and outraged that anyone could be silenced in the land of free speech. Cartoons of Michael visiting Catherine with his mouth gagged generated more publicity for the Karolyis's cause than all of Catherine's speeches put together. Petitions demanded that the ban be lifted, and the couple was besieged with offers: book contracts, speaking engagements, even roles in a Broadway play if Catherine recovered.

Catherine recovered but at a terrible cost: her gall bladder and all but a half of one of her lungs. Forced to stay in New York until Catherine was well enough to travel, the Karolyis made a point of appearing conspicuous and silent at a number of public events. Then the newspapers discovered that the Hungarian Embassy had hired detectives to follow them. There was nothing illegal in this but, once again, the American people were outraged. Reprints of Catherine's speeches began appearing in newspapers and magazines. When the couple left the country in April of 1925, an army of reporters followed them across the Canadian border. They wanted to record what so many people had become so anxious to hear.

Michael didn't mince his words. They began: "Now that I am on the free soil of Canada . . ."

Back in London, the Karolyis received the verdict in Michael's trial for treason. The Horthy government had charged him with negotiating with the Allies in Switzerland in 1917, helping the Entente defeat Austria-Hungary, forming a National Council, and preventing the King from exercising his rights. None of Michael's witnesses were given a hearing and no evidence supporting his side was admitted. Nor were any condemning documents entered. Michael was found guilty on the grounds that all the charges were a matter of public record. No proof was necessary.

The Karolyis decided to move to Paris. It was cheaper than London and, as the center of political activity in Europe, Paris had a large Hungarian community that had been forced into exile by the Horthy government. If Michael could organize support there, he could establish a base from which to influence his standing among Hungarians in other countries. Catherine joined The League of the Rights of Man to

spread the Karolyi word by protesting against
governments that persecuted individuals, and Michael,
when not speaking to Hungarians, worked on *The Big
Lie*. A manifesto as well as a drama, the two-act play
tells the story of a man who attempts to live as if he
were dead and, in the end, actually dies to validate his
existence.

The main character, Ravelski, is a revolutionary
whose party is preparing to overthrow a government.
The government wants Ravelski killed. When Ravelski
secretly travels to negotiate with revolutionaries in a
neighboring country, news of his assassination spreads
quickly through his own capitol. The people revolt, the
government falls, and Ravelski's party prepares to take
over.

Ravelski then returns the same way he left—in
secret—but his party's leaders ask him to continue to
pretend he's dead because his death was the catalyst for
the revolution. Ravelski agrees. For the rest of his life
he must be someone other than who he is.

Like Michael, Ravelski moves to a foreign
country where he is deprived of his citizenship, his
property, and, most importantly, his revolution. In
short, his life suddenly has no context. Everything he
does seems grotesque or absurd. Finally, he can take it
no longer. He returns home to discover that his
martyrdom is only a cover. The government has built a
great mausoleum in his honor but shelved all his
revolutionary ideals. Seeing the mausoleum as the
cornerstone for a whole edifice of lies, Ravelski decides
to show up at his own memorial service. His former
comrades have already prepared for this possibility,
however, and send to a mental hospital the madman
who thinks he is Ravelski.

Completed in 1926, Michael wanted the play
distributed in Hungary through the underground
communist press. To do this, he needed the help of Bela
Kun, now living illegally in Vienna. Michael met with
Kun, but Kun dismissed the play as irrelevant to the

proletariat's immediate needs. He did, however, accept Michael's pamphlet on land reform and published it in 1927.

The pamphlet, which received widespread distribution in the West, established Michael as an authority in the field and, in 1928, President Obregon of Mexico invited him to examine the country's land reform program.

The trip began badly. American reporters on the ship from Havana to Mexico City badgered him about an article he had written condemning the execution of Sacco and Vanzetti in Boston. Michael claimed that Governor Fuller had allowed the Italian immigrants to be falsely convicted of murder because they were enemies of capitalism. Although this interpretation of the radical workers' trial is common today, Michael was among the first to voice this opinion in his time. He compared the plight of immigrants from the Mediterranean countries to that of blacks in the United States. Both were kept behind "symbolic barbed wires," both were targets of the Nordic ruling classes, and both were victims of America's "Sheriff Complex." The "pure races"—those with the power—didn't have to worry about the guilt of two Italians or the persecution of millions of black people "to believe in their semi-divine right to destroy them."

Nevertheless, Michael refused to use Sacco and Vanzetti as an indictment of the American people. "The case shouldn't cause us to confuse America with Governor Fuller," he told the *New York World*. "In 1925, when my freedom of speech was the issue in a fight between reaction and progress, I experienced the strength and conviction of progressive American sympathy."

Michael arrived in Mexico to discover that President Obregon had been assassinated a week earlier. His successor, President Calles, needed a favorable report from Michael to divert leftist criticism from his fascist military policies. Michael not only

criticized the government's program of land
reform—that it looked good on paper was his highest
praise—but he warned Mexicans about the rising tide
of fascism.

Fascism, according to Michael, is the middle
class's reaction to a revolution which began with World
War I. The war took people's respect for life and law
and turned them on their heads. Kindhearted people
were taught to murder, lies became a patriotic
occupation, laws no longer protected people from their
own governments, and God was called on to bless
everything that caused death and destruction. After the
war, people realized what they had lost and headed in
one of two directions: the left or the right. Those who
moved toward the left sought a new, more equitable and
egalitarian social structure; those who headed toward
the right sought to bring back what they had lost. But
fascism provided conservatives with something else: a
way to return from the war, hold on to their social
positions, and not work.

Michael cited Italy's Blackshirts as a good
example. As mercenaries for the big industrialists,
Italian farmers had the excuse that they needed to use
weapons to keep those beneath them in their place. In
other words, fascism was a kind of dole for unemployed
bourgeoisie desperate enough to turn to violence to stop
the world's evolution towards socialism. The result
would be a never-ending series of wars such as the one
that broke out in 1914.

While Michael worked hard at telling the
Mexican government what they didn't want to hear,
Catherine entertained an old fascist of her own: Uncle
Duci. It was the first time they had seen each other in
over eight years. Ill and very much older, Julius
Andrassy, Jr. asked Catherine's forgiveness for the way
he treated her and Michael after the Republic collapsed.
A lot of harm had been done by gossip and intrigue.

Most of the Andrassys—now members of the fascist Red Arrow Society—still believed the Karolyis would destroy them if they got the chance.

But Uncle Duci hadn't come to Paris to talk politics. He wanted a reconciliation. His world—the world of principle—had foundered. A distinguished refugee in his own country, he wanted to restore some of the humanity that had slipped away from him in the last days of the Hapsburg monarchy. Catherine gave him more than he needed. When he died several months later, she fully realized how difficult and important seeing her meant to him.

In 1931, Lucien Vogel asked Michael and Catherine to visit the Soviet Union and write a series of articles for a special issue of *Vu*. They enthusiastically accepted. Neither had been to the only country in the world that based its economy on principles they could believe in.

They weren't disappointed. No unemployment, no exploitation by private industry, no showing off for the tourists, and no homeless people. All these were signs of progress. And all had been accomplished in less than ten years! What Western nation could boast as much?

Not many. But Michael and Catherine also chose to see things as they wanted to see them. Religious persecution, for example, was viewed as an effort to enlighten the backward population. And it never dawned on them that separating the minority population into republics tightly controlled by a centralized state was an effective policy of divide and conquer. Nor did they have to look hard in any direction to see signs of repression. Gorky's imprisonment and Trotsky's banishment to Siberia were well known as was Stalin's violent suppression of the kulaks.

And what differences the Karolyis chose to recognize, they often rationalized. "How could we expect

the Soviets to guide us through the miserable quarters
of Moscow or to the concentration camps?" Michael asks
in *Vu.* "What government in the world would make a
show of its slums, prisons, or black markets?"

Again, not many. But Michael's rationalizations
became increasingly strained as he rhetorically
answered the questions he knew his readers would ask:
"Is not human suffering inevitably linked up with
progress? And why do those who assail the Soviets on
grounds of inhumanity accept the cruelty of modern
warfare? Why is hardship acceptable for the sake of
imperialism but not acceptable in the cause of
progress?"

What the Karolyis didn't rationalize, they
blamed on the West. Certainly there is more than a
little truth to this. The capitalist nations had been
working for years to undermine the Soviet Republic,
and the resulting policies of Soviet expediency—Real
Politik—were bound to shake the foundation of
communist principles. But did the state need foreign
currency so badly that it had to recruit prostitutes to
entertain tourists and diplomats in the Western hotels?
How much revenue could these prostitutes generate?
And at what expense to themselves?

Nevertheless, the Karolyis weren't the only ones
to put the best light on what they saw. Writing for the
New Statesman, Catherine describes a reception for
George Bernard Shaw at the British Embassy.
Everybody who is anybody in the Soviet Union is there.
Shaw is introduced in Russian. A translator tells
Catherine the crusty Irishman is a "precursor of the
proletarian dictatorship, the 'Voltaire' of the Russian
Revolution, the destroyer of individualism, and the
inspirer of the new collective ideology."

A thunderous applause welcomes Shaw to the
podium.

"*Tovarichi . . .*"

A storm of cheers prevents him from
continuing. When the noise dies down, Shaw explains it

is the only Russian word he knows.

"My traveling companions are all capitalists, very rich capitalists."

Lady Astor claps her hands so quickly at this they look like the wings of a hummingbird. The audience, not understanding English, thinks something revolutionary has been said and bursts into another round of prolonged applause.

Shaw doesn't understand. He tries to say something about being a communist before Lenin was born but, when the audience doesn't respond, he falters. He tells the Russians, "I can't talk to you as I generally do. I see in your eyes something I have never met in the audiences of other countries." An uncharacteristic earnestness takes over. He tells the Russians: "It is a real comfort to me, an old man, to be able to step into my grave with the knowledge that the civilization of the world will be saved. It is here in the Soviet Union that I have actually been convinced that the new communist system is capable of leading mankind out of its present crisis and saving it from complete anarchy and ruin."

Ironically, Shaw outlived most of the Bolsheviks cheering him on. Ardent Stalinists, they were either executed or shipped off to Siberia within the next eight years.

Among those fated to die was Bela Kun. He had settled in Moscow to write and edit works on Hungarian affairs. Relations between him and Michael were still strained, and it didn't help that Kun had recently rejected an article he had personally asked Michael to write for *Izvestia*. When Kun's eyes moistened at the name of the New York Cafe in Budapest, however, Michael could see only the stereotyped blending of the patriotic but despised Hungarian Jew.

Michael and Catherine wrote several laudatory stories about their trip to the Soviet Union, but the most vivid impression they carried away with them was a banquet honoring a delegation of fascist businessmen. In the middle of the room was a table covered with huge sturgeons, shining caviar, steaming pancakes, and a mountain of red, white and green ice cream topped with Soviet and Italian flags. A band in the corner alternated between "Giovanezza" and the "Internationale." It was a sign of things to come.

In an effort to make people more aware of the fascist threat, Michael convinced the editors at *Vu* to run a series of articles on Germany. He would write on agriculture, while Catherine surreptitiously searched for evidence relating to the Reichstag fire, dug up evidence of the reported concentration camps, and tried to measure the extent of Hitler's rearmament policy. When she was discovered and denounced by her cousin, Louis Windischgraetz, she handed over everything she had gathered to the French Embassy.

Back in Paris, the Karolyis joined the campaign to save Dimitrov, the Bulgarian communist charged with setting fire to the Reichstag. The campaign ended successfully: though sentenced to death by a Nazi court, Dimitrov was deported to the Soviet Union.

Not nearly so successful was the Karolyis' attempt to publish the facts about Hitler's rearmament program. People didn't want to hear them. Story after story was turned down in Paris and London on the grounds that the Karolyis' views, even if correct, would only hasten a conflict. One editor called Michael a warmonger, and another told Catherine the West wasn't going to risk war in order to oblige expatriates.

Then, in 1935, the problem of the Saar was to be solved by a plebiscite. The people of the region would decide whether they would remain under the League of Nations' control or return to Germany. The Karolyis campaigned against the return because the Saar's mines and heavy industry would only help Hitler's rearmament program.

They lost. Fearing a Nazi reprisal if the French

were defeated in the war everyone knew was coming, the people voted for German rule. One year later, Hitler marched into the Rhineland. The French government did nothing, and the Karolyis realized France was doomed. In 1939, they returned to London.

Michael and Catherine settled near Winchester to be with their son. Adam was twenty now, had been brought up in England, and was training pilots in the Royal Air Force. A week before the fighting started, however,his plane crashed. The student was pulled from beneath the fiery wreckage without a scratch, but no one noticed Adam. Thrown into a nearby ditch, he burned to death.

Michael and Catherine moved back to London. If they weren't able to create a new world order for their children, they would do their best to prevent a reactionary one. They began by uniting the Hungarian refugeess who opposed Horthy's pro-German policies, but this proved easier said than done. The British Broadcasting Company, the agency through which the Karolyis hoped to reach their fellow expatriates, was sympathetic to Hungary. Horthy was presented as having no choice but to support Germany. Rather than win Horthy over to the Allies' side, however, the broadcasts made him feel confident and secure. Why should he give the Nazis any trouble? If Hitler lost, the British would stop the Russians from bombing or occupying Hungary.

The Karolyis responded by forming the New Democratic Hungarian Movement. With chapters in Mexico, Canada, Switzerland, Palestine, Algiers, Brazil, and the United States—Bela Lugosi headed the Hollywood contingent—Michael and Catherine pressured the British government to broadcast their messages. In them, they encouraged Hungarians to join

Tito in Yugoslavia and fight against the Germans. While Catherine called for the withdrawal of Hungarian troops from Soviet territory, Michael offered to lead an army recruited from the 70,000 Hungarian prisoners in Russia.

As the outcome of World War II became increasingly obvious, the Horthyites rallied to the Karolyis' side. So did the leftists who, without orders from Moscow, didn't want to miss out. The result was a united if tenuous front.

But the Germans didn't know that. They saw the New Democratic Hungarian Movement as a first sign of their world exploding from within as well as caving in from without. A sense of panic and doom seized the German press.

Then the Soviets stepped in. They resented the Karolyis' interference in their war policy and asked the BBC to stop the broadcasts.

The BBC complied.

The Karolyis were disappointed, but the Soviet request came too late to stem the tide of Michael's popularity. Wires and messages from inside Hungary arrived daily. The Social Democrats wanted him to lead their party, the communists wanted to nominate him for President of the First Soviet Hungarian Republic, and the House of Deputies elected him as one of four non-party members. How soon could he return to Budapest to take up his duties?

As soon as he heard from the Hungarian government and all the parties in the National Front. For twenty-five years, a generation of Hungarians had been raised on anti-Karolyi propaganda. To return without a unanimous call would be a mistake. If Parliament wanted him to return, it could begin the process by reversing Michael's conviction for high treason.

May 8th, 1946. The Karolyi Palace. The

Minister of Justice hands Michael a huge key. He apologizes to the Karolyis for all the wrongs Hungary has done to them. Not all of their stolen property will be returned—only a wing of the seventy-two room palace—but Michael will receive an exalted position in the new communist state.

Michael and Catherine aren't listening. They're thinking of the bullet holes in the wall, the smashed windows, and the library that once held the 20,000 books Elizabeth had to sell at auction. They're remembering Adam, who was born in the palace, and the National Council that was formed in the dining room that October night in 1918. They're also wondering if what they had tried and failed to do could be achieved now that Hungary was backed by a great power.

Stepping onto a balcony, the Karolyis are shown what used to be a private garden. It's now a public park with a statue in the center.

"Who is it?" Michael asks.

"Bishop Prohaszka."

The patron of Horthy's White Terror, Prohaszka had started out as a liberal. Michael had asked him to marry him and Catherine.

"It will have to go," Michael tells the Minister of Justice.

May 9th, 1946. Parliament. More speeches like the ones the day before. Again the Karolyis only half listen. Tisza, Andrassy, and Apponyi—their presence is still felt. Michael is introduced by Laszlo Rajk, the hero of the Spanish Civil War, leader of the Hungarian Resistance, and Secretary of the Communist Party. He alone seems to understand Michael's role in the country's history.

Michael rises to the podium. He speaks for more than an hour, but there is only one thing he really wants to say: "Without Catherine's help, her love, and her courage, I would not be here today."

The whole house stands, faces the gallery where Catherine sits, and gives her the day's longest ovation. Michael has never felt more proud or happy. He and Catherine have won their race with history.

But the new government doesn't know what to do with the Karolyis. Although never critical of the Soviet Union, they were not communists. What position could they hold in a Russianized state?

Michael and Catherine didn't waste any time waiting for an answer. Believing that little good could come from the generation that had lived through the White Terror, Horthyism, Fascism, and the German occupation, the Karolyis decided to focus their attention on the young. Many children had lost their families during the war. Caught stealing to stay alive, they had been sent to prisons because there were no institutions for young people. Small cells, tiny windows, straw mattresses on the floor, a jug of water, and a stinking pail in the corner to be shared by four boys were the norm. A mug of watery broth and a piece of bread twice a day passed as food.

Catherine visited the boys in Marko Utca Prison. Peeping through a spyhole, she saw a pile of boys moving in a heap on the floor. She recoiled in obvious embarrassment. "That's what they do all day long," the warden told her. "The bastards."

Michael and Catherine published articles and gave lectures to draw attention to the plight of these young prisoners. Of particular interest to them was a reformatory for girls. Before the war, they had sewn twelve hours a day to keep the institution from going under. Then the Red Army entered Budapest and the girls found another way to make money.

Catherine decided to establish a home that combined the reforms of the famous Russian "Bolshevo" with the kind of education her children received in

England. She started with five boys. The children were told they were not serving sentences and that their future would not be affected by their past. Everything was done to raise their self-esteem. On Sundays, they went to the movies and, in the summer, swam daily in the Danube. Michael, meanwhile, convinced Parliament to place the country's reformatories under the control of the Welfare Minister. He also introduced the idea of the probationary system to Hungary. When Catherine's home reached its capacity of seventy boys, the state took it over.

During his exile, Michael had established himself as a leading authority on land reform. It was only natural, then, for the new government to seek his opinion. Michael pointed out that any reforms implemented too quickly would be counterproductive. To announce the immediate distribution of all the estates into small holdings, for example, meant finding over 400,000 homes for the new proprietors. The government, of course, didn't listen, and its reforms caused unnecessary discontent. Farm workers, however much they might have been exploited by the aristocrats, at least had a pigsty to sleep in and some food to eat. As proprietors, they had neither food nor shelter—a situation the overthrown rulers were quick to exploit through their agent in the Catholic Church: Cardinal Mindszenty. Agrarian reform then turned into a humanitarian issue when large members of neglected Troglodytes refused to settle on the land the government had provided for them. They preferred the safety and comfort of their caves.

Traveling through Hungary for the Ministry of Agriculture, Michael visited his ancestral homes in Parad and Kalkapolna. There was no trouble with distribution at Parad. Over 250 workers from the estate

had emigrated to Ohio. But Kalkapolna, the estate
where Michael had announced the distribution of his
own estate in 1919, was a different story. These were
not the same people who looked in wonder at the crazy
count who gave them the land they had worked for
centuries. These people were harder, more demanding.
They had been robbed of what Michael had given them
and learned that only something as powerful as the Red
Army could defeat their new landlords. But the Red
Army wasn't all it was cracked up to be either. They
had carried off the peasants' sons and daughters to
work as slaves in the Ukraine, the area most damaged
by the Hungarian army. Then the new government gave
the best land to the fascists who had joined the
communist party to save their lives. The peasants, who
were mostly apolitical, lost out. And now that Michael
was there, they were going to lose out again. They
expected him to do something about the injustices they
had suffered for hoping to lead a better life, but the
truth was he could do nothing. Or rather, he could do
nothing more than fill out a report that everybody knew
would be ignored.

So was Michael's request to be named
Anbassador to Czechoslovakia. Having eliminated
himself from consideration for the Presidency with the
announcement that he wouldn't return to Hungary to
be Stalin's Quisling, Michael hoped to work for a united
Eastern Europe with Jan Masaryk. Moscow rejected the
request, however, and Michael was offered the
Ambassadorship in France. There were several reasons
for this: the cold war had already started and Moscow
didn't think diplomatic representation in the West
mattered very much, it was better to have the Karolyis
out of the country as they had a tendency to act on their
own when they were in it, and the ambassadorship gave
the Karolyis their due while minimizing their influence
and popularity.

But the Karolyis saw the Ambassadorship as an
opportunity to advertise their policies. That Moscow

considered the past of little importance was all the more reason for accurate and unprejudiced information. The communist ambassadors—Michael was the government's only independent—were all "yes men."

Michael soon learned, however, that one ambassador telling the truth as he saw it was one too many. Cardinal Mindszenty had been arrested for endangering the state. His pastoral letters to the powerful clergy directly attacked the government's agrarian policy and encouraged the peasants to defy the new system. Moreover, his negotiations with Cardinal Spellman exceeded his duties as Primate. The Crown of St. Stephen, which many Hungarians believed no ruler could rule without, had been given to the Americans by escaping fascists in return for their freedom and protection. Mindszenty wanted Cardinal Spellman to convince the Americans to keep the crown or send it to Rome until Hungary's anti-religious government was overthrown.

The West used Mindszenty's trial to sway public opinion against the communist bloc countries, and Michael pulled no punches in explaining the extent of the damage. He also granted visas to the French and Australian Ambassadors so they could see for themselves that Mindszenty hadn't been murdered and wasn't being tortured. He then suggested that Mindszenty be deported to Rome.

When the government granted the visas but denied the ambassadors' request to visit Mindszenty in jail, Michael realized that his influence was marginal and his presence in Paris superfluous. But he couldn't tender his resignation because he knew the West would interpret it as a protest against the treatment of Cardinal Mindszenty.

Michael decided to call on Laszlo Rajk, the Hungarian war hero now Minister of the Interior. He didn't know Rajk, but he intuitively felt he could trust him. Rajk begged Michael not to resign. The Karolyis' support was needed now more than ever.

Michael said he would resign but would stay in his post until a successor could be found.

Rajk was arrested the next morning. A rumor spread that he had been taken to Moscow.

Other arrests followed.

Michael realized that there was a lot going on that he didn't know about.

A representative from the government told him that Rajk had been a Horthy informer since 1933, an American agent since the liberation, and a spy for Tito for the last two years.

Michael observed that this was an odd resume for someone entrusted with Interior Ministry, but he knew that what the messenger was saying had nothing to do with truth. His job was to deliver the message.

"And what about Rajk's courageous behavior in the Spanish Civil War?" Michael asked.

"His wounds were accidental."

Rajk's crime, the Karolyis realized, was being a communist rather than a Stalinist. His popularity and his views stood in the ways of Hungary's Russianization. To get rid of him by connecting his him with the independent Tito discredited two heroes at the same time. At Rajk's trial, no plot was discovered and no new evidence was introduced. All the witnesses were either police agents or prisoners. The defense called no witnesses and the judge was more aggressive than the chief prosecutor.

There was, however, a signed confession. Rajk and seven of his comrades were sentenced to hang.

XI.
THE BATTLE NEVER LOST

Of course there were appeals. When Michael read the court's report, he noticed that Rajk had confessed to granting a visa to an "enemy of the People's Republic." Fortunately, Michael was present when Deputy Minister Rakosi told the former Prime Minister that he had issued the visa to this "enemy" because Hungary was better off with him out of the country.

It was a small point but, if Michael could get a stay of execution, other false statements might come to light. People would realize that Rajk had been tortured into signing what he wasn't responsible for. Public pressure could then be brought to bear from inside as well as outside the country. If he failed, Michael knew he could never return to Hungary. The people would be told he had betrayed them.

What the people were told was that Michael had sided with the capitalists because he was too old and too ill to resist their influence. His appeal for a new trial for Rajk went unanswered.

The Karolyis had no illusions about saving Rajk, but they couldn't live with themselves without protesting against the continued violation of socialist principles. Socialism for them was an ethical as well as an economic issue. To eliminate capitalism would serve little purpose unless a higher, freer, more egalitarian order took its place—precisely the kind of attitude that led Rajk to his death.

But where would the Karolyis go? To have confused Stalinism with communism was one mistake; to believe that America would save the world by propping up fascist regimes in exchange for military bases would be worse.

They decided to stay in France. There was a strong socialist movement there, and the government did what was necessary to keep out of America's pocket. Or at least not be all the way in it.

Catherine found an old farm house on the outskirts of Vence. A small town overlooking the Cote d'Azur, Vence was, and is, the refuge of many artists and writers.

In 1950, Michael began rewriting the memoirs he had published in 1923. There was a lot to add, but there was still much he left out. Unable to protest in Hungary, he also refused to manufacture ammunition for the West's propaganda machine. Nevertheless, he made some stunningly accurate predictions: "As long as the rearmament of Europe continues, producing poverty and the proletarianization of its citizens, as long as it becomes more and more enslaved economically to the United States, so long will Russian mistrust and apprehension continue to grow and her grip on her satellites become fiercer." Had Michael lived a little longer, he would have seen Stalinism reveal its violent nature in another Hungarian revolution, but he died in Vence on March 19, 1955.

Three years later, Catherine established in Vence the Michael Karolyi Memorial Foundation. The foundation provides housing and studio space for writers and artists from all over the world. During residencies of three to six months, the foundation's fellows confirm Catherine's belief that communication through the arts is an effective way to break down the barriers of prejudice.

But Catherine wasn't content with merely running a foundation in Michael's memory. She singlehandedly launched a campaign to "rehabilitate" his reputation in Hungary by writing articles and letters, giving speeches and interviews, appearing at conferences, and contacting influential people. By 1962, the Janos Kadar government transferred Michael's remains from the Isle of Wight—he had been buried next to Adam—to the Hungarian Pantheon in Budapest, commissioned a huge statue to be erected in his honor outside the Parliament building and overlooking the Danube, turned the wing of the Karolyi Palace where Michael and Catherine lived during World War I into the Karolyi Museum, renamed the street in front of the palace to Michael Karolyi Utca, and published Michael's memoirs. They were censored, of course, but Michael's rehabilitation in Hungary seems as if it will last.

So will Catherine's. On her ninetieth birthday, she received Hungary's highest honor: the Order of the Flag. A cosmonaut and a Noble Prize winner are the only other recipients. In 1984, the most popular film in Hungary was a biography of her life.

Catherine died shortly after the Michael Karolyi Memorial Foundation celebrated its twenty-fifth anniversary. Supported in part by the French and Hungarian governments—or at least kept from going under by them—the foundation is now run by the Karolyis' youngest daughter, Judith. Eva is married and lives with her family in England.

The Karolyis' critics have called them inconsequential and labeled Michael an Hungarian Kerensky. In the sense that the Karolyis failed to establish a democracy after the first world war and were unable to moderate the communists after the second, the critics are probably right. But the Karolyis were never indifferent or apathetic to the problems of their time. They believed that everyone is responsible for the evil that takes place in the world and that those who are not actively working against evil are, in fact, perpetuating it.

The Karolyis beliefs were shared by many people before World War I, but what separates them from so many of the others is their commitment to humanistic ideals despite increasing sacrifices and disappointments. Their efforts did not bring happiness, but happiness was never their aim. Justice was. And though they never realized the justice they sought, they learned that the battle for justice is never lost either. Nor is it in vain. This particular struggle has an existence of its own and, in time, will be realized even if those who gave their lives for it are no longer with us.